THE RULE OF LAW IN THE UNITED STATES

What is the American rule of law? Is it a paradigm case of the strong constitutionalism concept of the rule of law or has it fallen short of its rule of law ambitions?

This open access book traces the promise and paradox of the American rule of law in three interwoven ways.

It focuses on explicating the ideals of the American rule of law by asking: how do we interpret its history and the goals of its constitutional framers to see the rule of law ambitions its foundational institutions express?

It considers those constitutional institutions as inextricable from the problem of race in the United States and the tensions between the rule of law as a protector of property rights and the rule of law as a restrictor on arbitrary power and a guarantor of legal equality. In that context, it explores the distinctive role of Black liberation movements in developing the American rule of law.

Finally, it considers the extent to which the American rule of law is compromised at its frontiers, and the extent that those compromises undermine legal protections Americans enjoy in the interior. It asks how America reflects the legal contradictions of capitalism and empire outside its borders, and the impact of those contradictions on its external goals.

For more, please visit http://rulelaw.us

The eBook editions of this book are available open access under a CC BY-NC-ND 4.0 licence on www.bloomsburycollections.com. Open access was funded by Northwestern University Pritzker School of Law and the Northwestern Open Access Fund, provided by Northwestern University Libraries.

Volume 1 in the series The Rule of Law In Context

The Rule of Law In Context

By exploring the rule of law in different jurisdictions around the world, the series makes an original and insightful contribution to the rule of law scholarship by moving past intractable debates over what the rule of law should mean to find out what it actually means and how it works 'on the ground', with an implicitly comparative objective as it explores these issues in the context of different legal systems.

Series Editors

Lorne Neudorf
Gabrielle Appleby

Associate Editors

Rosalind Dixon
David Landau
Lawrence McNamara
Arun Thiruvengadam

The Rule of Law in the United States

An Unfinished Project of Black Liberation

by
Paul Gowder

·HART·
OXFORD · LONDON · NEW YORK · NEW DELHI · SYDNEY

HART PUBLISHING

Bloomsbury Publishing Plc

Kemp House, Chawley Park, Cumnor Hill, Oxford, OX2 9PH, UK

1385 Broadway, New York, NY 10018, USA

29 Earlsfort Terrace, Dublin 2, Ireland

HART PUBLISHING, the Hart/Stag logo, BLOOMSBURY and the Diana logo are
trademarks of Bloomsbury Publishing Plc

First published in Great Britain 2021

Open Access was funded by Northwestern University Pritzker School of Law and the Northwestern Open
Access Fund, provided by Northwestern University Libraries.

A catalogue record for this book is available from the British Library.

Library of Congress Cataloging-in-Publication data

Names: Gowder, Paul, author.

Title: The rule of law in the United States : an unfinished project of Black liberation / by Paul Gowder.

Description: Oxford ; New York : Hart, 2021. | Series: The rule of law in context ; volume 1 |
Includes bibliographical references and index.

Identifiers: LCCN 2021035363 (print) | LCCN 2021035364 (ebook) |
ISBN 9781509939992 (hardback) | ISBN 9781509954667 (paperback) |
ISBN 9781509940011 (pdf) | ISBN 9781509940004 (Epub)

Subjects: LCSH: African Americans—Legal status, laws, etc.—History. | Rule of law—United States—History.

Classification: LCC KF4757 .G659 2021 (print) | LCC KF4757 (ebook) | DDC 342.7308/73—dc23

LC record available at https://lccn.loc.gov/2021035363

LC ebook record available at https://lccn.loc.gov/2021035364

ISBN: HB: 978-1-50993-999-2
         ePDF: 978-1-50994-001-1
         ePub: 978-1-50994-000-4

Typeset by Compuscript Ltd, Shannon

Acknowledgements

M Y DEEPEST THANKS to a number of kind colleagues, both at Northwestern and elsewhere, who read and provided helpful comments on parts or all of the manuscript, including (in alphabetical order) Charles Barzun, Josh Bowers, Steve Calabresi, Jack Chin, Mark Graber, Craig Green, Llezlie Green, Jonathan Hafetz, Kevin Johnson, Jennifer Koh, Andy Koppelman, Anthony Kreis, Matt Lister, Jessica Lowe, Steve Lubet, Matthew Mirow, Kali Murray, Emily Ryo, Rich Schragger, Micah Schwartzman, Brian Tamanaha, Hannibal Travis, and Howard Wasserman. I am grateful to the hosts and attendees of workshops on this manuscript at Florida International University and at the Karsh Center for Law and Democracy at the University of Virginia for facilitating many of these conversations. This book has immensely benefitted from their assistance, although, as is customary, I have ignored enough of their wise comments to ensure that they bear no blame for its errors.

For assistance in finding some of the more obscure sources described herein, I thank the dedicated and talented librarians at Northwestern, including Sarah Reis and Tom Gaylord, as well as Leah Regan-Smith, a research assistant working for the library. My research assistant Lawrance Choi has offered invaluable help in making sense of numerous aspects of the problems posed by this volume. My former colleagues Stella and Bram Elias and my current cross-departmental colleague Jackie Stevens have been endlessly kind and patient sounding boards on questions of immigration law and practice.

Some of the material in chapter four on criminal justice was drawn from a separate project that I have on policing; that material benefitted substantially from comments on an in-progress paper in that other project by Amna Akbar, David Barnett, Shima Baradaran Baughman, Kevin Baum, Hannah Bloch-Wehba, Sharon Brett, Cyra Choudhury, Billy Christmas, Zach Clopton, Frank Rudy Cooper, Raff Donelson, Felipe Jimenez, Andrew Johnson, Orin Kerr, Colin Levy, Ben McJunkin, Eric Miller, Jamelia Morgan, Justin Murray, Enzo Rossi, Alan Rozenshtein, Nirej Sekhon, David Skarbek, Etienne Toussaint, and Daniel Wade. Some of my remarks on administrative law benefitted from discussions surrounding an earlier administrative law book review I wrote, for which I additionally thank Erin Delaney, Jim Speta, and Matt Spitzer.

I also thank Kate Whetter, Rosie Mearns, Linda Staniford, and Claire Banyard from Hart for fabulous editorial work and patience, and Gabrielle Appleby and

Lorne Neudorf for their leadership and creativity as series editors in initiating this entire enterprise.

For Leonidas, my best friend.

This book is published Open Access thanks to funding by Northwestern University Pritzker School of Law and the Northwestern Open Access Fund, provided by Northwestern University Libraries.

Table of Contents

Introduction: Is America the Paragon of the Rule of Law?

THE UNITED STATES presents itself to the world and to its own citizens as the global paragon of the rule of law. Its Supreme Court has been among the most trusted parts of the federal government for decades.[1] Day to day political debate features near-constant appeals to the Constitution and close watching of the courts. Abroad, the American government as well as private nonprofits have vigorously promoted American legal institutions as a model for the world.

Yet the United States has always fallen short of its own vision. Even as the framers claimed to be building a state modelled after Montesquieu's republican ideals, they held thousands of humans in a bondage that placed them utterly outside the regard of the law. In the nineteenth century, it ignored its treaties with Native American nations with abandon – it violated one within two weeks of negotiating it.[2] For decades in the beginning of the twentieth century it permitted a regime of mob domination to operate in the South in which Black Americans received not the protection of the law but the terror of the noose. Since the start of the War on Terror, the United States has operated legal black holes in which those accused of terrorism are held without trial. And its immigration system locks up and deports countless noncitizens with the barest pretence of judicial process. The 45th President of the United States took to Twitter to publicly threaten to have his political opponents arrested for treason and to scold his own Attorney General for having the temerity to enforce the criminal laws against his political allies in advance of an election.[3]

---

[1] S Sinozich, 'The Polls – Trends: Public Opinion on the US Supreme Court, 1973–2015' (2017) 81 *Public Opinion Quarterly* 173.

[2] CF Wilkinson and JM Volkman, 'Judicial Review of Indian Treaty Abrogation: As Long as Water Flows, or Grass Grows upon the Earth – How Long a Time is That' (1975) 63 *California Law Review* 601, 611.

[3] DJ Trump, (*Twitter*, 30 September 2019) twitter.com/realdonaldtrump/status/1178643854737 772545 [perma.cc/S42N-XRUZ] ('Rep. Adam Schiff illegally made up a FAKE & terrible statement, pretended it to be mine as the most important part of my call to the Ukrainian President, and read it aloud to Congress and the American people. It bore NO relationship to what I said on the call. Arrest for Treason?'). DJ Trump, (*Twitter*, 3 September 2019) twitter.com/realdonaldtrump/ status/1036681588573130752 [perma.cc/3Q47-EU8V] ('Two long running, Obama era, investigations of two very popular Republican Congressmen were brought to a well publicized charge, just ahead of the Mid-Terms, by the Jeff Sessions Justice Department. Two easy wins now in doubt because there is not enough time. Good job Jeff ...... '). (NB: Since Twitter's ban of Trump's account, the original links for those two tweets are no longer available, but have been archived at the two perma.cc locations noted; the archive URLs were last accessed on 20 April 2021.)

This book attempts to make some sense of this mixed record. American legal and political institutions, and their development through its history, represent a kind of aspirational rule of law ideal – but an aspiration that the United States has yet to meet. Hence, I try to draw out the paradoxes embedded in the American rule of law – how have our claims to lawful government carried within them both the ambition to genuinely deliver equal justice under law and the seeds of lawlessness and terror?

The account revolves around two ideas. First, the US rule of law has been marked by a history of conflicts over inclusion within the protections of legal order, conflicts which continue to the present. Those conflicts have revolved around race, and around race-adjacent categories such as ethnicity and nationality. At the founding, the enslaved were completely outside the ambit of the law – prohibited from testifying in court, holders of no rights. Likewise, Native Americans were represented as foreigners rather than members of the legal community and, until 1871, the objects of treaty rather than regulation (although the Native American case is somewhat more complicated, as, of course, the independence of the Native American nations was valuable to them as well, whereas the outlawry of the enslaved was a pure disadvantage). Both Black Americans and Native Americans ultimately became at least partially included in the legal community as the American rule of law has progressed.

Over time, the Black struggle for inclusion has built the foundations of our rule of law – it is that struggle for legal membership that has brought us the Fourteenth Amendment, our most direct textual representation of the ideal of the rule of law, as well as the rules of constitutional criminal procedure that are the foundations of such protections as we have from arbitrary police action. But, even today, the lack of full legal inclusion of Black Americans has persisted through egregious disparities in criminal justice. Moreover, the full-fledged exclusion of a class of people from the legal community persists in immigration law's plenary power doctrine, whose origins are in the openly racist Chinese Exclusion period, but which has recurred as recently as 2018 to permit Donald Trump to enforce his infamous Muslim ban.

Conflicts over membership are inextricable from the United States interpreted as an *empire*. In the early days of the United States, the lawless treatment of the Native American nations was occasioned by the imperial drive to expand its territory. Today, the consequences of this imperialism remain in the second-class legal status of Native Americans, who are the only substantial group of people born on American soil whose citizenship is not constitutionally guaranteed but merely a creature of statute, and whose capacity to engage in collective self-governance as well as to make decisions entrusted to other citizens such as the management of their own property has been subject to erratic federal supervision. Native American nations are also addressed by the plenary power doctrine, and in that domain it traces back to Chief Justice Marshall's open acknowledgement that the United States courts stood with respect to those nations as 'the courts of the conqueror'.[4]

At the same time, the United States runs a system of global political and economic hegemony in which it pressures other nations to adopt forms of economic liberalisation that permit the free movement of capital – and rule of law institutions meant to preserve the security of multinational investment – while aggressively restricting the movement of labour through its immigration laws. This is so even though many migrants are fleeing nations whose devastation is partly attributable to the United States' own military adventures – such as its destabilising Middle East warfare – or its economic hegemony. In the future we are very likely to be required to add refugees from the climate change caused in part by its irresponsible environmental policy to the list.

Nor are the international and the domestic independent. The techniques and habits of arbitrary imperial power have a tendency to leak into the domestic sphere through phenomena such as police militarisation.[5] We can see this in, for example, the revolving door that one torturer passed through between the Chicago Police Department and the lawless War on Terror black hole at Guantanamo Bay, and in the deployment of Border Patrol units among federal officials sent by the Trump administration to beat protesters in Portland.[6] In the economic sphere, the legal subordination of foreigners supports the domestic availability of noncitizen workers in jobs considered undesirable by citizens. That, in turn, is the same mechanism that was used to impose undesirable 'dependent' types of labour on legally subordinated groups including the enslaved, and, to a less dire degree, women, at the dawn of the republic.[7]

That point leads into the second theme of this book's account: the idea of property (and with it, economic independence) has a kind of propulsive force in the American rule of law; but also a contradictory force, sometimes serving as the foundational basis for other legal rights-claiming, but other times

[handwritten margin note: Passavant property connects to Commerce + neoliberalism]

---

[4] *Johnson v M'Intosh* 21 US 543, 588 (1823).

[5] CJ Coyne and AR Hall, *Tyranny Comes Home: The Domestic Fate of U.S. Militarism* (Stanford University Press, 2018).

[6] S Ackerman, 'Bad Lieutenant: American Police Brutality, Exported from Chicago to Guantánamo' (*The Guardian*, 18 February 2015) www.theguardian.com/us-news/2015/feb/18/american-police-brutality-chicago-guantanamo; E Pilkington, '"These Are His People": Inside the Elite Border Patrol Unit Trump Sent to Portland' (*The Guardian*, 27 July 2020) www.theguardian.com/us-news/2020/jul/27/trump-border-patrol-troops-portland-bortac; S Olmos, M Baker and Z Kanno-Youngs, 'Federal Agents Unleash Militarized Crackdown on Portland' (*The New York Times*, 17 July 2020) www.nytimes.com/2020/07/17/us/portland-protests.html; J Ismay, 'A Navy Veteran Had a Question for the Feds in Portland. They Beat Him in Response.' (*The New York Times*, 20 July 2020) www.nytimes.com/2020/07/20/us/portland-protests-navy-christopher-david.html; T Jawetz, PE Wolgin and C Flores, '5 Immediate Steps To Rein in DHS in the Wake of Portland' (*Center for American Progress*, 2 September 2020) www.americanprogress.org/issues/immigration/reports/2020/09/02/489934/5-immediate-steps-rein-dhs-wake-portland/.

[7] A Rana, *The Two Faces of American Freedom* (Harvard University Press, 2014) 163, 188, 340–42.

as the signal of a person's status as beyond or beneath the protections of law. At its dawning, we can fruitfully see property as both the core legal right of an American and as the legal face of the tension between liberal and republican conceptions of the political community popularised by historians such as Gordon Wood. Yet the idea of property was also the legal foundation for the subordination of the enslaved, and one of the chief post-emancipation struggles of the freed was to acquire property, and with it republican independence.

Property is also the face that the American rule of law presents to the outside world. The so-called 'Washington Consensus' school promotes the free movement of capital in part by insisting that a conception of the rule of law that revolves around the security of property for foreign investors is a key component of the normative path of economic development.[8] This conception has been central to American foreign relations ideology for longer than the Washington consensus has had a name – its roots can be seen, for example, in the US government support for Augusto Pinochet combined with the 'Chicago Boys' economists' development plan adopted by Chile during that period – an entirely investor-focused conception of what the rule of law might be and do.

Placing property in the driver's seat imposes inegalitarian pressure on a legal system: if property is a fundamental legal interest to be protected, then reforms that might give the poor a stake in the system start to seem like affronts to the rule of law itself. However, over time, property began to reveal the potential to serve as a liberating role – first abortively, as the potential basis for inclusion of the freed slaves into the ranks of full-fledged republican independent citizens under the failed 40 acres Reconstruction land distribution plan, and then more firmly in the Warren Court's due process revolution, when the economic interests of the poor were for the first time treated as legitimate property interests just like the economic interests of the rich.

Nonetheless the foundational dichotomy between the rule of law interests of individual persons and the rule of law interest in capitalist property persists. For example, harsh policing policies are often motivated by the desire to protect property, but such policies have also driven America's racial disparities in criminal justice and the segregation at its foundation. On the theoretical level, the most visible criticism of excessive discretionary executive power in the American context today is dominated by libertarians, who focus on the failure of the United States to provide fair hearings in cases involving things like patents and securities regulation.[9] At the same time some of the same scholars claim that the

---

[8] B Tamanaha, 'The Dark Side of the Relationship Between the Rule of Law and Liberalism' (2008) 3 *New York University Journal of Law & Liberty* 516, 537–41.

[9] eg, G Lawson, 'Appointments and Illegal Adjudication: The America Invents Act through a Constitutional Lens' (2018) 26 *George Mason Law Review* 26; RA Epstein, 'Structural Protections for Individual Rights: The Indispensable Role of Article III – Or Even Article I – Courts in the Administrative State' (2019) 26 *George Mason Law Review* 777.

idea of treating welfare benefits like property and hence amenable to the protections of procedural due process is 'quite laughable and wrong'.[10]

Ultimately, the two lodestar features of the American rule of law come together in the idea that the possession of secure property rights is a core attribute of legal inclusion itself: those whose economic interests get counted as property and protected are, for that reason, shielded from much of the arbitrary power that American government as well as powerful private entities might inflict. Those who are the subjects of arbitrary power often experience it in the form of unstable property rights. But the inegalitarian implications of America's property-first conception of the rule of law are its greatest weakness. The rule of law requires the support of the community as a whole if it is to be maintained; but a legal system which consistently attaches the core of its protections to the kinds of legal interests held primarily by its richest and its most powerful members is one which is continually under pressure from both the top and the bottom. The rich have continual incentives to capture legal institutions to reinforce their own supremacy. The poor have continual incentives to abandon them or seek extra-legal change. The result is a legal order that is permanently vulnerable to, well, precisely what the United States saw in the recent presidency of Donald Trump: a demagogue who in many ways personified the rejection of law as a way of organising American public life.

THE METHODOLOGICAL PROBLEM:
WHAT IS THE RULE OF LAW, ANYWAY?

The rule of law, much like democracy, is a complex normative concept, frequently invoked by scholars as a criterion for a morally legitimate state, but which is the subject of little academic consensus – indeed, it has been described as an 'essentially contested concept'.[11] Still, most rule of law scholars and practitioners accept a few core claims, such as that the relevant contrast against which we might judge the rule of law is the rule of persons, and particularly, the arbitrary

---

[10] G Lawson and S Calabresi, 'The Depravity of the 1930s and the Modern Administrative State' (2018) 94 *Notre Dame Law Review* 821, 865. This view is defensible, but only if one grants broad deference to the history of American conceptions of property, according to which it feels perfectly natural that a government-granted monopoly (ie, a patent) can be a real kind of property, but a government-granted annuity (ie, welfare) cannot. Thus Lawson's (n 9) argument revolves around an analogy between intellectual property patents and land patents dating from the era of Westward Expansion. RE Zietlow, 'Giving Substance to Process: Countering the Due Process Counterrevolution' (1997) 75 *Denver University Law Review* 9, insightfully contextualises the background and aftermath of the expansion of due process rights to welfare benefits as a kind of brief moment of 'communitarian' as opposed to an individualist (or liberal, we might say) reading of the scope of constitutional rights which had the never fully realised potential to promote the poor to full constitutional membership.

[11] J Waldron, 'Is the Rule of Law an Essentially Contested Concept (In Florida)?' (2002) 21 *Law and Philosophy* 137.

will of those persons; as well as that inherent in the rule of law is a kind of neutrality, in which a person may not be judge in her own case and the application of law is independent of private passions and interests.

Another fairly well-accepted description of the basic conceptual core of the rule of law is Lon Fuller's eight principles of legality.[12] While Fuller saw those principles – which focus on what we might think of as operational criteria of a legal system, such as the prospectivity, publicity, and stability of laws, their rule-like (as opposed to command-like) character, and the extent to which what officials enforce is the same as what is written down – as the basic criteria for a legal system to be functional, they are also widely seen as closely related to the idea of the rule of law itself.

These abstract ideas also come associated with some concrete institutional commitments that are fairly well-accepted, at least as a baseline. Rule of law scholars and advocates typically are committed to, for example, legal rules that do not leave excessive room for official discretion in their application, and fair trials with neutral judges especially (but not exclusively) in the criminal law.

Beyond that uncontroversial core, however, there is little consensus about what the rule of law is. And I do not come to the task of elucidating the (or a) American conception of the rule of law from a blank slate: in my previous work, I've defended several positions about the concept of the rule of law.[13] For present purposes, the key claims are as follows. First, the rule of law consists in principles requiring procedural legal justice and the control of state power (what I have called 'regularity' and 'publicity') and in a principle requiring substantive legal equality ('generality'). Secondly, it is conceptually possible to have a state that achieves the rule of law as procedural legal justice/control of power but not substantive legal equality, but such a legal order is unstable: the lack of legal equality undermines the ability to achieve the more formal principles. Thirdly, the rule of law is an egalitarian principle but it is distinct from the demands of egalitarian justice as a whole: it is possible for there to be an unjust rule of law state. Finally, in the face of the ineluctable controversy about what the rule of law is, the correct way to give an account of the concept is to draw on the experiences of actual rule of law states and of the people who have fought to achieve the rule of law in real-world politics.[14]

Apart from the final methodological claim, this book does not assume the theoretical framework elucidated in my prior work. Quite the contrary: consistent with the methodological claim, the prior work rested in substantial part on

---

[12] LL Fuller, *The Morality of Law*, revised edn (Yale University Press, 1969) 39; see discussion in C Murphy, 'Lon Fuller and the Moral Value of the Rule of Law' (2005) 24 *Law and Philosophy* 239.

[13] P Gowder, 'Equal Law in an Unequal World' (2014) 99 *Iowa Law Review* 1021; P Gowder, 'The Rule of Law and Equality' (2013) 32 *Law and Philosophy* 565; P Gowder, *The Rule of Law in the Real World* (Cambridge University Press, 2016).

[14] On this last claim, see also P Gowder, 'Institutional Values, or How to Say What Democracy Is' (2014) 30 *Southwest Philosophy Review* 235.

having reflected on the American system; this book fills out the reflections that grounded the theoretical claims I previously made on their basis. For example, the theoretical claim that procedural justice goes together with substantive legal equality in part responds to the fact that in the American tradition, their constitutional instantiations live side-by-side in the Fourteenth Amendment, frequently coincide in real-world constitutional litigation, and indeed have been made explicitly to depend on one another when the Supreme Court 'reverse incorporated' the Equal Protection Clause as an aspect of due process.[15] It also responds to much of the historical and present experience with <u>legal caste</u> recounted in this book, in which legally-enforced subordination repeatedly finds itself accompanied by procedural injustice – as when the rightslessness of the enslaved was implemented in the kangaroo courts of the Fugitive Slave Act of 1850 and the contemporary rightslessness of immigrants is implemented in kangaroo immigration courts and 'expedited removals' – and then that procedural injustice in turn <u>leaks out</u> to people who are putatively outside the subordinated caste – as *spillover effects* when the Fugitive Slave adjudications facilitated the kidnapping of free Black Northerners, or when citizens get deported in expedited removals.

The work of this volume also rests on a refinement of the methodological claim noted above. I have previously argued that what we might call our abstract concept of the rule of law depends on reality from a general perspective, ie, on our observations of the variety of societies with and advocates for the rule of law across history; here I further contend that the same point applies in elucidating a particular country's conception of the rule of law. When attempting to say what the American rule of law is, it is not correct merely to look at the country's formal institutions as they've been written down in legal documents – and this book does very little of that. Rather, what really matters are the boundaries where the rule of law has been tested and contested in that country: where some have been denied access to the forms of law to vindicate their claims to rights and status, and how they have understood that denial as contrasted with how those who did the denying understood it. In those interstices, the 'law on the <u>books</u>' and the '<u>law in action</u>' meet one another, as state and society are forced to resolve a conflict over the scope of the legal system's protections, and, in doing so, more fully articulate for themselves what those protections mean.

Such an account – we might call it critical Hegelian – is a natural fit for the United States, which is distinctive both for having begun with a set of very broad stated ideals about things like human equality and inalienable rights and for having violated those ideals with vigour for all of its history. By examining how those ideals played out from the standpoint of contestation over their boundaries, we can see both the value and the victories of those ideals – with respect to the rule of law, the way that American institutions have genuinely provided the basis to deliver something like legal justice – and the way in which those

---

[15] *Bolling v Sharpe* 347 US 497 (1954).

victories are compromised, and in which the American rule of law continues to be surrounded by a core of lawlessness. Only in that way can an honest account of the American rule of law be given.

These claims are not to exclude the possibility of a coherent and useful account of the American rule of law more focused on its formal institutions, the statements of its constitutional founders, and the like. While this book is not that account (although the founders receive substantial attention in the first two chapters), such an account would also have value. The material of the constitutional framing period contains numerous references to classic formulations of identifiably rule-of-law oriented ideas. Madison's declaration in Federalist 47 that the accumulation of legislative, executive, and judicial power in a single branch is the 'very definition of tyranny,' for example, is an obvious reference to Montesquieu's rule of law-centric theory of republican liberty.[16] The 1780 Massachusetts Constitution, written by John Adams, declares that its establishment of the principle of separation of powers is done 'to the end it may be a government of laws, and not of men'.[17] In Federalist 10, Madison gives a nod to that other early modern rule of law paragon, John Locke, and his principle that '[n]o man is allowed to be a judge in his own cause, because his interest would certainly bias his judgment, and, not improbably, corrupt his integrity'. In Federalist 78, Alexander Hamilton argues for judicial independence and judicial review 'to secure a steady, upright, and impartial administration of the laws'. And a Pennsylvania judge in 1786 argued against judicial discretion in punishments on the ground that 'It is a distinguishing mark of a free government, that the people shall know before hand, the penalty which the laws annex to every offense; and, therefore, such a system is called a government of laws, and not of men.'[18] That sentence could just as well have been written by a rule of law scholar today.

But I am more interested in what the American government did than what its framers said, and for that we must attend to the voices of those other than James Madison.

THE BLACK LIBERATION RULE OF LAW

One of the key organising principles of this book is an emphasis on the role of subordinated groups in American society in the development and articulation of the American conception of the rule of law. This includes discussions of the US

---

[16] The source of all quotations to the Federalist Papers in this volume is Yale University's Avalon Project, at avalon.law.yale.edu/subject_menus/fed.asp.

[17] Massachusetts Constitution (1780), Part I, Art 30; *cf* SB Benjamin, 'The Significance of the Massachusetts Constitution of 1780' (1997) 70 *Temple Law Review* 883.

[18] MJ Horwitz, *The Transformation of American Law, 1780–1860* (Harvard University Press, 1977) 12.

legal system's treatment of immigrants and of those within the criminal justice process, as well as some attention to US legal colonialism with respect to Native American nations. But the primary conflict around which this book revolves is the Black American struggle for inclusion.

This emphasis has a sound historical and structural basis. Black enslavement was the original and most drastic failing of America's rule of law. Enslavement also operated as a pivot around which debates about what the rule of law meant turned: Black Americans and abolitionists claimed (rightly, in my view) that slavery was inherently lawless, but, at the same time, slaveholders argued that something like the rule of law with its central American focus on the protection of property against expropriation justified (indeed, required) infamies like the Fugitive Slave Acts and *Dred Scott v Sandford* – the fight to end slavery can be usefully interpreted as in part a fight over what it might mean to operate government under law in the American sense.

There is also a broader methodological point to this focus. The American legal realists largely punctured the notion that the legal domain can ever be wholly autonomous from politics early in the twentieth century. In the late twentieth century, scholars in the tradition of critical legal studies (CLS) and critical race theory (CRT) attempted to take the next step and puncture the notion that the law can be independent from broader structures of social and economic power – but those puncturings, unlike the legal realist one, didn't so fully take over the broader academic community. Of the two modern puncturings, CRT is far more vital, and has heavily influenced this book.

The conversation between CRT and the rule of law has been particularly fruitful because leading scholars within the CRT tradition have articulated sophisticated conceptions of the relationship between the social standpoint of people of colour and liberal legalism. Polemicists on the right have frequently run critical legal studies and critical race theory together, and accused both of sharing a disdain for the rule of law.[19] It is true that many CRT scholars do count CLS as one of their intellectual influences, and CRT scholars such as Derrick Bell have made extremely productive use of the CLS insight that many supposedly neutral legal rules contain deeply embedded political and social hierarchies. It is also true that CLS scholars have typically rejected the rule of law as an ideal worth pursuing.[20] But it's a serious mistake to think that CRT scholarship necessarily rejects the rule of law. Quite the contrary, one of the most important intellectual moves made early on by some (though not all) of the most prominent scholars in the tradition was to reject the CLS abandonment of the rule

---

[19] eg, DE Bernstein, *Lawless: The Obama Administration's Unprecedented Assault on the Constitution and the Rule of Law*, 1st American edn (Encounter Books, 2015) 5–6.

[20] eg, MJ Horwitz, 'The Rule of Law: An Unqualified Human Good?' (1977) 86 *Yale Law Journal* 561; D Kennedy, 'The Critique of Rights in Critical Legal Studies' in W Brown and JE Halley (eds), *Left Legalism/Left Critique* (Duke University Press, 2002); M Tushnet, 'An Essay on Rights' (1984) 62 *Texas Law Review* 1363.

of law. Most influentially, Patricia Williams argued that the CLS and Marxist
dismissal of the rule of law and legal rights itself represents a privileged white
standpoint: only those who have sufficient reserves of social power to draw on
can abandon the protections of law, and it's no coincidence that CLS scholars
tended to be people who had never had to rely on thin legal protections as their
only shield against social oppression.[21] Sometimes, some critical race scholars,
like some Black liberation activists, have taken a cynical stance toward American
legal institutions.[22] But even a kind of 'cynical legalism' is still a legalism, that
recognises at least the rhetorical power of law and hence its capacity to serve as
a tool for liberation.

Simultaneously considering the United States through a critical race theory
lens and through a rule of law lens allows us to see how the rule of law as
rhetoric can be used to promote lawless ends while simultaneously seeing how
the institutions that rhetoric built represent a genuine ideal to which our legal
system can aspire. This is a 'dual consciousness' strategy long associated with
critical race theory, and with Black Americans more generally.[23]

Moreover, the conjunction of rule of law ideology with extreme inequality –
which is most vividly manifested in the United States on the dimension of race,
and on race conjoined with class – can help us see the unavoidable dependence
of rule of law ideals on genuine social equality.

The warping of a legal system in the face of race-class inequality can be seen
even at its most granular implementation levels. I recall my own first job out of
law school, as a low-income legal services lawyer in a community in rural Oregon
that was starkly divided along socioeconomic as well as racial grounds, with a
substantial mostly-Latino underclass of agricultural workers and other labourers and a dominant middle-class of mostly-white business owners and social
service providers. My job was essentially to represent the former against the
latter, but the social positioning of a lawyer in the face of such inequality meant
that I was largely perceived by both sides as an ally of the powerful – the welfare
office staff and the business owners routinely tried to demand that I work with
them to regulate the workers, while my clients often feared and distrusted me.
One pro se business owner whom I was suing demanded to *speak to my manager*
after settlement negotiations were insufficiently conciliatory for his tastes. Both
sides of the class/racial divide recognised that, given the underlying inequality,
the position of a legal aid lawyer forced me to resist endless incentives and temp-
tations to serve the underlying power structure of the community rather than
my clients.

---

[21] P Williams, 'Alchemical Notes: Reconstructing Ideals from Deconstructed Rights' (1987) 22 *Harvard Civil Rights-Civil Liberties Law Review* 401.
[22] DE Roberts, 'The Meaning of Blacks' Fidelity to the Constitution' (1997) 65 *Fordham Law Review* 1761.
[23] MJ Matsuda, 'When the First Quail Calls: Multiple Consciousness as Jurisprudential Method' (1989) 11 *Women's Rights Law Reporter* 7.

My positioning in Oregon as a lawyer was merely a manifestation of a broader power-contingency of the implements of American legal order. The distortion of the function of the lawyer is probably most widely noticed and decried in the large literature on the 'access to justice' gap, perceived at least in substantial part as an access to legal representation gap.[24] But it has many other manifestations. Consider, for example, the notion of a 'contract', conventionally understood as a tool of individual autonomy. In reality, scholars have observed that contract serves to undermine autonomy in the face of vast economic power disparities: corporations use the form of contract to impose what Radin calls 'rights-deletion' on consumers and employees.[25] Or consider LaToya Baldwin Clark's research on the Individuals with Disabilities Education Act as an exemplar of a broader phenomenon in which groups lacking social, economic, and cultural capital experience disparate legal outcomes in contexts where individual initiative is required to make use of legal entitlements.[26] The focus on subordination in this book is in part consciously chosen to make visible the contingency of American legal institutions on social inequality.

A focus on the subordinated also serves a more banal evaluative purpose. To the extent part of the task in a work such as this is to figure out the extent to which the United States actually meets its rule of law ideals, the place to look as a test for that achievement is to its treatment of those who are most vulnerable to failures of the rule of law – that is, to those who have been subject to discrimination and oppression.

A further theoretical reason to focus on Black liberation movements relates to the idea, which I have defended elsewhere, that the rule of law typically requires collective action, or the threat thereof, against powerful public officials to keep the legal constraint of power together.[27] For this reason, the movement-building activity of subordinated groups itself facilitates the rule of law for everyone. I contend that this has been true of Black organising: by expanding both Black organisational capacity and the scope of the people encompassed within American law's orbit (and hence the scope of the people who have an incentive to defend the legal constraint of the powerful), the very fact of robust and successful Black social movements that have won victories for themselves creates positive legal externalities in supporting the preservation of the legal protections enjoyed by others.

There is also an epistemic reason for focusing on Black agency. As Anderson has persuasively argued with respect to moral discourse in the abolitionist movement, abstracted moral critique of social injustice by members of groups

---

[24] RL Sandefur, 'Access to Civil Justice and Race, Class, and Gender Inequality' (2008) 34 *Annual Review of Sociology* 339.

[25] MJ Radin, *Boilerplate* (Princeton University Press, 2012).

[26] L Baldwin Clark, 'Beyond Bias: Cultural Capital in Anti-Discrimination Law' (2018) 53 *Harvard Civil Rights-Civil Liberties Law Review* 381.

[27] Gowder, *The Rule of Law in the Real World* (n 13) chs 6, 8.

privileged by that injustice has a built-in efficacy disadvantage because of the way that power and privilege introduce bias into moral reasoning.[28] By contrast, concrete political contestation rooted in a claim of right by the subordinated can unsettle pre-existing power relations and provide room for genuine engagement with the moral claims at issue.

Finally, constitutional theory itself, properly understood, recommends specifically emphasising the Black role in the development of the American rule of law. To the extent the US Constitution is democratically legitimate, it is so because the Constitution is rooted in the authorial autonomy of the people. Thus, for example, the flavour of originalist constitutional interpretation known as 'original public meaning' posits a public whose linguistic understandings are the source of constitutional meaning – which to me seems to rest on the democratic claim that the people are the lawmakers. More broadly, the tradition of appealing to history to fill out American constitutional doctrine, which has been around much longer than some articulated scholarly concept called 'originalism', has also often rested on an implicit public whose understanding of the law they were making and the social environment in which their law was made was relevant to understanding the meaning of the Constitution. Yet until all too recently constitutional law has rested on an implicit presupposition that the views and interests of the public are exclusively the views and interests of whites.

By emphasising the agency of Black Americans – of those who were members of the community from the get-go but excluded from formal recognition of legal personality – part of the project of this book is to unsettle those assumptions of white constitutional authorship. This is a longstanding project of a tradition of Black scholarship that begins with WEB Du Bois's *Black Reconstruction in America*, which pioneered the understanding of emancipation as Black self-liberation. And as I have argued at length elsewhere, Black Americans have always been constitutional authors.[29]

In recent years, scholars have done substantial, though incomplete, work to remedy the neglect within the academy of the role of the histories of Black and Brown people, the enslaved, Native Americans, and migrants in our legal doctrine.[30] But this work needs to continue, and this book aims to contribute to remedying at least some of the longstanding erasure of subordinated groups in American law. This goal is an element of the critical Hegelian methodological approach of this book, as applied both to our legal doctrines and to the concepts underlying them. In this, I am inspired by Neil Roberts, who brilliantly asks

---

[28] E Anderson, 'Moral Bias and Corrective Practices: A Pragmatist Perspective' (2015) 89 *Proceedings and Addresses of the American Philosophical Association* 21.

[29] P Gowder, 'Reconstituting We the People: Frederick Douglass and Jürgen Habermas in Conversation' (2019) 114 *Northwestern University Law Review* 335.

[30] K-S Park, 'This Land Is Not Our Land' (2020) 87 *University of Chicago Law Review* 1977, 1992–2004.

what our concept of 'freedom' would be if we began with the experience of the enslaved in seizing it.[31]

It seems to me to be a disastrous form of intellectual negligence – and a form of institutional racism – to operate a system of law under the assumption that those whose oppression has been foundational to its creation have not said or done anything relevant to its meaning. Consider, for just a single example, the following passage from the (truly poorly-named) *Civil Rights Cases* – a collection of consolidated Supreme Court cases which held that Congress did not have authority, under the Fourteenth Amendment, to regulate private discrimination:

> When a man has emerged from slavery, and, by the aid of beneficent legislation, has shaken off the inseparable concomitants of that state, there must be some stage in the progress of his elevation when he takes the rank of a mere citizen and ceases to be the special favorite of the laws, and when his rights as a citizen or a man are to be protected in the ordinary modes by which other men's rights are protected. There were thousands of free colored people in this country before the abolition of slavery, enjoying all the essential rights of life, liberty and property the same as white citizens, yet no one at that time thought that it was any invasion of his personal status as a freeman because he was not admitted to all the privileges enjoyed by white citizens, or because he was subjected to discriminations in the enjoyment of accommodations in inns, public conveyances and places of amusement. Mere discriminations on account of race or color were not regarded as badges of slavery. If, since that time, the enjoyment of equal rights in all these respects has become established by constitutional enactment, it is not by force of the Thirteenth Amendment (which merely abolishes slavery), but by force of the Fourteenth and Fifteenth Amendments.[32]

The unwillingness to think about the role of Black Americans as constitutional co-creators begins with the very first sentence, which declares that the legislation passed during Reconstruction to regularise the civil and political condition of Black Americans was some kind of 'beneficent' gift from whites, rather than something that the freedpeople had fought for. It then acknowledges the legal inequality to which free Black Americans were subjected prior to the Civil War, but asserts that 'no one at that time thought that it was any invasion of his personal status as a freeman'. To this proposition, one must ask: 'who is in the no one?' Maybe white people didn't think that, but Black people certainly did. But there is no evidence that the Court thought it necessary to examine any record of the numerous assertions of legal, political, social, and economic rights made by antebellum free Black Americans.[33]

---

[31] N Roberts, *Freedom as Marronage* (The University of Chicago Press, 2015).

[32] *Civil Rights Cases* 109 US 3, 25 (1883). The 'Fourteenth' in the last clause might actually be 'Thirteenth' – there is some confusion, likely due to a typesetter's error, however, the most plausible reading is 'Fourteenth', and this is, apparently, what the historical record should suggest. G Rutherglen, 'Textual Corruption in the *Civil Rights Cases*' (2009) 34 *Journal of Supreme Court History* 164.

[33] See eg MS Jones, *Birthright Citizens: A History of Race and Rights in Antebellum America* (Cambridge University Press, 2018).

There is copious evidence of Black Americans recognising that economic discrimination was inextricable from slavery. In the North Black abolitionists had long made it clear that ending exclusion from and segregation in churches, schools, restaurants, and transportation was part of the abolitionist quest.[34] Consider the following statements by two of the most prominent Black leaders. The first argument for affirmative action of which I am aware was made in 1852 by Martin Delany, who scolded white abolitionists for failing to employ Black Americans at high levels in their newspapers and the like, on the grounds that the abolitionist position entailed promoting the 'elevation' of Black people, including in the economic sphere.[35] And on 11 May 1858, Frederick Douglass gave a speech against race discrimination in New York City streetcar carriages in which he declared that this economic discrimination was part of 'the cruel and malignant spirit of caste, which is at the foundation, and is the cause, as well as the effect of our American slave system' and went hand-in-hand with '[t]he denial of our citizenship', and with such core wrongs of slavery as exclusion from suffrage; Douglass went on to contrast the condition of Black men in the United States with those in Brazil, highlighting that the latter were truly free because they had access to high posts in law, medicine, the army, the church, and private business.[36]

If the Court had been aware that Black Americans had been claiming all along that emancipation meant economic inclusion rather than merely having a status other than chattel, the argument of the *Civil Rights Cases* may not have been sustainable. At least the Court would have had to offer an argument about how the position of Black abolitionists didn't entail permitting Congress to destroy private economic discrimination. But because the justices utterly failed to attend to the advocacy of Black Americans – failed to treat Black Americans as constitutional framers and as part of the people whose beliefs about the meaning of concepts like freedom, slavery, and citizenship bear on constitutional interpretation – the Court could just wave it away with a 'no one at that time thought', and, in doing so, hand down a pallid interpretation of the Fourteenth Amendment that buttressed generations of failure to defend the full access to property and contract, those foundations of American legality, for Black Americans.

As the *Civil Rights Cases* illustrate, to neglect Black constitutional authorship is to get one's legal analysis wrong. And likewise, to neglect Black action in

---

[34] M Sinha, *The Slave's Cause: A History of Abolition* (Yale University Press, 2017) 313–16, 325–30; see also M Peeples, 'Creating Political Authority: The Role of the Antebellum Black Press in the Political Mobilization and Empowerment of African Americans' (2008) 34 *Journalism History* 76, 80–82.

[35] M Robison Delany, *The Condition, Elevation, Emigration, and Destiny of the Colored People of the United States Politically Considered* (Published by the Author, 1852) 26–29.

[36] F Douglass, 'Citizenship and the Spirit of Caste' in JW Blassingame (ed), *The Frederick Douglass Papers. Ser. 1 Vol. 3: Speeches, Debates and Interviews 1855–63* (Yale University Press, 1985) 208–12.

the building of the American rule of law is to leave aside key material that would help us understand what the rule of law means in this country.

However, the analysis in this book is still partially incomplete even with respect to that critical mission. In particular, emphasising the Black liberation movement through American history not only neglects the voices of other activists for liberation and constitutional authors – particularly the distinctive voices of Native Americans and of women – including Black women – speaking as women rather than or (intersectionally) in addition to as subjects of racial ascriptions – but also in a deeper sense provides a partial view even of Black liberation itself; for Black freedom movements have often adopted self-consciously solidaristic forms, both appealing to international freedom movements (starting at least since Haiti tore off the chains of slavery) and defending the rights of others who have been subject to American oppression. It is no coincidence, for example, that Douglass supported women's suffrage and opposed Chinese Exclusion, which he connected to the exclusion of Black Americans and Native Americans.[37] That solidarity was strategic as well as moral: consider that Delany advocated Black emigration to Central America in part on the basis of the recognition that those who currently lived in that region were natural allies, for both had been victims of American empire, and both had been disenfranchised on account of race.[38] I have done what I can to reflect this broader framework of liberation constitutional authorship, but there is more to be done.

WHERE WE'RE GOING

The first several chapters are broadly historical in orientation, although not in methodology. Chapter one begins with the intellectual framework of America's rule of law at its origins, offering a reading of the founding-era rule of law through the idea of property rights as the fulcrum around which legal personality and membership turn and of slavery as the foundational paradox of property rights and the rule of law. Chapter two continues the discussion of slavery through an interpretation of the Fugitive Slave Acts as defiance of the American rule of law ideals of judicial independence, due process, and empowered juries, but also as inevitable consequences of the incentives created by a system of legal caste.

The next portion of the book turns to a close examination of the relationship between Black American constitutional agency and the American rule of

---

[37] N Knowles Bromell, *The Powers of Dignity: The Black Political Philosophy of Frederick Douglass* (Duke University Press, 2021) 159–60; J Hooker, '"A Black Sister to Massachusetts": Latin America and the Fugitive Democratic Ethos of Frederick Douglass' (2015) 109 *American Political Science Review* 690, 696–97.

[38] MR Delany, 'Political Destiny of the Colored Race on the American Continent' in RS Levine (ed), *Martin R. Delany, A Documentary Reader* (University of North Carolina Press 2003) 245–79, 268.

• law. Chapter three focuses on the most significant innovation in the actual text of our Constitution driven by the Black struggle for inclusion: the Fourteenth Amendment's written guarantees of both the procedural/formal and the substantive sides of the rule of law. Chapter four discusses the failed promise of Reconstruction and the demands and achievements of the Civil Rights Movement through the lens of the rule of law.

The final two chapters focus on problems of the rule of law and executive power. Chapter five discusses the overall critique of executive power in the United States through the lenses of police and prosecutors and their arbitrary power in the criminal justice system – and its continuation of lawless Black oppression – and of the President's power arbitrary power over anything that might be characterised as 'foreign affairs' or 'national security'. Chapter six is an extended examination of immigration law and its reproduction of older patterns of legal exclusion from both slavery and Indian removal, as well as its status as a kind of limit case of arbitrary executive power.

This book's conclusion looks forward to the future. The United States also has a vigorous programme of promoting the rule of law abroad; can we view that programme as credible given its own struggles to achieve lawful governance? Can it even maintain such legal order as it has? This volume concludes by calling for egalitarian reforms to permit the United States to fulfil its own ambitions as well as its global image to truly become a community under law.

This book is simultaneously impossible and necessary. Impossible because it attempts to provide a panoptic view of that thing which we might call the American rule of law both in its contemporary instantiations and failures and in its historical roots – such a task can't be done right in a lousy couple of hundred pages, and I apologise to the reader who will be forced to fill in many gaps in the exposition. But necessary because only such an approach can throw a badly-needed bucket of ice water on a variety of mistaken ideas about the contemporary status of the United States as a rule of law state.

Most importantly, I hope this book can contribute to the end of a conventional narrative which represents prominent US failures of legality – most notably those associated with the post-2001 War on Terror – as a kind of aberrant departure from a long and consistent tradition of legal fidelity. In fact, the best understanding of the American rule of law recognises that it has long reflected contestations over the bounds of the legal community in which persons and associated places defined as outside the scope of American legality are not entitled to the protections of the rule of law at all.

For the most salient example of that continuity: in *Boumediene v Bush*, the Supreme Court rejected the government's argument that the writ of habeas corpus did not extend to accused terrorists held in Guantanamo Bay.[39] But the attempt to use Guantanamo as a legal black hole was no novelty: a decade

---

[39] *Boumediene v Bush* 553 US 723 (2008).

before 9/11, the government had successfully convinced the Eleventh Circuit to permit it to deprive Haitian refugees whom it had interdicted at sea and held at Guantanamo of any procedural rights under either immigration law or general administrative law.[40] A full century before the Bush Administration resorted to 'waterboarding', US soldiers were court-martialled for administering the 'water cure' in their occupation of the Philippines.[41] The theory of 'unlawful combatants' used by the Bush Administration to justify deviation from the laws of war was pioneered by an American general in the Philippines who said that 'those who engaged in guerrilla warfare divested themselves of the character of soldiers, and if captured could be denied the privileges of prisoners of war'.[42]

It's impossible not to think that the government took lessons from the legal exclusion of Haitian refugees and its colonial adventures in the Philippines when it violated the Constitution and detainees' fundamental human rights in the War on Terror; only a panoptic view of the American rule of law and its connection to the borders of membership can permit us to see the further debts that the legal tools for the exclusion of migrants like the Haitian refugees owe to the legacy of slavery and Indian removal.

---

[40] *Haitian Refugee Center v Baker* 953 F3d 1498, 1505-09 (11th Cir 1992); see GL Neuman, 'Anomalous Zones' (1996) 48 *Stanford Law Review* 1197; W Kidane, 'The Alienage Spectrum Disorder: The Bill of Rights from Chinese Exclusion to Guantanamo' (2010) 20 *Berkeley La Raza Law Journal* 89. Further illustrating the possibility for theoretical continuity between slavery, immigration, and the war on terror, Kato uses Neuman's theory of anomalous zones to characterise the South under lynch law. D Kato, *Liberalizing Lynching: Building a New Racialized State* (Oxford University Press, 2016) 124–31.

[41] RE Welch Jr, 'American Atrocities in the Philippines The Indictment and the Response' (1974) 43 *Pacific Historical Review* 233, 235; G Mettraux, 'US Courts-Martial and the Armed Conflict in the Philippines (1899–1902): Their Contribution to National Case Law on War Crimes' (2003) 1 *Journal of International Criminal Justice* 135, 143–46.

[42] Mettraux (n 41) 145.

1

Madison's Theory of General Law versus Property and Slavery

IN FEDERALIST 57, James Madison articulated a version of the rule of law demand of generality that would be echoed almost two centuries later by Friedrich Hayek: freedom is preserved by preventing legislators from passing laws that do not apply to themselves.[1] But Madison tied his 'Constitution of Liberty' to popular sovereignty:

> I will add, as a fifth circumstance in the situation of the House of Representatives, restraining them from oppressive measures, that they can make no law which will not have its full operation on themselves and their friends, as well as on the great mass of the society.

> This has always been deemed one of the strongest bonds by which human policy can connect the rulers and the people together. It creates between them that communion of interests and sympathy of sentiments, of which few governments have furnished examples; but without which every government degenerates into tyranny. If it be asked, what is to restrain the House of Representatives from making legal discriminations in favor of themselves and a particular class of the society? I answer: the genius of the whole system; the nature of just and constitutional laws; and above all, the vigilant and manly spirit which actuates the people of America, a spirit which nourishes freedom, and in return is nourished by it. If this spirit shall ever be so far debased as to tolerate a law not obligatory on the legislature, as well as on the people, the people will be prepared to tolerate any thing but liberty. Such will be the relation between the House of Representatives and their constituents. Duty, gratitude, interest, ambition itself, are the chords by which they will be bound to fidelity and sympathy with the great mass of the people.

The American Founders had recent experience with legislators who enacted oppressive laws that didn't apply to themselves: one of the main precipitating factors of the American Revolution was special taxation for the colonies, even though Parliament was entirely composed of representation from the English metropole. (Every American schoolchild learns 'no taxation without representation' as the slogan of the Revolution.) The Stamp Act of 1765 is the most famous example. It imposed a fee on effectively every legal act to be done by an

---

[1] FA Hayek, *The Constitution of Liberty* (University of Chicago Press, 1960) 155.

American by requiring tax stamps to be on every piece of paper used for such ordinary tasks as filing a document in court, accepting a public office, carrying out a land survey, giving a bond of debt, and many other acts.[2] Strictly speaking, stamp taxes themselves were not novel or unique to the colonies, as there had been stamp taxes in England proper at least since 1694.[3] However, it appears that the American stamp act was somewhat broader in scope, and, at any rate, the real novelty, and the piece which would not have been permitted in England, was the use of the vice-admiralty courts to enforce such an internal tax – a point which I will discuss further in the next chapter.[4]

To understand Madison's Federalist 57 argument, we must attend to a classical theoretical binary in the intellectual history of the American founding. In that historical period, the United States occupied a position of intellectual tension between two ways of viewing a citizen's relationship to the state that are traditionally called 'republican' and 'liberal' – and many of the complexities of our constitutional institutions can be seen as the product of the cross-pollination of those two sets of ideas and their development through time.[5]

On the republican way of thinking, reaching the constitutional framers through the likes of Harrington and Montesquieu, the individual citizen is a

---

[2] ES Morgan, *Prologue to Revolution: Sources and Documents on the Stamp Act Crisis, 1764–1766* (Norton, 1973) 35 et seq.

[3] S Dowell, *A History and Explanation of the Stamp Duties: Containing Remarks on the Origin of Stamp Duties, a History of the Duties in This Country ... An Explanation of the System and Administration of the Tax, Observations on the Stamp Duties in Foreign Countries and the Stamp Laws at Present in Force in the United Kingdom, with Notes, Appendices, and a Copious Index* (Butterworths, 1873) 16.

[4] The use of admiralty jurisdiction for tax enforcement 'was a principle, however, that Englishmen had successfully resisted in the past and that could not have been applied in England itself without raising a storm of protest'. ES Morgan and HM Morgan, *The Stamp Act Crisis: Prologue to Revolution* (University of North Carolina Press, 1995) 73.

[5] By making that statement, I begin this book with a framework that may seem obsolete, even passé, to cutting edge constitutional scholars and historians: this chapter situates the intellectual tension at the founding of the United States in a theoretical binary between republicanism and liberalism largely following mid-20th-century historians such as Gordon Wood, Bernard Bailyn, and John Pocock; a historical tradition which spawned a kind of 'republican revival' in constitutional scholarship toward the end of that century. Since then, however, historians have complicated the question rather substantially, and constitutional scholarship has partly moved on. See discussion in J Gienapp, 'Beyond Republicanism, Back to Constitutionalism: The Creation of the American Republic at Fifty' (2020) 93 *The New England Quarterly* 275. As early as the 1990s, historians were already shaking their head sadly at the belated adoption by academic lawyers of the republican framework. GE White, 'Reflections on the Republican Revival: Interdisciplinary Scholarship in the Legal Academy' (1994) 6 *Yale Journal of Law & the Humanities* 1. Yet I heavily rely on Gordon Wood in this chapter, and – perhaps also disappointing to cutting edge constitutional scholars steeped in modern techniques such as corpus linguistics – also rely heavily on the Federalist Papers. But to the extent constitutional theory has moved past a previously myopic emphasis on those sources and theories, it is only because of their strength – they have receded into the background of more contemporary work. In examining a particular dimension of American constitutionalism and politics, its orientation toward the rule of law, which has not yet been the subject of focused attention through such an analytic lens, recourse to the previously hegemonic framework in combination with modern rule of law theory is appropriate.

kind of repository of civic virtue who would subordinate his (with, alas, the pronoun used intentionally) private interests to the public interest; elected representatives would share a universal conception of the public good with the people. Traditionally, republican theory is associated with a civic conception of liberty according to which the most important sense of freedom is political freedom.[6] It is also associated with ideas such as separation of powers and the 'mixed' or 'compound' republic; small, homogeneous states; and the simultaneous endorsement of property qualifications for voting to ensure independence and civic virtue in the electorate and egalitarian efforts to promote equal property ownership to mitigate the corrupting influence of wealth. At heart, republicanism is the ideology of the yeoman farmer-citizen. The people are an organic whole with substantial common interests, the duty of the individual is to suppress their private interest in favour of the public interest, and the conception of liberty that most matters is the political liberty of a self-governing people, not individual liberty in the sense of the freedom to pursue one's private good.[7] The republicanism of the framers of America's constitution can be seen, for example, in John Jay's Federalist 2, an encomium to 'one united people – a people descended from the same ancestors, speaking the same language, professing the same religion, attached to the same principles of government, very similar in their manners and customs' which declares that the land and the people 'seem to have been made for each other'.

An important recent gloss on the republican view of the founding, and one which has heavily influenced this book, is Aziz Rana's account of settler ideology.[8] For Rana, American civic (ie, republican) freedom as independence rested on an imperial expansionist drive – one which could secure the predicates of republican citizenship for all (white men), where those predicates are understood in terms of a high-status economic role revolving around landownership. Such a conception of freedom rests on the unfreedom of others, for the land, and the people to do the low-status, dependent, work on it, must come from somewhere – ie, from Native Americans and the enslaved, respectively.

By contrast, the liberal way of thinking, which reached the framers primarily through writers such as John Locke, is more familiar as the dominant ideology of the contemporary United States. It sees the individual as having a right to pursue his or her private interests without interference from the state, and, in conjunction with that idea, emphasises a conception of liberty as non-interference with those private interests and, in effect, the capacity to ignore the state if one desires just so long as one obeys the rules it lays down. The contemporary literature on the rule of law is replete with liberal assumptions; most famously,

---

[6] Although modern neorepublican historians have argued that it ought to be associated with a conception of liberty as nondomination.

[7] GS Wood, *The Creation of the American Republic, 1776–1787*, 2nd edn (University of North Carolina Press, 1998) 57–65.

[8] A Rana, *The Two Faces of American Freedom* (Harvard University Press, 2014).

Frederich Hayek's account of the importance of the rule of law to liberty in *The Constitution of Liberty* is liberal through and through, and does much to drive the contemporary emphasis on ideas such as predictability as core aims of the rule of law. The liberal view is rather more compatible with a diversity of views and interests in the public, and rather less demanding on civic virtue. Property rights are important on liberal views as well, because property, when guarded by robust liberal protections, provides a determinate sphere of autonomy through which individuals can pursue their private goals. At heart, liberalism is the ideology of the aspirational wealthy merchant. And its influence on America's constitutional framers can also be seen in the Federalist Papers, perhaps most saliently in Federalist 10, Madison's famous disquisition on faction, which emphasises not the unity of the American people but their unavoidable differences, in religion, in abilities, and in wealth, and the conflicts which arise among 'A landed interest, a manufacturing interest, a mercantile interest, a monied interest, with many lesser interests.'

In Federalist 57, Madison appears to straddle the liberal/republican binary. His account of how the rule of (general) law is to be preserved rests on the presumption of a common interest between the people and their representatives – and hence implicitly, on a fairly homogenous conception of the public, like the one traditionally associated with classical republican political thought. For a liberal with a presumption of social diversity, it's hard to see how the argument from democratic representation to laws protecting the interests of minorities could possibly work: imagine, for example, a House of Representatives composed entirely of Christians and the application of a law requiring work on Saturday and rest on Sunday to Jews. But a republican who assumes a homogenous English Protestant civic community would not naturally focus on that sort of diversity. Yet, in the same document, Madison appears to move in a more liberal direction in his conception of the value of this generality, via the articulation of a kind of libertarian fear of oppressive laws that might regulate the behaviour of the people but not of the government.

From the rule of law standpoint, we can read Federalist 10 as an answer to that worry, and to another obvious objection to the republican side of Federalist 57. To wit: a dominant view of the period, following Montesquieu, suggested that large countries could not sustain republican governments because republicanism depended on close relations among the people and their representatives (a kind of dense social capital, in contemporary terms), which would be much harder to achieve in a large country.[9]

But Madison was not ignorant of the diversity in his political world – particularly the diversity between rich and poor, which could easily lead either group to pass laws perceived as oppressive by the other (land reforms for the

---

[9] See CM Kenyon, 'Men of Little Faith: The Anti-Federalists on the Nature of Representative Government' (1955) 12 *The William and Mary Quarterly* 3, 6–10.

first, debtor's prisons for the second, perhaps). The framing generation was also obviously aware of disparate interests between the states.[10] Federalist 10 is taught to American schoolchildren as Madison's theory of how the Constitution prevents 'faction'. But, in the context of Federalist 57, we can understand it as a second take at why Congress could be trusted to act like a genuine representative of the public good as a whole in enacting general laws. Not, on this particular Madisonian argument, because the people in fact have homogeneous interests, for Madison recognises in Federalist 10 that this is not the case. Thus, he draws on the Lockean rule of law objection to a person being judge in their own case to explain the risk of abuses like steep taxes on the property of other factions but not on the faction represented by a majority of Congress. Instead, his response to the worry is his theory of enlargement, according to which larger constituencies are safer against faction, because they are more likely to have qualified representatives available and because demagoguery and conspiracy are harder to pull off in larger constituencies. Moreover, he argues that larger constituencies are likely to contain a larger variety of interests, and hence to be more likely to resist capture by a single interest controlling a majority of voters. The same argument applies at least in principle for Congress's representation of the entire nation: because it contains representatives from a vast number of interest groups, it might arguably be more resistant to capture, and hence more obliged to enact truly general laws.

THE SPECIAL POSITION OF PROPERTY

There's still an obvious problem. Even if we grant republican assumptions about common fundamental interests, and even if 'enlargement' could prevent faction within the various classes who elected the House of Representatives, the Federalist 57 claim is quite implausible. After all, the American constitutional structure manifestly failed to prevent caste legislation: the entire country began as one giant legal discrimination in favour of whites against the enslaved, against Native Americans, and, in different respects, against women as well. Even among white men, early American suffrage (and hence access to the representative mechanisms that were supposed to protect the generality of legislation) was notoriously exclusionary – property qualifications were widespread in the early constitutional period, and even when those were repealed, they were replaced with laws that excluded 'paupers'.[11] There were unquestionably differences in interest between the enfranchised and all those classes of persons.

The case of the propertyless is particularly important. From the modern point of view, we intuitively think of those without property as full members

---

[10] Wood (n 7) 356, 527.
[11] RJ Steinfeld, 'Property and Suffrage in the Early American Republic' (1989) 41 *Stanford Law Review* 335.

of the political community. And while it's easy to recognise the moral failures of the framers in excluding women, Native Americans, and Black Americans from suffrage, and hence from the democratic guarantee of general law – we're familiar with misogyny and racism – the exclusion of the propertyless isn't as comprehensible in 2021. For that reason, unpacking it will be particularly fruitful in making sense of how property was and continues to be foundational to the American conception of the rule of law.

The rhetoric surrounding property qualifications for the electoral franchise drew on a republican conception of independence according to which holding property shields a citizen from domination by others, and only the vote of such an independent citizen can be trusted. Hence, justifications for the exclusion of the propertyless from the franchise referred to their lack of an independent will.[12] At least in some of the early state constitutions, higher amounts of property also permitted the identification of a wiser or more virtuous class of citizens, as well as and eventually standing in for an interest in itself – and for both reasons seemed suitable for justifying the existence of a quasi-aristocratic legislative upper house.[13] Enfranchisement of the propertyless could be seen as futile as well as pernicious – pernicious because the propertyless were likely to simply vote how their patrons commanded, but also futile because, already being under the domination of others, there's a sense in which they already lacked the autonomy which representative democracy as well as well as the rule of law were meant to protect.[14]

The conception of property as independence and, with that independence, a kind of civic virtue had longstanding origins, tracing at least back to Florentine humanist republicanism and then Harrington. Pocock explains:

> The Englishman had begun to envisage himself as civic individual through the use of Aristotelian and civic humanist categories, which required among other things that there be a material foundation, the equivalent of Aristotle's oikos, for his independence, leisure and virtue. The nature of this equivalent had been described for him, first by Machiavelli in terms of arms, second by Harrington in terms of property; and the realities of the seventeenth-century social structure had established as paradigmatic the image of the freeholder, founded upon real or landed property which was inheritable rather than marketable, was protected by the ancient sanctions of the common law, and brought with it membership in the related structures of the militia and the parliamentary electorate, thus guaranteeing civic virtue.[15]

[12] ibid 337–44; Wood (n 7) 168–69.
[13] Wood (n 7) 218, 244.
[14] See also B Young Welke, *Law and the Borders of Belonging in the Long Nineteenth Century United States* (Cambridge University Press, 2010) on how the concept of property wove through the inequalities and exclusions of early America, encompassing not just race but also gender, nativity, and abledness.
[15] JGA Pocock, *The Machiavellian Moment: Florentine Political Thought and the Atlantic Republican Tradition*, 2nd pbk edn (Princeton University Press, 2003) 450.

This conception of the republican importance of property also contributes to an explanation of why the framing generation's individual rights so often seem to be oriented around the protection of property, as with the formulation 'life, liberty, and property', as in the Due Process clauses of the Fifth and (later) Fourteenth Amendments, and, in thinly veiled form, in the Declaration of Independence.[16]

Because property was a precondition of independence and full citizenship, its protection was a paramount concern of the rule of law. A state that could deprive a citizen of their property could reduce them to a subordinate social, economic, and political status.

Property was not only a precondition for full citizenship, citizenship was originally a precondition for property ownership. At the dawn of the United States, the states applied common-law doctrines restricting alien rights to own real property.[17] In a kind of yeoman republic, this makes some intuitive sense: if property ownership is a marker of citizenship and civic virtue, extensive property ownership by non-members may seem to threaten the integrity of that relationship – or may simply deprive citizens of the opportunity to attain full status through pricing them out of landownership. Perhaps unsurprisingly (given the lack of land scarcity and need for labour) such laws began to fall away with the growth of the west, before rising again with nativist prejudices in the Chinese Exclusion era.[18] As late as 1923, the Supreme Court appealed to republican ideas about land and civic virtue in upholding a Californian law excluding Japanese people (and others ineligible under openly race-based federal law of the time for citizenship) from land ownership:

> We agree with the court below that 'It is obvious that one who is not a citizen and cannot become one lacks an interest in, and the power to effectually work for the welfare of, the State, and, so lacking, the State may rightfully deny him the right to own and lease real estate within its boundaries. If one incapable of citizenship may lease or own real estate, it is within the realm of possibility that every foot of land within the State might pass to the ownership or possession of noncitizens.'... The quality and allegiance of those who own, occupy and use the farm lands within its borders are matters of highest importance, and affect the safety and power of the State itself.[19]

---

[16] For an account of the 'pursuit of happiness' which centres property and, indeed, even reaffirms in modern times the claim that possession of property makes one independent and hence particularly capable of serving as a democratic citizen, see LW Levy, 'Property as a Human Right' (1988) 5 *Constitutional Commentary* 169, 175–76.

[17] A Brownell Tirres, 'Property Outliers: Non-Citizens, Property Rights and State Power' (2012) 27 *Georgetown Immigration Law Journal* 77, 91–2; PJ Price, 'Alien Land Restrictions in the American Common Law: Exploring the Relative Autonomy Paradigm' (1999) 43 *American Journal of Legal History* 152; A Brownell Tirres, 'Ownership without Citizenship: The Creation of Noncitizen Property Rights' (2013) 19 *Michigan Journal of Race & Law* 1. According to Justice Story's discussion of the common-law rule inherited from England in *Fairfax's Devisee v Hunter's Lessee* 11 US 603, 619–20 (1812), an alien could purchase but not inherit land, and the sovereign had the right to dispossess the alien's land at will.

[18] Tirres (n 17) 94–95. Of course, the 'growth of the west' was nothing more than the removal of one particular category of noncitizens, namely the Native Americans, from their land and replacing them with citizen settlers.

[19] *Terrace v Thompson* 263 US 197, 220–21 (1923) (internal citation omitted).

Vestiges of these laws persist today. As recently as 1980, the John Marshall Law Review could publish an article calling for federal legislation restricting foreign land ownership, and there are alien-restrictive land laws on the books in the majority of states even into the twenty-first century.[20]

However, even as property provided the foundation (as it were) of citizenship, there's also an inherent tension between some of the revolutionary and founding-era ideas surrounding property and the rule of law and a republican conception of equal citizenship. For legal equality even among property holding citizens – especially if that equality is protected by equal shares of democratic suffrage, as on the Federalist 57 argument – may also pose a threat to concentrations of property.

The tension between legal and civic equality and the protection of property was a basic background problem of the Constitution (and much of the rest of this book traces it through to the present). Consider state senates, sometimes openly understood to be a way to provide substantial property holders with special representation and a veto over legislation that might otherwise expropriate them – Madison himself characterises state senates that way in Federalist 54. On the one hand, surely such a protection against expropriation is itself part of the rule of law. But on the other, because that protection against expropriation entailed giving the wealthy disproportionate power in government, it also gave them the prospect of using that power to oppress the less wealthy, and undermined the notion of equal citizens on which republican conceptions of civic virtue and common interest rested.[21]

The same fundamental conflict was the constitutional heart of the problem of slavery from the standpoint of many Northerners: by giving the slave states disproportionate power in government to protect their 'property' in humans – such as with the three-fifths clause, which granted the slave states Congressional representation on the partial basis of the enslaved people whom they held, although the slaves obviously could not vote – the Constitution also gave them the power to dominate the North. This is what abolitionists came to call the 'slave power': the fact that their government was structurally rigged to empower slaveholders to preserve slavery-as-property.[22]

Another way to think about the problem is that strong property rights protections and popular government can only be wholly compatible under conditions of relative economic equality – but the revolutionary generation recognised that the aggressive protection of private property leads to the creation of wealth, which undermines the equality on which republican virtue is founded.[23]

---

[20] RL Bell and JD Savage, 'Our Land is Your Land: Ineffective State Restriction of Alien Land Ownership and the Need for Federal Legislation' (1980) 13 *John Marshall Law Review* 679; Tirres (n 17) 97–101.

[21] Wood (n 7) 221.

[22] LL Richards, *The Slave Power: The Free North and Southern Domination, 1780–1860* (Louisiana State University Press, 2000).

[23] Wood (n 7) 65.

Perhaps it is for this reason that classical republican influences like Harrington had favoured land reform legislation to distribute property on an egalitarian basis, and prominent members of the framing generation such as Adams and Jefferson favoured similar legislative measures, such as the reform of inheritance laws and the distribution of western lands.[24] Such policies were implemented at least in part and at some points, by the early Americans.[25]

The Affinity between Republican Property and Liberal Property

For a country whose normative foundations oscillate so noticeably between republicanism and liberalism it is notable that the legal protection for property might shift seamlessly between them as well. In liberalism's emphasis on individual rights to pursue a person's independent conception of the good, property can serve as the primary means by which those individual conceptions of the good may be pursued – and hence American solicitude toward property also invites interpretation as a built-in bias toward more capitalistic versions of individual legal rights, which emphasise the liberties of the market over those of the forum.[26]

In one of his more liberal moods, Madison even saw other individual rights as mere flavours of property. In a 1792 essay simply entitled 'Property', he claims that property has both narrow and broad senses, the narrow sense being the conventional physical things over which one exercises 'dominion'; and the broad sense something like a modern conception of equal liberty: 'every thing to which a man may attach a value and have a right; and which leaves to every one else the like advantage'.[27] For Madison, it was possible to understand even the most historically salient noneconomic liberal right, religious toleration, as a subspecies of property: a person 'has a property of peculiar value in his religious opinions, and in the profession and practice dictated by them'. Accordingly, he argues that governments should protect freedoms like individual religious liberty because a government that fails to do so violates property rights just as if it expropriated their land or burgled their houses.

Madison's caveat about 'like advantage' resembles Locke's famous proviso, which permits the acquisition of private property in a state of nature just so long

[24] GS Alexander, 'Time and Property in the American Republican Legal Culture' (1991) 66 *New York University Law Review* 273, 291–99.

[25] ibid 313.

[26] Alexander, ibid 328, associates the shift from republican to liberal views of property in American law with the Scottish Enlightenment and the shift from land to more commercial conceptions of property. On the influence of Locke's conception of property as well, see Schultz, 'The Locke Republican Debate and the Paradox of Property Rights in Early American Jurisprudence' (1991) 13 *Western New England Law Review* 155.

[27] J Madison, 'Property', available in *The Founders' Constitution*, Vol 1, ch 16, Document 23, press-pubs.uchicago.edu/founders/documents/v1ch16s23.html (The University of Chicago Press).

as 'there is enough, and as good, left in common for others'.[28] Madison also sounds quite Lockean when he says that 'Government is instituted to protect property of every sort', and also offers a kind of foreshadowing of the early twentieth century *Lochner*-era constitutional rejection of economic regulation, arguing that government violates property rights when it legislates anticompetitive market regulations and high taxes – in part on the basis that such regulations amount to invasions of a person's property right in their own labour.

In the contemporary period, from the fully-fledged liberal standpoint of the contemporary American rule of law, property rights are widely seen as at its centre.[29] Thus, in the United States, more so than many other countries, there is a real sense that private property comes with a domain of rights not just against other citizens, but against certain kinds of government regulation. We can see this, for example, in our 'regulatory takings' doctrine, under which government land use rules for things like environmental purposes are sometimes classified as 'takings' of property under the Fifth Amendment – that is, expropriations of property in the traditional language of the rule of law – and hence as requiring compensation.[30] Leading 'classical liberal' Richard Epstein has argued that strong private property rights are instrumental in achieving the constraint of state power by reducing the scope of discretionary government decision.[31]

Republican Property and Slavery

But the unjust face of property and its threat to the popular protections of the rule of law cannot be ignored. Whether through a liberal or a republican lens the limitation of representation to property holders – let alone the far more dramatic exclusions, particularly of slaves – undermined the claim that 'communion of interests and sympathy of sentiments' could ensure that Congress would only make general laws. It is true, perhaps, that thanks to the House of Representatives Congress could not make law that applied to ordinary property holders but not to elected officials. But they easily could make law that applied to non-property holders but not to property holders. And, of course,

---

[28] Second Treatise, ch 5, s 27.

[29] This began early: Scheiber suggests that the protection of 'vested rights', centrally including vested property rights, was 'an absorbing concern for the Supreme Court in the early history of the republic'. H Scheiber, 'Public Rights and the Rule of Law in American Legal History' (1984) 72 *California Law Review* 217, 218–19. Tamanaha views the protection of property as the central ideal of the 'classical liberal'/laissez-faire period of American jurisprudence. B Tamanaha, 'The Dark Side of the Relationship Between the Rule of Law and Liberalism' (2008) 3 *New York University Journal of Law & Liberty* 516, 519–21.

[30] eg, *Lucas v South Carolina Coastal Council* 505 US 1003 (1992). See J Waldron, *The Rule of Law and the Measure of Property* (Cambridge University Press, 2012) for discussion.

[31] R Epstein, *Design for Liberty: Private Property, Public Administration, and the Rule of Law* (Harvard University Press, 2011) 95.

they could make law that brutally oppressed people who were held as property. Regardless of what Madison believed would happen when he wrote Federalist 57, the representative character of the government did not keep the Slave Power from enacting the Fugitive Slave Act of 1850, widely and correctly believed in the North to be oppressive and to savagely disregard the interests of free Black Americans and also the political liberties of all Northerners who wished to make their own decisions in their own states about such things as freedom and kidnapping.

Alas, the framers' vision of themselves as creating a system that could generate laws applicable to all rested ineluctably on their foundational unwillingness to actually think of the enslaved and the subordinated as members of the political community. Again Wood's account of American republicanism casts the problem into sharp relief: he attributes to the revolutionary generation a self-image of themselves, drawn from European perceptions of America, as egalitarian and free of social caste, a society in which 'almost every man is a freeholder' and in which '[n]o man held his land by feudal tenure, for "every cultivator" was "lord of his soil"'.[32] But that self-image was total nonsense, as the South was politically and economically dominated by a class of massive landowners relying on enslaved labour to carry out the actual cultivation.[33] And this contradiction existed in the very persons of the founders – most infamously, in Thomas Jefferson, who simultaneously defended republican theories of the relationship between property ownership, equality, and civic virtue while owning an immense wealth in plantation land and slaves.[34]

From the contemporary point of view, it seems bizarre that Thomas Jefferson could write a letter contrasting the inherent virtue of 'those who labor in the earth' with the 'dependence' of those who were employed in manufacturing, even while those who laboured on the earth he owned were kept in the most abject state of dependence known to humanity.[35] It's understandable from the standpoint of Rana's theory of settler ideology, but only if we force ourselves to remember that the enslaved weren't even eligible for republican virtue on that ideological framework. Similarly, it requires a kind of wilful self-delusion to, with John Adams, contrast a slave state with a feudal 'tyranny' and conclude that the former somehow comes out ahead.[36] While many in the revolutionary generation were aware that the vision of America as a bunch of hardy virtuous smallholder farmers didn't match the reality, and particularly didn't match the

---

[32] Wood (n 7) 100.

[33] Evidence from economic history shows an immense concentration of wealth in large slaveholders in 1860; evidence from the end of the 18th century is scarcer, but L Soltow, 'Economic Inequality in the United States in the Period from 1790 to 1860' (1971) 31 *The Journal of Economic History* 822, argues that the degree of inequality was similar.

[34] SN Katz, 'Thomas Jefferson and the Right to Property in Revolutionary America' (1976) 19 *The Journal of Law & Economics* 467, 467, 473–74, 483.

[35] ibid 473.

[36] Alexander (n 26) 309–10.

reality of the Southern planter elite, their worries focused on things like monarchical influences and extravagant fashion.[37] One would have hoped that they might be a bit more worried about the fact that the people who did the actual work in their economy were not counted as members of the republican polis at all, except, of course, in the infamous proportion of 3/5 for the purposes of representative apportionment to their masters. And even when they favoured land redistribution, that hardly seemed to show any solicitude to the enslaved, or to Native Americans, or to women excluded from political power.[38]

The deepest contradiction of all between the republican and later liberal emphasis on property as the bulwark of a free society and the institution of slavery was not merely that slaves were disenfranchised and denied (with some complications) the capacity to hold property. Rather, it is that slaves *were* property. And property, in the framing conception, was a kind of 'absolute dominion', what Blackstone described as 'despotic'.[39] Madison, too, used that term 'dominion' in his essay on property. Necessarily, then, slaves could not be the independent republican agents deemed suitably virtuous for citizenship – if being subject to the will of an employer or the regulations of a pauper made one unfit for republican citizenship, how much more so if the control another was definitionally entitled to exercise over one was outright 'despotic'?

There's a vicious kind of circularity at the heart of republican slavery: a slave was dependent, so they couldn't be a citizen with the power to hold property or otherwise protect their interests under law; the slave's lack of citizenship and property in turn made them dependent. Indeed, the republican character of the United States made slavery more robust as well as more brutal. This is a core insight of recent comparative work by Alejandro De La Fuente and Ariela Gross: in a regime like Cuba where traditional monarchical social hierarchies ruled, slaves could be permitted to obtain freedom on an individual basis (and, as I read their account, some degree of softening of the treatment of the enslaved as a group) without threatening the overall hierarchical status of the master class; by contrast, in the United States, such measures appeared to pose the risk of raising the formerly enslaved to the same status of free and equal citizenship as whites, and hence was more robustly resisted.[40]

---

[37] Wood (n 7) 109.

[38] To be sure, some antifederalists at least identified the corruption of the idea of representation captured in the three-fifths clause. D Waldstreicher, *Slavery's Constitution: From Revolution to Ratification* (Hill and Wang, 2009) 116–24.

[39] I take the phrase 'absolute dominion' from KJ Vandevelde, 'The New Property of the Nineteenth Century: The Development of the Modern Concept of Property' (1980) 29 *Buffalo Law Review* 325, 330–31, who also quotes the relevant part of Blackstone, and who notes, ibid, that 'Blackstone divided all legal rights into two categories: rights over persons and rights over things. The law of property concerned only the latter'. So, on the Blackstonian conception, slaves would be things to the early Americans.

[40] A de la Fuente and AJ Gross, *Becoming Free, Becoming Black: Race, Freedom, and Law in Cuba, Virginia, and Louisiana* (Cambridge University Press, 2020) 130, 180–81, 221–23.

SLAVERY AS LAWLESSNESS

I contend that slavery as a regime was incompatible with the rule of law from the start. This is a conceptual claim: to have slaves is to identify a class of persons who are wholly excluded from legal personality and protection. As Patterson argued in his influential account of the institution, socially and legally a slave is a kind of walking dead: the condition of slavery is inevitably represented as an alternative to the death which would have otherwise been the slave's lot, where the master holds that death in abeyance; as a result, 'the slave had no socially recognised existence outside of his master, he became a social nonperson'.[41] Unsurprisingly, the legal texts of the antebellum period are replete with the parallel proposition that the enslaved (and those racially liable to enslavement) were legal nonpersons as well, most famously captured in the claim of *Dred Scott v Sandford* that Black Americans had been understood by the Constitution's authors as having 'no rights which the white man was bound to respect', and hence could not avail themselves of the protection of the federal courts.

But the generalisation of that claim immediately faces a challenge from the fact that the enslavers understood themselves as a people of law. And even the organisation of slavery helped itself to the forms of law: contracts for the hire of slaves could be enforced in court, slaves could be punished by law for their crimes. Moreover, slaveholders also asserted claims to slaves and defences of slavery against political challenges in the language of the rule of law.

Even the implementation of the slave system's most brutal provisions was wrapped in the language of legalism. Thus, Harriet Jacobs recounts that one would-be slavecatcher characterised his activity not as the kidnapping for profit that it was in reality, but as an act of noble self-subordination to the laws (in terms that eerily resemble Socrates's explanation in Plato's *Crito* of why he must submit to execution): 'There are enough of us here to swear to her identity as your property. I am a patriot, a lover of my country, and I do this as an act of justice to the laws.'[42] Antislavery judges who saw themselves as forced to enforce the enactments reinforcing that institution expressed a (perhaps more sincere, but misguided) version of the same idea.[43]

Yet the intellectual framework of the period also identified the fundamental lawlessness of slavery. Even as the American colonists were brutalising their slaves, they were conducting a revolution under the influence of an idea that intellectual historians have since named 'antityrannicism'. As the term suggests, the rhetoric of antityrannicism identifies slavery and lawlessness in the form of tyranny, but puts the focus in the opposite direction from the one we might

---

[41] O Patterson, *Slavery and Social Death: A Comparative Study* (Harvard University Press, 1982) 5.

[42] H Jacobs in L Maria Child (ed), *Incidents in the Life of a Slave Girl* (Pub For the Author, 1861) 270 (written under the pen name Linda Brent).

[43] See RM Cover, *Justice Accused: Antislavery and the Judicial Process* (Yale University Press, 1975); R Dworkin, 'The Law of the Slave-Catchers' (1975) *Times Literary Supplement* 1437.

expect: revolutionaries under the influence of antityrannicism fought against forms of government identified as tyrannical by wielding the claim that to live under lawless government is to be delivered into a state of slavery.

Antityrannicism was an important part of the intellectual background to the American Revolution.[44] Mary Nyquist has written the most important book on the subject, and she identifies that John Locke was deeply invested in antityrannicism – and that for Locke, a key objection to lawless government was the impossibility of voluntarily agreeing to the 'Absolute, Arbitrary Power' associated with enslavement.[45] On the other side of the race divide, the great Black abolitionist and revolutionary David Walker directly engaged with the intellectual framework of antityrannicism in his famous Appeal to the Coloured Citizens of the World, in which he deployed American rejection of tyranny to motivate a demand for the end to slavery.[46]

Notwithstanding the fact that even the framing generation could identify slavery with lawless tyranny, some contemporary scholars resist the idea that slavery was incompatible with the rule of law. For example, Tushnet accused legal scholars who claim that slavery and basic legal values are incompatible of spouting 'nonsense' and 'Whigishness' on the basis of 'contemporary standards of fairness and justice.'[47]

I disagree with Tushnet: even if the forms of the legal system are used to organise a relationship, to the extent that relationship gives one person the effectively unlimited capacity to do violence to another, then it is force that regulates that relationship, even if a court occasionally decides to describe it in legal terms. As North Carolina Chief Justice Thomas Ruffin said in the infamous case of *State v Mann*:

> We cannot allow the right of the master to be brought into discussion in the Courts of Justice. The slave, to remain a slave, must be made sensible, that there is no appeal from his master; that his power is in no instance, usurped; but is conferred by the laws of man at least, if not by the law of God.[48]

Ruffin further explained that such legally unconstrained power was necessary in order to achieve the 'uncontrolled authority over the body' (ie, unlimited right to do violence) that was in turn necessary to bring it about that the slave 'surrenders his will in implicit obedience to that of another', which in turn was necessary to compel the labour of a person 'doomed in his own person, and his posterity, to live without knowledge, and without the capacity to make any thing

---

[44] eg, L Benton, 'Just Despots: The Cultural Construction of Imperial Constitutionalism' (2013) 9 *Law, Culture and the Humanities* 213.

[45] M Nyquist, *Arbitrary Rule: Slavery, Tyranny, and the Power of Life and Death* (2015) 329–52.

[46] E Duquette, 'Tyranny in America, or, the Appeal to the Coloured Citizens of the World' (2021) 33 *American Literary History* 1.

[47] M Tushnet, *The American Law of Slavery, 1810–1860: Considerations of Humanity and Interest* (Princeton University Press, 1981) 25–26.

[48] *State v Mann* 13 NC 263 (1829).

his own, and to toil that another may reap the fruits'. The mere fact that Ruffin announced that doctrine from the bench of a courtroom while wearing a robe does not make its content any less lawless.

Another way to think of the problem is that 'slave law' was only coherent from what Williams called the 'experiential perspective' of masters.[49] For slaves, there was no such thing; indeed, slaves could not be allowed to know that there might be such a thing or to integrate it into their plans and their lives, and Ruffin explained exactly why: even if there were legal rules constraining masters, the enslaved couldn't be allowed to perceive them lest the totality of enslaver power be undermined thereby.

I will fill out the lawlessness of slavery in more detail. At the grossest level, American slavery could be described as the conjunction of four legal/social facts about the relations between slaves and their masters as well as the rest of the society. First, slaves were considered the property of their masters, and, as property, could be deprived of all other social ties at will, such as by selling them away from their families. Secondly, was the radical unfreedom of slaves, who were subject to the absolute command of their masters and were further denied the social and legal prerequisites of freedom, such as the right to own property or to be literate.[50] Thirdly was the complete or near-complete subjection of the slave to violence at the unrestrained will of the master, a subjection necessary in order to enforce the other facts about slavery, as, of course, no human not subject to extreme violence would ever submit to such a regime (as Ruffin explained). Fourthly was the status hierarchy between masters and slaves; and between those who were subject to slavery and citizens as a body; a hierarchy constituted in part by the prior three facts, but also by a broad-based exclusion of the enslaved from legal rights, and even of free Black Americans in the North from most of the rights of citizenship. The conjunction of those facts achieved Patterson's 'social death': 'the permanent, violent domination of natally alienated and generally dishonored persons'.[51]

Practically (as opposed to legally) speaking, the most important of those facts is the pervasive threat of arbitrary violence. On Patterson's analysis, the 'social death' of slavery is a substitute for (and a social simulacrum of) the physical death to which a slave is subject: the traditional theory of justifiable enslavement is that those who were subject to permissible killing (as in war) may be enslaved instead.[52] Accordingly, across slave societies, slaves typically had

---

[49] P Williams, 'Alchemical Notes: Reconstructing Ideals from Deconstructed Rights' (1987) 22 *Harvard Civil Rights-Civil Liberties Law Review* 401, 417.

[50] Property holding by slaves is further discussed below. On literacy, and on many other legal disabilities, see AB Mitchell, 'Self-Emancipation and Slavery: An Examination of the African American's Quest for Literacy and Freedom' (2008) 2 *Journal of Pan African Studies* 78; J Cornelius, '"We Slipped and Learned to Read": Slave Accounts of the Literacy Process, 1830–1865' (1983) 44 *Phylon* (1960–) 171; B Brander Rasmussen, '"Attended with Great Inconveniences": Slave Literacy and the 1740 South Carolina Negro Act' (2010) 125 *PMLA* 201.

[51] Patterson (n 41) 13.

[52] ibid 5, 38–44.

death continually hanging over their heads, to be inflicted at the master's will – some 75 per cent of slave societies in Patterson's study imposed no or minimal penalties on a master who killed their slave.[53] To the extent American slaves were protected from violence by whites, it was primarily from violence by whites who were not their masters, for, after all, a master may destroy his own property but some third person may not.[54]

Because of the linkage between slavery and status, the power of arbitrary violence necessarily extends, at least in part, to the entire free community against the entire slave community – susceptibility to violence becomes the mark of the enslaved. This is also true of slavery across cultures. The first reference to it of which I am aware comes from Pseudo-Xenophon (also known as the Old Oligarch), in his Constitution of the Athenians, where he contrasts ancient Athens to other (implicitly more virtuous – and implicitly meaning Sparta) polities with reference to the unusual fact that Athenians were not allowed to generally hit slaves: 'Now among the slaves and metics at Athens there is the greatest uncontrolled wantonness; you can't hit them there, and a slave will not stand aside for you.'[55] In other words: Athens was aberrant in virtue of the fact that arbitrary public violence could not be used to demarcate the line between free and slave and enforce subordinate behaviour in slaves by terror. Colonial Virginia did not share Athens's aberration: a law of 1680 provided for 30 lashes for any enslaved person who 'shall presume to lift up his hand in opposition against any christian' – thus suggesting, as Morgan plausibly interprets it, 'that it allowed servants [ie, poor whites] to bully slaves without fear of retaliation'.[56] Similarly, in French colonial Louisiana the law outright instructed whites to do violence to presumptively-enslaved Black strangers encountered on the street who seemed insufficiently respectful.[57]

If the rule of law prohibits anything at all, it prohibits the law authorising one class of people to engage in violence against another for any reason, or no reason at all. Indeed, doing so is the essence of what, in other work, I have called

---

[53] ibid 190–93.

[54] More on this below; for some nuances see A Fede, 'Legitimized Violent Slave Abuse in the American South, 1619–1865: A Case Study of Law and Social Change in Six Southern States' (1985) 29 *American Journal of Legal History* 93.

[55] From the EC Marchant translation, online at the Perseus Project, www.perseus.tufts.edu/hopper/text?doc=Perseus%3atext%3a1999.01.0158.

[56] ES Morgan, *American Slavery, American Freedom: The Ordeal of Colonial Virginia* (2005) 331. This vesting of a de facto arbitrary power of violence in every white person against every slave was not, however, entirely unproblematic even in the South. After all, if one white person could do violence to another white person's slave, they might accidentally or intentionally damage that other's 'property'. This is an important contrast between a system of individually-owned chattel slavery and something like publicly-owned Spartan helotage. T Figueira, 'Helotage and the Spartan Economy', *A Companion to Sparta* (John Wiley & Sons, Ltd, 2017) 566. There was at least the potential, even, sometimes for slave self-defence, albeit under disadvantageous conditions relative to that of whites and with the caveat that random whites were permitted to do violence to slaves owned by another as punishment for 'insolence', as in *State v Jarrott* 23 NC 76 (1840).

[57] Fuente and Gross (n 40) 35.

terror: the use of the power of violence to reduce another to submission and force the other to act out their subordinate status.[58] Although the conventional form of terror is a power vested in state officials – consider the Gestapo or KGB secret police – slave societies are distinctive in part by their formal separation of the class who gets to inflict arbitrary violence from the state. Slave terror is inflicted by owners rather than by lords or soldiers, but it is nonetheless authorised by the state and backed up by the force of the state such that the slaveholder and the state operate hand in hand upon the body of the slave as a person wholly without legal protections.

The dynamic of terror explains why the ability of slaves to sometimes defend themselves could be seen as deeply transformative – a kind of simulacrum of the rule of law. This is the lesson of Frederick Douglass's famous fight with the vicious overseer Covey: 'I found my strong fingers firmly attached to the throat of my cowardly tormentor; as heedless of consequences, at the moment, as though we stood as equals before the law.'[59] That one sentence captures the essence of slavery's lawlessness. In essentially every society there's a right to self-defence against violence from others. Recall that Thomas Hobbes saw it as the one inalienable natural right; on his theory one can fight back even against the sovereign if he comes to kill you. Not so a slave. The law stripped Douglass of that right, and thus enabled the notoriously brutal overseer. By standing up for himself with violence, Douglass claimed legal equality and legal personhood.

Another important recognition of the relationship between the slave's potential capacity not merely to receive but also to inflict violence and a claim to even humanity itself comes from none other than James Madison. In Federalist 43, Madison defended that clause of the Constitution which permitted the federal government to militarily intervene to put down rebellions in the states (the Guarantee Clause, Art IV, Sec 4) on the basis that, after all, the citizens of a state could get overwhelmed by the military force of a majority of noncitizens:

> May it not happen, in fine, that the minority of CITIZENS may become a majority of PERSONS, by the accession of alien residents, of a casual concourse of adventurers, or of those whom the constitution of the State has not admitted to the rights of suffrage? I take no notice of an unhappy species of population abounding in some of the States, who, during the calm of regular government, are sunk below the level of men; but who, in the tempestuous scenes of civil violence, may emerge into the human character, and give a superiority of strength to any party with which they may associate themselves. In cases where it may be doubtful on which side justice lies, what better umpires could be desired by two violent factions, flying to arms, and tearing a State to pieces, than the representatives of confederate States, not heated by the local flame? To the impartiality of judges, they would unite the affection of friends.

---

[58] P Gowder, 'The Rule of Law and Equality' (2013) 32 *Law and Philosophy* 565; P Gowder, *The Rule of Law in the Real World* (Cambridge University Press, 2016).

[59] F Douglass, *My Bondage and My Freedom* (Miller, Orton & Co, 1857) 242.

That passage is an astonishing confession on a number of levels. First, of course, is that Madison openly admits that the framing vision of a republic encompasses the possibility of rule by force rather than consent – that citizens or some faction thereof might make up a minority yet still claim, and militarily enforce, the right to rule over the rest. But for present purposes the most important part is the next sentence, in which the 'unhappy species of population' obviously refers to slaves.[60] That sentence agrees with Douglass that the capacity for the violent defence of one's own personhood is indeed a precondition of that personhood, and hence identifies that under 'regular government', the enslaved are subhuman because of the asymmetry in violence in their condition. He then cynically appeals to the rule of law value of judicial impartiality to suppose that the United States would step in as a partisan of one side – including, at least implicitly, the side of the slaveholders – in such a case, and hence once again reduce the enslaved to the status of sub-persons overawed by the power of violence held over their heads – while delicately admitting some uncertainty as to the justice of such a course. (Left unexplained is precisely how the impartiality of judges and the affection of friends are meant to be compatible.)

So what was the theory according to which the masters convinced themselves that they still ran a legal state? It was all about property.

SLAVERY AS PROPERTY

The law of slavery might be summarised in the words of Justice William Tilghman of the Pennsylvania Supreme Court: 'I know that freedom is to be favored, but we have no right to favor it at the expense of property.'[61]

Even as property was the heart of classical republican citizenship and freedom, it was also the material out of which the chains of the enslaved were built. From the legal perspective, perhaps the foundational principle of American slavery was the idea that a person could be property. Foundational, that is, because we can cogently trace the other evils of slavery to property – if not necessarily in a historical or a causal sense then certainly analytically, logically, doctrinally. In the words of Moses Finley: 'All forms of labor on behalf of another, whether "free" or "unfree", place the man who labors in the power of another; what separates the slave from the rest, including the serf or peon, is the totality of his powerlessness in principle, and for that the idea of property is juristically the key – hence the term "chattel slave".'[62] Abolitionists recognised this connection;

---

[60] Waldstreicher (n 38) 136 agrees.
[61] *Marchand v Peggy* 2 Serg & Rawle 18, 1815 WL 1280 (Pa 1815).
[62] MI Finley, 'Slavery' in DL Sills (ed), *International Encyclopedia of the Social Sciences*, vol 14 (Macmillan Co and Free Press, 1968) 307. Jagmohan has convincingly argued that the property nature of American chattel slavery is the foundation of the natal alienation that Patterson identified as the key feature of slavery in the abstract. D Jagmohan, 'Peculiar Property: Harriet Jacobs on the Nature of Slavery' [Forthcoming] *Journal of Politics* 25.

for just one example, William Goodell in his *American Slave Code* organised the entire book around the notion of slaves as property, with chapter headings like 'Slaves can possess nothing: being Property themselves, they can own no property nor make any contract.'[63]

The logical passage from status as property to bearer of no rights is inexorable. Start with the susceptibility to violence that makes the primary factual rather than legal condition of the enslaved: the property owner is traditionally considered to have the power to waste or destroy his or her property – this is the *jus abutendi* of Roman law. Thus, a slaveholder had the perfect legal right to do immense physical harm, sometimes (although not always) onto death, to his slaves, and the protection of slaves' physical persons, to the extent it had any kind of standing in law at all, was rooted in the slaveholder's right to protect his 'property' against harm from third persons.[64] Sometimes third parties who had 'hired' slaves were liable to their owners because they were put to excessively dangerous work – essentially on the same sort of theory according to which you or I might be held liable for negligently wrecking a rented car.[65]

In addition to providing legal justification for violence, the idea of the slave as property also supplied an economic story to explain it away. Morgan quotes a particularly striking 1669 Virginia statute 'about the causall killing of slaves' which purported to excuse a master's murder of his slave in the course of punishment with reference to the slave's status as property, and hence as valuable asset: 'it cannot be presumed that prepensed malice (which alone makes murther Felony) should induce any man to destroy his own estate'.[66] In other words: if a master killed their slave, the law would presume that they had no real choice about the matter – because the slave was a valuable piece of property, subject to rights of use and of alienation, and so what master in his or her right mind would destroy such property without good reason? Moreover, the law recognised that because masters had this economic investment in their slaves, they might actually *lack* sufficient incentive to use potentially damaging violence to control them – and hence laws were enacted permitting any person to kill runaway slaves, and the master would receive compensation for the loss out of the public purse, thus guaranteeing that masters' economic incentives would not undermine the social interest in controlling loose slaves who might otherwise start rebellions or encourage others to escape, and partially reconciling the

---

[63] W Goodell, *The American Slave Code in Theory and Practice: Its Distinctive Features Shown by Its Statutes, Judicial Decisions, and Illustrative Facts* (American and Foreign Anti-Slavery Society, 1853).

[64] For a summary of the *jus abutendi*, see L Strahilevitz, 'The Right to Destroy' (2005) 114 *Yale Law Journal* 781. For further discussion of the right to harm slaves, and its limits in North Carolina, see PS Brady, 'Slavery, Race, and the Criminal Law in Antebellum North Carolina: A Reconsideration of the Thomas Ruffin Court' (1979) 10 *North Carolina Central Law Journal* 248.

[65] TD Morris, *Southern Slavery and the Law, 1619–1860* (University of North Carolina Press, 1996) 142.

[66] Morgan (n 56) 312.

tension between property rights and the universal violent enforcement of white supremacy noted above.[67]

Property owners also have the right to alienate their property. The susceptibility of the slave to being sold or rented and the susceptibility of the slave to violence come together in the slave's status as property, which made the slave permanently vulnerable, not merely to the person who happened to be their owner, but to any other such person who they might happen to sell or lend the slave to. The formerly enslaved James Pennington, in the preface to his narrative, fleshed this idea out in the form of what he called 'the chattel principle'.[68] In Pennington's words, 'The being of slavery, its soul and body, lives and moves in the chattel principle, the property principle, the bill of sale principle; the cart-whip, starvation, and nakedness, are its inevitable consequences to a greater or less extent, warring with the dispositions of men.' By this, Pennington means to suggest that by making the slave chattel, it held out against even those with supposedly 'mild' masters the ever-present possibility of being sold 'down the river' into more extreme brutality.[69]

Finally, property owners have the right to the use and the fruits of their property. The combination of the right to alienate and the right to the fruits provides a legal ground for the power of the slaveowner to rent out his slave and take the wages that would otherwise be due even from a third party, as well as to seize property which would under normal circumstances be owned by the slave.

The *usus* right and the *fructus* right came together to reward one of American slavery's most notorious evils. One way in which masters 'used' their human property was to rape them – a point that Pennington also emphasises in talking about the 'degradation' to which women in slavery were subject.[70] The property character of slavery supplied a financial incentive: the children of an enslaved woman were the 'fruits' who were themselves enslaved, so a master could increase his own wealth by raping the women held in bondage to him.[71]

---

[67] ibid 312–13. Moreover, as Harriet Jacobs saw, see discussion in Jagmohan (n 62), a master's incentive to protect his property could give way: if he were sufficiently wealthy, he needn't worry so much about maiming or killing one slave, and it might be worth doing so in order to terrify more productive work out of the others.

[68] JWC Pennington, *The Fugitive Blacksmith, or, Events in the History of James W.C. Pennington, Pastor of a Presbyterian Church, New York, Formerly a Slave in the State of Maryland, United States*, 2nd edn (Charles Gilpin, 1849) iv–v.

[69] I take this interpretation from Johnson's introduction to an edited volume on slave trading. W Johnson (ed), *The Chattel Principle: Internal Slave Trades in the Americas* (Yale University Press, 2004) 1. Morris notes that there was an early debate about whether slaves were attached to real property – and hence essentially tied to the land like serfs – rather than chattel, and that some argued that had slaves been defined as realty, at least they could have been free of cruelties like the separation of families by sale. Morris (n 65) 63–65.

[70] Pennington (n 68) v–vii.

[71] CI Harris, 'Whiteness as Property' (1993) 106 *Harvard Law Review* 1707, 1719–20; Jagmohan (n 62).

Internal Tensions in the Law of Slavery as Property

Notwithstanding the foregoing, it was not possible to fully transpose the laws pertaining to property to the enslaved, because slaves when given the opportunity behaved like persons they were rather than like the property the law saw them as.[72] In particular, they had the capacity to work collectively and assert their human interests. Thus, even though formally speaking slaves were not able to hold property, and the law certainly wouldn't defend them in any property claims, there were informal arrangements under which they did hold property.[73] Some slaves even managed to buy their own freedom, though there was inconsistency across both time and space in whether courts would enforce such bargains.[74] Hahn suggests that the *de facto* capacity of many slaves to hold property was a product of self-assertion of rights rooted in social ties among slaves and their latent capacity for coordinated action.[75] Even their presence as property within the courts sometimes undermined the stark contrast between persons and property, for disputes about slaves sometimes required evidence of their behaviour and characteristics, which in turn necessarily presented their personhood to the court.[76]

However, when the law or the rhetoric of the time made concessions to the personhood of slaves, it was often only to inflict further wrongs on

---

[72] It is on the basis of the unavoidable dissonance between how slaves were treated and how they behaved, particularly as people who needed incentives, reasons, albeit supplied by coercion, to be induced to do what they were told, that Cohen offers slavery as an illustration of the instability of extreme injustice. J Cohen, 'The Arc of the Moral Universe' (1997) 26 *Philosophy & Public Affairs* 91. It was particularly challenging when slaves committed crimes and needed state punishment; punishment which was premised on the idea of humans addressed by the law, eg cases described in Tushnet (n 47).

[73] DC Penningroth, *The Claims of Kinfolk: African American Property and Community in the Nineteenth-Century South* (The University of North Carolina Press, 2004); DC Penningroth, 'The Claims of Slaves and Ex-Slaves to Family and Property: A Transatlantic Comparison' (2007) 112 *The American Historical Review* 1039, 1054–55; J Forret, 'Slaves, Poor Whites, and the Underground Economy of the Rural Carolinas' (2004) 70 *The Journal of Southern History* 783.

[74] AL Higginbotham and BK Kopytoff, 'Property First, Humanity Second: The Recognition of the Slave's Human Nature in Virginia Civil Law' (1989) 50 *Ohio State Law Journal* 511, 526–27; JEK Walker, 'Racism, Slavery, and Free Enterprise: Black Entrepreneurship in the United States Before the Civil War' (1986) 60 *The Business History Review* 343, 364–70; KM Kennington, *In the Shadow of Dred Scott: St. Louis Freedom Suits and the Legal Culture of Slavery in Antebellum America* (The University of Georgia Press, 2017) 128–32; Fuente and Gross (n 40) 128; S Lubet, *The 'Colored Hero' of Harpers Ferry: John Anthony Copeland and the War Against Slavery* (Cambridge University Press, 2015) 35; G Binder, 'The Slavery of Emancipation Bondage, Freedom and the Constitution: The New Slavery Scholarship and Its Impact on Law and Legal Historiography' (1995) 17 *Cardozo Law Review* 2063, 2086–93.

[75] S Hahn, *A Nation Under Our Feet: Black Political Struggles in the Rural South, From Slavery to the Great Migration* (Belknap Press of Harvard University Press, 2003) 24–33. This seems to me to be an instance of the general truth that rules, even *de facto* rules, protecting the powerless from the powerful only ever exist in the context of a credible threat of collective action, see discussion in P Gowder, 'What the Laws Demand of Socrates – and of Us' (2015) 98 *The Monist* 360.

[76] AJ Gross, *Double Character: Slavery and Mastery in the Antebellum Southern Courtroom* (Princeton University Press, 2000).

them. For example, in one infamous court case, *US ex rel John Wheeler v Passmore Williamson*, a slaveowner turned no less an institution than the writ of *habeas corpus* to the purposes of slavery, using it to demand the return of his slaves who were held by an abolitionist who had spirited them away when he entered Philadelphia with them.[77] The slaveowner claimed that the slaves were held involuntarily by the abolitionist, and convinced a district court judge to hold him in contempt for refusing to bring them to court to be turned over.

In the same cynical vein is a statement of Madison's in Federalist 54. In that essay, he took it upon himself to defend the three-fifths clause against the Northern Anti-Federalist argument that 'Slaves are considered as property, not as persons. They ought therefore to be comprehended in estimates of taxation which are founded on property, and to be excluded from representation which is regulated by a census of persons.' In response, he puts into the mouth of a hypothetical Southerner the claim that:

> But we must deny the fact, that slaves are considered merely as property, and in no respect whatever as persons. The true state of the case is, that they partake of both these qualities: being considered by our laws, in some respects, as persons, and in other respects as property.
>
> In being compelled to labor, not for himself, but for a master; in being vendible by one master to another master; and in being subject at all times to be restrained in his liberty and chastised in his body, by the capricious will of another, the slave may appear to be degraded from the human rank, and classed with those irrational animals which fall under the legal denomination of property. In being protected, on the other hand, in his life and in his limbs, against the violence of all others, even the master of his labor and his liberty; and in being punishable himself for all violence committed against others, the slave is no less evidently regarded by the law as a member of the society, not as a part of the irrational creation; as a moral person, not as a mere article of property.

The claim that slaves were protected against a master's violence was just a lie – and a lie that blatantly contradicted the previous sentence according to which a slave may be 'chastised in his body, by the capricious will of another'. Even if the law occasionally protected slaves from outright murder, that was merely a deviation from their general vulnerability to arbitrary violence. But more telling for present purposes is the way that Madison strategically used the argument that slaves were not *pure* property to defend the undemocratic empowering of the South to exercise disproportionate suffrage based on their slaves. Yet in practically the same breath, Madison also appeals to a kind of hyperactive republican

---

[77] *US ex rel John Wheeler v Passmore Williamson* 28 F Cas 686 (ED Pa 1855). LM Litman, 'The Myth of the Great Writ' (forthcoming 2022) 100 *Texas Law Review* discusses a number of additional cases in which the supposed great writ of freedom was used to facilitate the capture of alleged slaves.

preference for property, asserting that the existence of state senates and other special forms of representation for property justified the three-fifths clause:

> We have hitherto proceeded on the idea that representation related to persons only, and not at all to property. But is it a just idea? Government is instituted no less for protection of the property, than of the persons, of individuals. The one as well as the other, therefore, may be considered as represented by those who are charged with the government.

> Upon this principle it is, that in several of the States, and particularly in the State of New York, one branch of the government is intended more especially to be the guardian of property, and is accordingly elected by that part of the society which is most interested in this object of government. In the federal Constitution, this policy does not prevail. The rights of property are committed into the same hands with the personal rights. Some attention ought, therefore, to be paid to property in the choice of those hands.

There, ultimately, we see the slave's status as property and the American rule of law instinct to give special legal privileges to property holders to protect their property used to justify the political dominance of the South altogether, what abolitionists would aptly call the 'slave power'.

THE IMPOSSIBILITY OF HOLDING SLAVERY WITHIN ITS BOUNDS

A key challenge that slavery raises to the rule of law is that once a community admits of some who are without the protection of law, the legal tools used to institutionalise that rightslessness tend to promote the expansion of that rightslessness to more persons. Thus, slavery in the South inevitably posed a danger to freedom in the North.

For some Northerners, that worry was ideological; for example, Tewell interprets Lincoln before his presidency as opposing the expansion of slavery because making concessions in principle to the idea that people might be enslaved threatened the broader ideological content of documents like the Declaration of Independence, and hence the basis of American liberty more generally.[78] In Lincoln's words:

> Our defense is in the spirit which prized liberty as the heritage of all men, in all lands everywhere. Destroy this spirit and you have planted the seeds of despotism at your own doors. Familiarize yourselves with the chains of bondage and you prepare your own limbs to wear them. Accustomed to trample on the rights of others, you have lost the genius of your own independence and become the fit subjects of the first cunning tyrant who rises among you.[79]

---

[78] JJ Tewell, 'Assuring Freedom to the Free: Jefferson's Declaration and the Conflict over Slavery' (2012) 58 *Civil War History* 75.

[79] ibid 94; see also LE Morel, 'The Dred Scott Dissents: McLean, Curtis, Lincoln, and the Public Mind' (2007) 32 *Journal of Supreme Court History* 133, 143–44.

Frederick Douglass cogently explained how the risk of expansion also arose from the character of the slave as property, which necessarily impaired freedom in the North:

> Never, in our judgment, will the North be roused to intelligent and efficient action against slavery, until it shall become the settled conviction of the people, that slavery is anarchical, unconstitutional, and wholly incapable of legalization. While men admit that slavery can be lawful anywhere, they concede that it may be made lawful everywhere; the morality which concedes the legality of slavery in Missouri, is impotent as against slavery in Kansas or anywhere else. Slavery cannot be legal and illegal at the same time. It cannot be constitutional and unconstitutional at the same time. Grant that the constitution recognizes the right of slaveholders to their slaves in any State of this Union; and all the laws of comity, good neighborhood, and good faith, require that the parties to the constitution should respect the slaveholder's right of property everywhere in the Union. Free Soilism is lame, halt and blind, while it battles against the spread of slavery, and admits its right to exist anywhere. If it has the right to exist, it has a right to grow and spread. The slaveholder has the best of the argument the very moment the legality and constitutionality of slavery is conceded. There is much reason in the logic of the late John C. Calhoun. If slaves are property in the eye of the constitution of the United States, they are subject to the same condition of all other property contemplated in that instrument, and their owners are entitled to all the advantages of this property equally with other citizens in their property. We repeat, slaves are property, or they are not property. They are persons, or they are beasts of burden. The constitution must recognize them as one or the other. It cannot regard them as men and regard them as things at the same time. If it regards them as things, legitimate objects of property, then the laws that govern the rights and privileges of property must prevail in respect to them. But if it regards them as persons, then all the thunders of the constitution may be launched at the head of him who dares to treat them contrary to the rights sacred to persons in the constitution.[80]

There are many ideas embedded in this passage. First, the commercial character of slavery as property: the basic constitutional framework of the United States presupposed free economic interchange among the states, and required each state to respect property, contract, and other commercial rights established in others. Through Hamiltonian commercial ideas like the Full Faith and Credit Clause, slavery would inevitably leak out onto free soil. I think Douglass is making an ideological point as well: in a yeoman republic in which property is the central legal idea, calling slavery a form of property is a strong ideological endorsement of its compatibility with the legal mode of ordering society.

The character of slavery as property also promoted its expansion in more prosaic ways: like any other capital asset, slaves were the objects of investment. That investment gave slaveholders an incentive to promote the geographic expansion of slavery in order to increase or maintain the value of their slaves by

---

[80] From an 1855 editorial. F Douglass, *Frederick Douglass: Selected Speeches and Writings*, 1st edn (P Sheldon Foner and Y Taylor eds, Lawrence Hill Books, 1999) 374.

expanding their potential markets and the scope of the land on which they could be put to work.[81] Of course, there were political reasons for slaveholders to want expansion too: more slave territories meant more people with slaves on the land who would want to form slave states when they were fully incorporated into the Union; that in turn would reinforce the Slave Power dominance in Congress and the Electoral College.

Unsurprisingly, slaveholders argued from property rights to their continued right to own other humans even in territories outside the old South.[82] The infamous Lecompton Constitution of Kansas expressed the idea in the clearest terms: 'the right of property is before and higher than any constitutional sanction, and the right of the owner of a slave to such slave and its issue is the same and as inviolable as the right of the owner of any property whatever'.[83]

Dred Scott as the Triumph of Property Over Personhood

Douglass's fear that the property character of slavery would require its expansion proved prescient. Two years after his editorial which I quoted above, the Supreme Court, in *Dred Scott v Sandford*, used the constitutional protection of property to invalidate restrictions on slavery in the territories under the Missouri Compromise.[84] The Compromise was an Act of Congress under which Maine was admitted as a free state and slavery was prohibited in federal territory north of the 36'30 latitude in exchange for Missouri's admission as a slave state. But in

---

[81] J Clegg and D Foley, 'A Classical-Marxian Model of Antebellum Slavery' (2019) 43 *Cambridge Journal of Economics* 107. There is longstanding debate about the economics of slavery. However, there is no question that slaves represented a substantial investment for slaveholders. Random and Sutch, for example, estimated that a slave was worth 10 times the annual per capita crop production in 1860, and represented fully 44% of the wealth in the region in 1859. R Ransom and R Sutch, 'Capitalists Without Capital: The Burden of Slavery and the Impact of Emancipation' (1988) 62 *Agricultural History* 133, 135, 138–39. In at least one respect the economic investment in slaves turned out for the good: in order to protect the value of their slaves from external competition, the Southern states supported ending the overseas slave trade. G Wright, 'Slavery and Anglo-American Capitalism Revisited' (2020) 73 *The Economic History Review* 353, 370.

[82] EM Maltz, 'Fourteenth Amendment Concepts in the Antebellum Era' (1988) 32 *The American Journal of Legal History* 305, 309, 318–20. Such arguments persisted, with astonishing *chutzpah*, even after the Civil War. Southerners dared to demand compensation for the value of their emancipated slaves on the basis of the constitutional protections embedded in the Fifth Amendment – and even continued to petition for compensation after the enactment of the Thirteenth Amendment. A Laury Kleintop, 'Life, Liberty, and Property in Slaves: White Mississippians Seek "Just Compensation" for Their Freed Slaves in 1865' (2018) 39 *Slavery & Abolition* 383. (It's hard to see how that argument was supposed to work, since the Thirteenth Amendment as an after-enacted provision presumably prevails over the Fifth – as best as I can figure, the idea may have been that the Thirteenth Amendment could be read as one big act of eminent domain, ie, to divest slaveholders of their property right but not to deny their alleged entitlement to compensation. Section 4 of the Fourteenth Amendment ultimately precluded any such argument by explicitly prohibiting compensation for slaves.)

[83] Richards (n 22) 202.

[84] *Dred Scott v Sandford*, 60 US 393 (1857).

Dred Scott the Court turned property rights into the grounds to declare that Congress could not prohibit slavery in the territories.

Dred Scott was a slave who was allegedly owned by Sandford. The suit alleged his freedom on the grounds (with some simplification) that his prior owner had taken him to a military base north of the Missouri Compromise line before later taking him to Missouri and selling him to Sandford. The theory of the case (again, somewhat simplified) was that he was freed when he was taken to free territory, and hence could not be re-enslaved later on.

Technically speaking, the Court disposed of the case before even reaching the substance. Scott had brought suit in federal court, under the court's diversity jurisdiction; the complaint, in the Court's words, 'contain[ed] the averment necessary to give the court jurisdiction; that he and the defendant are citizens of different States; that is, that he is a citizen of Missouri, and the defendant a citizen of New York'.[85] And according to the Court only citizens could claim 'the rights, and privileges, and immunities, guaranteed by that instrument to the citizen, one of which rights is the privilege of suing in a court of the United States in the cases specified in the Constitution'.

But the Court held that because Scott was Black he could not be a citizen; therefore the federal courts could not exercise jurisdiction over his claim. It is this argument that occasioned Chief Justice Taney uttering what must be the most notorious and universally condemned statement ever produced by the Supreme Court: that, in the eyes of the legal tradition under which the US Constitution was built, Black persons

> had for more than a century before been regarded as beings of an inferior order, and altogether unfit to associate with the white race either in social or political relations, and so far inferior that they had no rights which the white man was bound to respect, and that the negro might justly and lawfully be reduced to slavery for his benefit.

So far, so bad. But under normal judicial standards, the Court should have stopped right there. No jurisdiction, the case is over. Instead – obviously motivated to maximise the legal defence of slavery, but perhaps further motivated by egregious executive interference in the courts, and hence by the violation of the core rule of law idea of judicial independence – the court went on to make an unnecessary bonus holding invalidating Congress's power to declare part of its territories to be free soil and hence striking down the Missouri Compromise.[86]

There were two key points the Court made in this legally extraneous part of the opinion. First, it denied that Congress had comprehensive legislative power over federal territories. Secondly, it argued that even with Congress's (limited)

---

[85] Apparently, Congress had not yet provided for general federal question jurisdiction in the federal courts. DT Hardy, 'Dred Scott, John San(d)ford, and the Case for Collusion' (2014) 41 *Northern Kentucky Law Review* 37, 46; R Berger, 'Congressional Contraction of Federal Jurisdiction' (1980) 1980 *Wisconsin Law Review* 801, 804.

[86] See DA Farber, 'A Fatal Loss of Balance: Dred Scott Revisited' (2011) 39 *Pepperdine Law Review* 13, 21, 39–40.

legislative power over territories, it could not violate individual constitutional rights established in the Bill of Rights – plausible enough so far, but here comes the unbelievable kicker – and that banning slavery violated the protection of property rights in the Due Process Clause of the Fifth Amendment:

> These powers, and others in relation to rights of person which it is not necessary here to enumerate, are, in express and positive terms, denied to the General Government, and the rights of private property have been guarded with equal care. Thus, the rights of property are united with the rights of person, and placed on the same ground by the fifth amendment to the Constitution, which provides that no person shall be deprived of life, liberty, and property, without due process of law. And an act of Congress which deprives a citizen of the United States of his liberty or property merely because he came himself or brought his property into a particular Territory of the United States, and who had committed no offence against the laws, could hardly be dignified with the name of due process of law.

and a few paragraphs later:

> Now, as we have already said in an earlier part of this opinion upon a different point, the right of property in a slave is distinctly and expressly affirmed in the Constitution. The right to traffic in it, like an ordinary article of merchandise and property, was guaranteed to the citizens of the United States in every State that might desire it for twenty years. And the Government in express terms is pledged to protect it in all future time if the slave escapes from his owner. This is done in plain words – too plain to be misunderstood. And no word can be found in the Constitution which gives Congress a greater power over slave property or which entitles property of that kind to less protection that property of any other description. The only power conferred is the power coupled with the duty of guarding and protecting the owner in his rights.

> Upon these considerations, it is the opinion of the court that the act of Congress which prohibited a citizen from holding and owning property of this kind in the territory of the United States north of the line therein mentioned is not warranted by the Constitution, and is therefore void, and that neither Dred Scott himself nor any of his family were made free by being carried into this territory, even if they had been carried there by the owner with the intention of becoming a permanent resident.

Thus were Douglass's fears immediately realised: property rights became the foundation for spreading slavery even into formerly free territory.

Some have understood this holding as an example of 'substantive due process' – that is, the Constitutional doctrine according to which the Supreme Court may find an unenumerated 'fundamental' individual right to be protected against governmental intrusion, such as the right to abortion.[87] Indeed, dissenting justices have criticised the Court's contemporary fundamental rights jurisprudence in part for hearkening back to *Dred Scott*. Perhaps the most egregious example is Chief Justice Roberts's dissent in *Obergefell v Hodges*, which

---

[87] eg, P Finkelman, 'Slavery and the Northwest Ordinance: A Study in Ambiguity' (1986) 6 *Journal of the Early Republic* 343, 355.

compares extending the long-established fundamental right of marriage to gay couples to *Dred Scott*.[88] Yet it seems to me to be an analytic mistake to assimilate the *Dred Scott* opinion to anything like the modern notion of substantive due process or the discovery of unenumerated constitutional rights. Property is unquestionably an enumerated right, and the Court was quite specifically invoking it. I discuss the general misuse of the notion of 'substantive due process' in chapter three; for present purposes, let's just note that the Court was treating the claim that Mr Scott was freed by operation of federal law when he was taken to free soil under the statute enacting the Missouri Compromise as a legislative expropriation, a concept within the core of due process in historical context, no 'substantive' gloss required – although it might perhaps have been more textually appropriate if it were treated as a federal taking of private property without compensation, unconstitutional under a different clause of the Fifth Amendment.

Yet that claim, whether due process or takings, should not have been terribly plausible in the *Dred Scott* case. After all, the possibility of property rights changing as a result of a voluntary change of jurisdiction is not an outrageous legal concept; nor is the idea that what sorts of things might be legal to own vary across jurisdictions. In the United States, as of this writing, marijuana is legal in some, but not all, US states. If I purchase marijuana in Colorado, I acquire a property right to it under Colorado law, but I am not free to transport it across the border to Idaho; should I do so, it's subject to confiscation by the Idaho state authorities (in addition to criminal consequences).[89] This hardly amounts to expropriation; rather, I am under a duty to learn in which states it's legal to possess marijuana and refrain from carrying any weed which I wish to keep into any other states. The same argument could have been applied to property in human beings. This concept surely would have been familiar to American law at the time, for it had been applied decades earlier in England: in *Somersett's Case* (1772), the Court of King's Bench is often understood to have decided that a slave purchased elsewhere and transported to England was free by virtue of setting foot on English soil. While much remains controversial and difficult to parse about the effect of *Somersett's Case* on American abolition and legal culture, the legal strategy, at least, of bounding property rights by territory could not have been totally novel.[90]

---

[88] *Obergefell v Hodges*, 576 U.S. 644, 695-6 (2015) (Roberts, CJ, dissenting). For a further discussion of the idea of *Dred Scott* as substantive due process, see Maltz (n 82) 319.

[89] This analogy leaves off some complexities with respect to federal marijuana prohibition as well as potential dormant Commerce Clause or similar issues should the federal prohibition be repealed; none of those federalism issues are relevant for the analogy with the Missouri Compromise, as under that legal regime it was the federal government that prohibited slavery in the Northern territories.

[90] P Hagler Minter, '"The State of Slavery": Somerset, The Slave, Grace, and the Rise of Pro-Slavery and Anti-Slavery Constitutionalism in the Nineteenth-Century Atlantic World' (2015) 36 *Slavery & Abolition* 603, has a very helpful discussion of the reception of *Somersett's Case* and subsequent caselaw surrounding the geographical boundedness of freedom and slavery. See also DA Webb, 'The Somerset Effect: Parsing Lord Mansfield's Words on Slavery in Nineteenth Century America' (2014)

To the extent the slaveholders had a serious argument, the best they could say is that while Dred Scott and his wife were free when they were on free territory, if they were transported to slave territory again, they could be re-enslaved; in effect, that the authority entitled to govern free territory (free states or Congress for unincorporated territories) could divest property rights only in that territory, to be reacquired in territories that allowed slavery. This was known as the doctrine of 'reattachment.'[91] Moreover, by the time of *Dred Scott*, the Supreme Court had already adopted the theory of reattachment in *Strader v Graham*, a case concerning two slaves who had been taken from Kentucky to Ohio with the permission of their owner and then been returned to Kentucky. After they escaped (from Kentucky), the owner sued the captain of the steamboat which they used to escape, and Taney, writing for the Supreme Court, rejected the steamboat captain's defence that their sojourn to Ohio made them free.[92]

As unfortunate as *Strader v Graham* was, it could have been a boon to Congress if Taney had taken his own prior opinion seriously, for it made totally unsustainable the argument that Congress's creating free soil in the territories amounted to a divestiture of Sandford's property. After all, under the rule of Strader, Sandford would have still prevailed: he was back in a slave state, that state's law permitted slavery, he could have his 'property' back – and therefore, Congress took away nothing to which Missouri law entitled Sandford. In other words, Congress would not have had any more ability to 'expropriate' a slave in the territories than any free state did in banning slavery on its own territory, so the Missouri Compromise could not be invalidated.

For that reason, the only way to redeem the due process argument in *Dred Scott* even accepting the notion that people could be property is to make it dependent on the limited federal power in the territories argument Taney also makes, that is, to suppose that the powers of the federal government to legislate for the territories did not encompass a right to make laws proscribing specific noxious kinds of property which couldn't be owned (a power which states clearly had, and which free states exercised); to hold, in effect, that persons entering the territories carried with them the property law of the states from which they'd departed.[93]

---

32 *Law and History Review* 455 and WM Wiecekt, 'Somerset: Lord Mansfield and the Legitimacy of Slavery in the Anglo-American World' (1974) 42 *University of Chicago Law Review* 86.

[91] See discussion in Minter (ibid) 604–06. The marijuana analogy also applies here: if I buy marijuana in Illinois, where it is legal, take it across the border to Iowa, where it is not, but escape detection of my contraband in Iowa and successfully take it back across the border to Illinois, I can probably expect Illinois law to respect my property right in my bag of weed notwithstanding the fact that I briefly took it to a state in which it is illegal and got away with it.

[92] *Strader v Graham* 51 US 82 (1851).

[93] Moreover, the perfectly plausible argument that Congress might have the power under the Commerce Clause to ban the transportation of slaves across state lines into free territory and to set the legal consequence of that unlawful transportation as freeing of the enslaved person apparently didn't even cross the Court's mind, although Justice Curtis vaguely hinted at it in dissent. 60 US at 622–23.

This seems like a fairly unbelievable argument. The closest thing to a plausible defence of it may be Graber's idea that excluding slavery from the territories amounted to excluding slaveowners from the territories.[94] But that view, notwithstanding the historical pedigree that Graber describes, seems too easily to fall prey to a kind of *reductio* under which the set of things that may be owned in the territories necessarily becomes the union of the sets of the things that may be owned in each individual state. Transposing it to the contemporary context for illustrative purposes, suppose one state went rogue and passed laws permitting all kinds of bizarre things to be owned in that state – corpses, heroin, nuclear weapons, the moon, a person's own grandmother, Ireland, the number seven. The viral property rights argument seems to entail that even though every other state rejects such property interests, Congress would be obliged to permit the residents of our rogue state to claim ownership of those things in Puerto Rico and Guam.[95] Perhaps that is the idea the framers had – but I'm reluctant to credit them with the notion that it was constitutionally required that territories would exist in a void of sovereignty until such time as they were incorporated as states – a void that seems to unavoidably follow from the notion that Congress lacks the power to sort out what kinds of property may be held in federal territory.[96]

Slavery, Land, and Territorial Expansion

Through an economic lens, slavery in the South followed from the easy acquisition of property in its more conventional sense: the availability of vast amounts of land, combined with the potential wealth to be made from tobacco, gave the new-formed planter elite strong incentives to turn to slavery to resolve their labour shortage problem.[97] By doing so, they could also ameliorate smallholders' disaffection, as smallholders could enjoy the benefits of republican equality on the backs of the capacity for all whites to own land and to rely on the labour of an oppressed group of outcastes.

[94] MA Graber, 'Desperately Ducking Slavery: Dred Scott and Contemporary Constitutional Theory' (1997) 14 *Constitutional Commentary* 271, 302–10.

[95] This is true, at least, unless state laws permitting property in slaves were somehow of higher constitutional status than hypothetical state laws permitting property in things like heroin. Against such a claim, see S Wilentz, *No Property in Man: Slavery and Antislavery at the Nation's Founding*, 2nd edn (Harvard University Press, 2019), arguing that the Constitutional Convention intentionally left off such a federal-level sanction for slaveholding.

[96] Such a view would disrupt even common law-style judging: what happens the first time someone shows up in Guam with a novel property claim, or two people from different states claim property in Guam under conflicting law from their home states? Could a federal judge constitutionally make any new doctrine at all to sort it out? On one reading of American history, these questions would not be resolved until the US Supreme Court was forced to deal with America's colonial possessions following the Spanish-American War, about which see further discussion in ch 6.

[97] Morgan (n 56) 296, 308–09, 380.

In more abstract terms, Domar argues that bonded labour arises from the incompatibility of three conditions: 'free land, free peasants, and non-working landowners'.[98] The essential logic of the argument is that when land is abundant, labour is scarce and demands a high price, because workers have the capacity to acquire their own land. Hence there cannot be a class of elite landowners who merely live off agricultural rents – at least not unless they can acquire the political power to reduce a labouring class to bondage.

But this casts a rather darker light on Thomas Jefferson's ambitions for land reform and indeed on the expansion of the United States westward more generally.[99] With the distribution of potentially productive agricultural land in the west to still more poor whites, one must ask: who would have worked that land? Westward expansion and land distribution both would, on Domar's logic, create even more of an incentive for southern whites to demand the further expansion of slavery, in order that those who benefited from enslaved labour could continue to so benefit, and those who did not yet benefit could begin to benefit on their newly acquired land. This is a point that also brings together slavery and the other great American crime of the period, namely, the policy of Indian Removal – which can be understood as driven in part by the motivation to make room for the further expansion of slavery.[100]

These points have a political valence too. Republicanism, as with all thick conceptions of political life, rests on a certain amount of economic independence and even leisure, insofar as a person whose life is organised around economic production cannot, for that reason, fully participate in politics – a fact known at least since the introduction of pay for jury and assembly service in Athens.[101] In an agrarian republic, that entails extending landownership to all citizens and finding ever more people reduced below the status of citizenship to do the actual work. This is what Aziz Rana identifies as the 'settler ideology': an entwined economic and political conception of freedom that ties together imperial expansion and unfree labour as the preconditions for establishing freedom for those who are considered the core members of society.[102] In the legal domain, a settler society is under continual pressure to permit the transfer of land from non-members (in this time period, Native Americans) as well as to

[98] ED Domar, 'The Causes of Slavery or Serfdom: A Hypothesis' (1970) 30 *Journal of Economic History* 18, 21.

[99] On Jefferson and land reform, see Alexander (n 24) 291–99. To be fair to Jefferson, he did introduce legislation to ban slavery from the west. W Cohen, 'Thomas Jefferson and the Problem of Slavery' (1969) 56 *The Journal of American History* 503, 510. Steve Lubet reminds me that the Northwest Ordinance of 1787 also serves as a counterexample to any theory according to which the relationship between expansion and slavery was conscious. On the other hand, Finkelman argues that the Northwest Ordinance wasn't actually all that anti-slavery, and may even have facilitated its expansion south of the Ohio River. Finkelman (n 87) 345.

[100] C Saunt, *Unworthy Republic: The Dispossession of Native Americans and the Road to Indian Territory*, 1st edn (WW Norton & Company, 2020).

[101] MM Markle, 'Jury Pay and Assembly Pay at Athens' (1985) 6 *History of Political Thought* 265.

[102] Rana (n 8) 12.

permit members to control the labour of non-members (ie, the enslaved); in both cases this goes through the deprivation of legal rights.

Thus, the economic incentives of property holding worked hand in hand with the law of property and the ideology of settler republicanism to make it difficult to keep slavery in its bounds. Because the economic and political benefits of slavery for the slaveholders were not in principle restricted to the South, there was substantial suspicion in abolitionist circles that the next step after the forced legalisation of slavery in federal territories would be the forced legalisation of slavery even in free states.[103]

But Black leaders realised that they had been effectively enslaved across the nation long before *Dred Scott* was decided – the Fugitive Slave Act of 1850 had removed the protections of law from them even in the North and rendered them vulnerable to kidnapping at the whim of an enslaver. That statute, and its role as the procedural face of slavery's lawlessness, is the subject of the next chapter.

---

[103] P Finkelman, *An Imperfect Union: Slavery, Federalism, and Comity* (University of North Carolina Press, 1981) 313; Richards (n 22) 15.

2

The Fugitive Slave Acts, Judicial Independence, and the Jury

ONE OF THE most prominent causes of the American Revolution, at least if one believes the rhetoric of the revolutionaries, was the system of enforcing colonial taxes in vice-admiralty courts without juries.

As the name suggests, these were naval courts whose original function in the colonies was the regulation of nautical matters such as salvage rights, the disposal of prizes captured in wartime, and disputes among sailors and merchants.[1] During the course of the controversies that led to the Revolution, however, the vice-admiralty courts (which I shall rename 'admiralty courts' for brevity) became important as a symbol of judicial lawlessness on behalf of the crown, as they were used first to enforce customs laws, and, later, to enforce general ('internal') taxation, most importantly the Stamp Act.

One can have some sympathy for the perspective of Parliament: overseas colonies naturally tend to have rather a lot of their economic activity within the jurisdiction of the naval courts, and it must have seemed quite natural to have them adjudicate tax evasion of all kinds when primary methods of revenue raising were monopolies and duties on sea-borne trade. Moreover, those seeking to regulate the colonies picked up on the idea that the admiralty courts were convenient tools to implement their policies not least because colonial juries had an inconvenient habit of refusing to convict their fellows for matters like smuggling and tax evasion, and moreover would sometimes go so far as to turn around and convict customs officials and admiralty judges themselves for illegally (by colonial lights) imposing taxes.[2] But Parliament's reaction clearly made the problem much worse: it began to expand the jurisdiction of the admiralty courts in the colonies beyond that which would have been permitted in the metropole, and stripped the common law courts of the power to interfere with their actions – in effect systematically depriving the colonists of the benefit of a

---

[1] C Ubbelohde, *The Vice-Admiralty Courts and the American Revolution* (University of North Carolina Press, 1960) 12.

[2] ibid 21, 31–36, 64; MP Harrington, 'The Legacy of the Colonial Vice-Admiralty Courts (Part I)' (1995) 26 *Journal of Maritime Law and Commerce* 581, 594; AW Alschuler and AG Deiss, 'A Brief History of the Criminal Jury in the United States' (1994) 61 *The University of Chicago Law Review* 867, 874–75.

jury of their peers with respect to some of the most infamous taxes that led to the revolution.

Rubbing it in, at one point Parliament created a centralised court in distant Halifax to handle some of these cases with more direct supervision from an officer sent over from England rather than hired from the colonies. The Sugar Act not only handed jurisdiction over to this new court, but also shifted the burden of proof so that the owners of goods which were seized for customs violations were obliged to prove their innocence.[3] While the centralised court in Halifax failed to catch on (largely because customs agents were too afraid of the citizens of the colonies to use it), the other admiralty courts may have been even worse, from a rule of law standpoint: the judge of the Halifax court at least earned a fixed salary, whereas the judges of the other admiralty courts earned a commission on the goods they ordered seized, rather obviously giving them a bias against defendants.[4]

To illustrate the degree of colonial offence taken at these courts and the rule of law valence of their objections, we need look no further than a particularly striking paragraph in the 'Braintree Instructions', a document, drafted by no less than John Adams, which the Braintree town meeting sent to the Massachusetts General Assembly in 1765:

> But the most grievous innovation of all, is the alarming extension of the power of courts of admiralty. In these courts, one judge presides alone! No juries have any concern there! The law and the fact are both to be decided by the same single judge, whose commission is only during pleasure, and with whom, as we are told, the most mischievous of all customs has become established, that of taking commissions on all condemnations; so that he is under a pecuniary temptation always against the subject. Now, if the wisdom of the mother country has thought the independency of the judges so essential to an impartial administration of justice, as to render them independent of every power on earth, – independent of the King, the Lords, the Commons, the people, nay, independent in hope and expectation of the heir-apparent, by continuing their commissions after a demise of the crown, what justice and impartiality are we, at three thousand miles distance from the fountain, to expect from such a judge of admiralty? We have all along thought the acts of trade in this respect a grievance; but the Stamp Act has opened a vast number of sources of new crimes, which may be committed by any man, and cannot but be committed by multitudes, and prodigious penalties are annexed, and all these are to be tried by such a judge of such a court! What can be wanting, after this, but a weak or wicked man for a judge, to render us the most sordid and forlorn of slaves? – we mean the slaves of a slave of the servants of a minister of state. We cannot help asserting, therefore, that this part of the act will make an essential change in the constitution of juries, and it

[3] Ubbelohde (n 1) 50–51.
[4] See Ubbelohde, ibid 6–7, 16, on the commissions, and ibid 69, 94, on the failure of the Halifax court. I'm eliding a little bit of complexity here – eventually the Halifax court was turned into four better-located courts, also with salaried judges, which at least partly superseded the old admiralty courts. ibid 133, 152.

is directly repugnant to the Great Charter itself; for, by that charter, 'no amerciament shall be assessed, but by the oath of honest and lawful men of the vicinage;' and, 'no freeman shall be taken, or imprisoned, or disseized of his freehold, or liberties of free customs, nor passed upon, nor condemned, but by lawful judgment of his peers, or by the law of the land.' So that this act will 'make such a distinction, and create such a difference between' the subjects in Great Britain and those in America, as we could not have expected from the guardians of liberty in 'both'.[5]

Observe the countless rule of law charges raised in this complaint – the absence of juries, the absence of judicial independence, the corrupting power of the dependence of the judge's payment on the result, as well as the special legal disabilities imposed on the colonists relative to the metropole – and the antityrannicism, along with the claim that Magna Carta itself had been violated by these measures.

It's worth unpacking precisely how judicial independence and the jury were supposed to support the rule of law, for these are key rule of law institutions that have been replicated in many other countries but also have been the subject of some controversy in them.

JUDICIAL INDEPENDENCE AND THE JURY

Contemporary rule of law scholars and advocates widely believe that there's a close relationship between the rule of law and judicial independence. This concern runs at least as far back as 17th century England: consider the *Case of Prohibitions*, in which no less a jurist than Edward Coke insisted that 'the King cannot take any cause out of any of his Courts, and give judgment upon it himself', in an effort to establish what in contemporary terms would be called the autonomy of law from politics.[6]

The most prominent feature of the American judiciary is, of course, its exercise of remarkably strong powers of constitutional judicial review. Historically speaking, a case can be made for the claim that judicial review itself arises from the protection of rule of law interests. Its first great appearance in Anglo-American jurisprudence was in Coke's opinion in *Bonham's Case*, in which he declared that the common law had the power to control acts of Parliament – a proposition that made sense largely because the specific control that Coke imposed on Parliament was the foundational rule of law principle that no person may be a judge in their own case – *Bonham's Case* was about the enforcement of

---

[5] J Adams in CF Adams (ed), *The Works of John Adams, Second President of the United States*, vol 3 (Little, Brown and Company, 1865) 466–67. Adams had direct experience in these courts, for that same year he was called upon to defend John Hancock (he of the gigantic signature) against a smuggling charge in them. Ubbelohde (n 1) 124–25.

[6] 12 Co Rep 64, 77 ER 1342, [1607] EWHC KB J23.

a ruling of the Royal College of Physicians in its own favour, under the authority of a statute that permitted it to serve as party and judge in a licensure dispute.[7]

More abstractly, the idea of judicial review represents the notion that a court, when it makes a legal ruling, must rule on *all* the law, that is, to reconcile the constitution, qua law, with the statute – which, in cases of unconstitutionality, simply means failing to enforce the statute – although this assumes a view about the nature of the constitution as fundamentally ordinary law which may be controversial, now or at the time of the framing.[8]

Juries as Popular Legalism

One important way to achieve both the constraint of officials by law and general law itself rather than factional legislation is to require the actual application of law to go through the agency of people who share key interests with those against whom the law would be applied. In this context, we must recall that for America's constitutional framers a key aspect of judicial independence was *jury* independence, and that juries were local and democratic.

Colonial and early American juries were substantially more active than contemporary juries and served as a check against arbitrary and oppressive government action.[9] Consider the notion of 'jury nullification' – the decision of a jury to free a guilty defendant of a crime due to its conviction that the law is unjust – or, for a less aggressive conception, to make its own decisions about what the law is. Nullification is today almost universally among the bench and the bar considered inappropriate, but in the framing generation this was seen as

---

[7] *Thomas Bonham v College of Physicians* (1610) 8 Co Rep 114. See JV Orth, *Due Process of Law: A Brief History* (University Press of Kansas, 2003) 18–27.

[8] Today, this debate has focused around S Snowiss, *Judicial Review and the Law of the Constitution* (Yale University Press, 1990), according to which judicial review was first seen as an extraordinary political as opposed to a basically legal act. For an example of more recent skepticism see G Leonard, 'Iredell Reclaimed: Farewell to Snowiss's History of Judicial Review' (2006) 81 *Chicago-Kent Law Review* 867. Regardless of what one thinks about Snowiss's theory, there are surely some unconstitutional acts which the courts would have had to police. For example, the Treason Clause of Article III, section III specifically defines what acts constitute treason and what evidence is required to procure a conviction. It would be somewhat bizarre if Congress could rewrite that crime, or the President could bring a prosecution for it, without a court applying the strictures of the Constitution when carrying out the core judicial function of interpreting and applying the criminal law. The same goes for the Suspension Clause, regulating when the writ of *habeas corpus* may be suspended.

[9] JN Rakove, *Original Meanings: Politics and Ideas in the Making of the Constitution* (Vintage, 1997) 300–01. In comparative context, there has been some scepticism in other countries in the contemporary world even of the *compatibility* of juries – who traditionally do not give reasons for their verdicts – with the rule of law. In 2010, the European Court of Human Rights ruled that Belgium had violated Article 6 of the European Convention on Human Rights (right to a fair trial) by convicting a defendant without making its reasons clear in the (incredibly controversial) case of *Taxquet v Belgium*. See P Roberts, 'Does Article 6 of the European Convention on Human Rights Require Reasoned Verdicts in Criminal Trials?' (2011) 11 *Human Rights Law Review* 213. The American framers would have seen this ruling as entirely backwards.

a vital function of the jury.[10] We can also think of jury nullification as a different kind of way in which the people could operate 'out of doors', ie, by collective action to directly control political outcomes, as a kind of alternative to the mobbing endorsed by some in the revolutionary period.[11]

From the standpoint of at least some in the Framing generation the jury and its power of nullification doubtless was seen as an important check on domineering government power. Importantly, this was not just about separation of powers and checks on executive power, but also as a direct popular check on judicial power. The colonial experience illustrated that judges themselves could be captured, and that judicial independence from the people posed its own risks of tyranny.[12] More broadly, the idea of jury nullification appears to have represented a kind of connection between participatory and representative institutions and the ideas that today come under the rubric of the rule of law.[13]

Jury nullification, or at least serious jury consideration about the legality of the charges having been brought, was also an important feature of the dispute over slavery: prosecutors and judges attempted to get juries to return treason convictions against those who violently resisted the Fugitive Slave Act of 1850, but, of course, such resistance happened in the North, and hence before Northern juries, and those juries weren't about to go along with it.[14] Contemporary scholars have suggested reviving the practice in the same tradition; most prominently, criminal law scholar and former prosecutor Paul Butler has called for Black jurors to engage in nullification in order to combat racial inequality in the criminal justice system.[15]

FUGITIVE SLAVE ACT OF 1850: THE RETURN OF THE VICE-ADMIRALTY COURT

The two Fugitive Slave Acts lent federal power to the enforcement by Southern slaveholders of their alleged property rights in the North. From the standpoint of Southern enslavers these could be seen as protections for the rule of law: the people and courts of the North were acting lawlessly in refusing to return fugitive 'property' to the South, and so federal intervention was required. Of course,

---

[10] See A Scheflin and J Van Dyke, 'Jury Nullification: The Contours of a Controversy' (1980) 43 *Law and Contemporary Problems* 51, for an extended overview of the historical shift in the United States from a celebration of jury nullification to its rejection.

[11] GS Wood, *The Creation of the American Republic, 1776–1787*, 2nd edn (University of North Carolina Press, 1998) 321.

[12] ibid 298–301.

[13] *cf* JE Carroll, 'Nullification as Law' (2014) 102 *Georgetown Law Journal* 579.

[14] HR Baker, 'The Fugitive Slave Clause and the Antebellum Constitution' (2012) 30 *Law and History Review* 1133, 1166–67.

[15] P Butler, 'Racially Based Jury Nullification: Black Power in the Criminal Justice System' (1995) 105 *Yale Law Journal* 677.

such an argument presupposes the possibility of slavery under law, a possibility that abolitionists (rightly, in my view) denied. But even assuming the Southern standpoint, the Fugitive Slave Acts illustrate the way that regimes of legal caste can ultimately undermine the protections of law for everyone.

The first – the Fugitive Slave Act of 1793 – permitted a person who claimed that another human was their slave to travel into free territory, arrest the alleged fugitive, and then appear before a judge or magistrate to prove that the person whom they captured was in fact their slave. It contained serious deviations from ordinary legal justice – for example, it purported to permit proof to be made of the slave status of a person seized as a fugitive by a mere affidavit from their purported owner.[16]

Free states tried to protect their people from this process, but, in *Prigg v Pennsylvania*, the Supreme Court held that federal legislation preempted state law attempting to protect fugitives – or alleged fugitives – and that Congress had exclusive authority over the law governing fugitive slave recapture.[17] The facts of *Prigg* illustrate the way in which even those who were free could be enslaved under the federal regime. In that case, the Supreme Court overturned the conviction of a kidnapper who seized a Black family in Pennsylvania and brought them to Maryland under the colour of a claim that they were fugitive slaves.

The victims were a woman named Margaret Morgan and her children.[18] Morgan's parents had been owned by a man named Ashmore, who claimed that he had freed them at least as of 1812. In 1832, Morgan married a free Black man and moved from Maryland to Pennsylvania; her children were born thereafter. Yet the kidnapper carried off Morgan's children along with her to slavery.

Even if Ashmore's freeing of Morgan's parents wasn't legally effective in Maryland (for whatever reason), and whatever we might think about Morgan's own status, it is highly dubious at best even under the law of the period to suppose that her children, born in a free state, to a woman who was herself born of people whose putative master had tried to free 30 years beforehand, would somehow still manage to inherit the status of slavery. But even if they had managed to inherit enslavement, it is patently absurd to suppose that they met the legal criteria to be subject to kidnapping under the text of either the 1793 Fugitive Slave Act ('a person held to labor in any of the United States, or in either of the Territories on the Northwest or South of the river Ohio, under the laws thereof, [who] shall escape into any other part of the said States or Territory') or the Constitution's Fugitive Slave Clause ('person held to service or labour in one state, under the laws thereof, escaping into another') – if for no other reason than they had never been held to labour anywhere to escape *from* and, as far as

---

[16] An Act respecting fugitives from justice, and persons escaping from the service of their masters, ch VII, 1 Stat 302 (1793).

[17] *Prigg v Pennsylvania* 41 US 539 (1842). *Prigg* is notoriously confusing, but P Finkleman, 'Sorting Out Prigg v Pennsylvania' (1993) 24 *Rutgers Law Journal* 605, has helpfully parsed out the various opinions.

[18] I take the facts in this paragraph from Finkleman, ibid 610–11.

we know, may never have set foot in a slave state until they were dragged there by a kidnapper.[19] They couldn't have escaped somewhere they never were in the first place. Nonetheless, these Black Northerners could be reduced to slavery. It should be unsurprising, in view of this kind of legal thumb on the scale in favour of the enslavement of the free, that kidnapping of free Black Northerners was a familiar occurrence.[20]

But *Prigg* provided one small comfort to the North: it permitted free states to decline to offer the aid of their own law enforcement in the recapture of 'fugitives'.[21] That tiny concession, however, was one of the drivers of the second act. Slaveholders complained of the costs associated with enforcing their claims against the hostility of Northern officials.[22] Hence, the second Fugitive Slave Act directly undermined *Prigg*, for while the states couldn't be commandeered, private citizens of the North could be, and were – and at least one Northern citizen was charged with treason for (in part) refusing to go along with the command to join a federal marshal's posse comitatus.[23]

The 1850 Act was much worse.[24] While the 1793 Act certainly undermined the basic right of a person to defend themselves, at least it required the recruitment of a real judicial officer as a precondition to deploying federal power on behalf of a putative slaveowner.

By contrast, the Fugitive Slave Act of 1850 made use of 'commissioners' – non-Article-III judges who sat in kangaroo courts to adjudicate the claims of slave-catchers with a number of very heavy thumbs on the scale in favour of slavery.[25] The slave-catchers could seize their victim 'without process' and bring

---

[19] There is at least one case where a slave-catcher was successfully convicted in Pennsylvania for kidnapping due to his seizure of the free-state-born children of an admitted fugitive slave. Carol Wilson, *Freedom at Risk: The Kidnapping of Free Blacks in America, 1780–1865* (University Press of Kentucky, 1994) 51.

[20] Wilson (n 19); Finkelman (n 17) 623.

[21] This was an early judicial recognition of the idea that today we call the 'anti-commandeering' doctrine. See *Printz v United States* 521 US 898 (1997). Similar commandeering issues exist today; in particular, 'sanctuary jurisdictions' prohibit their law enforcement officials from cooperating with the federal government in the holding of allegedly deportable immigrants, for example, by acceding to 'ICE Detainers' purporting to oblige or request state and local officials to hold prisoners beyond the term of their custodial sentence or trial in order to permit them to be turned over for deportation.

[22] SW Campbell, *The Slave Catchers: Enforcement of the Fugitive Slave Law, 1850–1860* (University of North Carolina Press, 1970) 14–15.

[23] G Rao, 'The Federal Posse Comitatus Doctrine: Slavery, Compulsion, and Statecraft in Mid-Nineteenth-Century America' (2008) 26 *Law and History Review* 1, 3. The defendant Rao mentions, Caster Hanaway, was also accused of being directly involved in the violent defence of the victim, Campbell (n 22) 153, so it's not completely clear to me that a treason charge would have worked for nonassistance alone.

[24] To amend, and supplementary to, the Act entitled An Act respecting Fugitives from Justice, and Persons escaping from the Service of their Masters, approved February twelfth, one thousand seven hundred and ninety-three, 9 Stat. 462 (18 September 1850).

[25] Abolitionist lawyers challenged the Act on the basis that commissioners were carrying out a judicial function without the protections of Article III independence. RM Cover, *Justice Accused: Antislavery and the Judicial Process* (Yale University Press, 1975) 177; Campbell (n 22) 35–44.

them before one of these commissioners. Thereafter, the commissioner was obliged 'to hear and determine the case of such claimant in a summary manner'. Commissioners upon receiving basically anything they viewed as evidence of the enslaved status of the victim would issue a certificate which counted as 'conclusive' proof sufficient to authorise the carrying of the victim back to the South and to 'prevent all molestation of such person or persons [ie, slave-catchers] by any process issued by any court, judge, magistrate, or other person whomsoever'. Moreover, much of this proof could be conducted entirely in the South and in advance (and hence thoroughly *ex parte*): the Act provided that a judge or magistrate in the state from which the person allegedly escaped could take testimony and that such a court's seal 'would be sufficient to establish the competency of the proof' of the escape.

Any interference with such a seizure was punishable by a 1,000 dollar fine, another 1,000 dollars in civil damages to the slave-catcher per victim rescued, and six months in jail.[26] Federal marshals were commanded to help out in any orders issued under the Act, and, as noted, were permitted to name deputies and to commandeer the service of local citizens to add to their force.

In principle, a kidnap victim who was legally free could then sue for their freedom in the courts of the slave state to which they were carried off.[27] But this probably would not have been an effective remedy, in view of the fact that such a person would be enslaved at the time, and likely under the heavy guard to which a kidnapper (for that they would be even under slave law if their victim was legally free) would naturally subject their victims – how is a person locked up in some plantation to even make it to a courthouse, let alone to find evidence to prove their freedom? If they would have any realistic shot at the protections of the law, it would have to be in some court in the North, and that's precisely what the Fugitive Slave Act of 1850 denied them.

I must be careful not to overstate the point there. The enslaved were not wholly defenceless; there were some successful freedom suits in the South. It's likely that the people who managed to achieve such feats were fairly extraordinary, but we cannot know precisely how extraordinary, as what we mostly have are historians' efforts to discover individual freedom suits rather than anything like quantitative data. Intuitively, such suits would have been difficult, but the degree of difficulty would depend on a victim's access to things like a social and informational network of other slaves, free people of colour, abolitionists, and the like. Physical access to the courts and to lawyers would have been a particular burden, except where slaves were taken to cities or the west, or after running away; and even for urban slaves, being sold down the river and away from the

---

[26] Based on consumer price index figures from the Minneapolis Federal Reserve Bank, *Consumer Price Index, 1800*, www.minneapolisfed.org/about-us/monetary-policy/inflation-calculator/consumer-price-index-1800-, the total fines and damages would be about $60,000 in 2019 dollars.

[27] Campbell (n 22) 35–36.

courts was a real danger, as was use of violence to deter litigation.[28] On the whole, in view of the fact that a kidnapper in particular would have very strong incentives to use force to keep their victims away from the courts, the notion that a person kidnapped in Pennsylvania and sold away to, say, some plantation in Georgia or South Carolina would have meaningful access to Southern courts to free them seems particularly implausible.

But we haven't even discussed the most egregious part of the act from the rule of law standpoint: commissioners were paid twice as much to rule in favour of the slave-catcher as to rule against them. That flagrant assault on the notion of judicial neutrality was written directly in the text of the statute:

> in all cases where the proceedings are before a commissioner, he shall be entitled to a fee of ten dollars in full for his services in each case, upon the delivery of the said certificate to the claimant, his agent or attorney; or a fee of five dollars in cases where the proof shall not, in the opinion of such commissioner, warrant such certificate and delivery.[29]

Such blatant built-in judge-bribing would have been particularly shocking if any of the revolutionary generation had been alive in 1850, for it is a vivid reprise of the 'pecuniary temptation always against the subject' for which Adams so vociferously condemned the admiralty courts. The commissioner system shared other features with the admiralty court too, most obviously the complete absence of a jury.[30] Apparently the American masters were not above using the same techniques of oppression against their enslaved – and against free Black Americans who were falsely alleged to be enslaved – as Prime Minister Grenville used on them.

In addition to the additional incentive and opportunity the 1850 law offered to kidnapping, even its process effectively enslaved free Black Northerners. If they were to be treated as free persons in the North, then the Bill of Rights would apply to them in proceedings conducted by the federal government. Those rights included the prohibition on unreasonable seizures of the person, and the right to due process of law, which, if nothing else, manifestly must include a minimally fair trial in front of a judge who isn't paid to rule against one. By denying those rights to any person brought before such a commission, the law effectively assumed that they were slaves not entitled to the protections of the Constitution from the get-go. Indeed, Martin Delany argued that the condition

---

[28] For discussion, see KM Kennington, *In the Shadow of Dred Scott: St. Louis Freedom Suits and the Legal Culture of Slavery in Antebellum America* (The University of Georgia Press, 2017) 44–47, 50, 53, 148, 192; L VanderVelde, *Redemption Songs: Suing for Freedom Before Dred Scott* (Oxford University Press, 2014) 4, 16–17, 29–30.

[29] It took 77 years for the Supreme Court to make clear that such a system was unconstitutional, at least in a criminal case. *Tumey v Ohio* 273 US 510 (1927). My colleague Steve Lubet informs me that there was at least a putative (albeit obviously pretextual) rationale for the difference in the Fugitive Slave Act: ruling in favour of enslavement supposedly required more paperwork.

[30] *cf* Campbell (n 22) 43–44.

of free Black Northerners was even worse than those of free Black Southerners, for at least the latter would have papers proving their status; because there was no slavery in the North, there was no bureaucratic mechanism by which a free Black Northerner could prove his non-slave status.[31]

Thus, the inevitable result of the 1850 Act was the expansion in the scope of slavery and the undermining of the capacity of the free states to keep it out of their territory. Unsurprisingly, those who were vulnerable to kidnapping recognised this fact: the Act sparked a vast migration of Black Americans in the North to Canada, illustrating with their feet the exclusion from the legal community that the statute inflicted on them; others took up arms for the protection the law would not give them.[32]

THE RULE OF LAW DEBATE ABOUT NORTHERN RESISTANCE TO SLAVERY

The claims of the Fugitive Slave Act to the status of 'law' – and the status of slavery as a form of property – drove the rhetoric of secession and Civil War. The statements issued by Southern states explaining their positions are replete with appeals to an alleged Northern lawlessness. Thus, South Carolina accused the North of having 'denied the rights of property' in slaves and of permitting 'open establishment ... of societies, whose avowed object is to disturb the peace and to eloign the property' of slaveholders.[33]

Georgia's statement includes a particularly revealing passage on the Fugitive Slave Act:

A similar provision of the Constitution requires them to surrender fugitives from labor. [...] In the fourth year of the Republic Congress passed a law to give full vigor and efficiency to this important provision. This act depended to a considerable degree upon the local magistrates in the several States for its efficiency. The non-slave-holding States generally repealed all laws intended to aid the execution of that act, and imposed penalties upon those citizens whose loyalty to the Constitution and their oaths might induce them to discharge their duty. Congress then passed the act of 1850, providing for the complete execution of this duty by Federal officers. This law, which their own bad faith rendered absolutely indispensable for the protection of constitutional rights, was instantly met with ferocious revilings and all conceivable modes of hostility. The Supreme Court unanimously, and their own local courts with equal unanimity (with the single and temporary exception of the supreme court of Wisconsin), sustained its constitutionality in all of its provisions. Yet it stands to-day a dead letter for all practicable purposes in every non-slave-holding State in

---

[31] M Robison Delany, *The Condition, Elevation, Emigration, and Destiny of the Colored People of the United States Politically Considered* (Published by the Author, 1852) 155–56.

[32] Campbell (n 22) 62–63.

[33] From the *Declaration of the Immediate Causes Which Induce and Justify the Secession of South Carolina from the Federal Union*, 24 December 1860, via Avalon Project, avalon.law.yale.edu/19th_century/csa_scarsec.asp.

the Union. We have their convenants, we have their oaths to keep and observe it, but the unfortunate claimant, even accompanied by a Federal officer with the mandate of the highest judicial authority in his hands, is everywhere met with fraud, with force, and with legislative enactments to elude, to resist, and defeat him. Claimants are murdered with impunity; officers of the law are beaten by frantic mobs instigated by inflammatory appeals from persons holding the highest public employment in these States, and supported by legislation in conflict with the clearest provisions of the Constitution, and even the ordinary principles of humanity. In several of our confederate States a citizen cannot travel the highway with his servant who may voluntarily accompany him, without being declared by law a felon and being subjected to infamous punishments.[34]

It was, it must be said, doubtless true that abolitionists used extra-legal means to resist the execution of the Fugitive Slave Act. Slave-catchers were met with violence on a number of occasions.[35] Northern officials who sympathised with abolition engaged in less dire and more amusing abuses of the legal system too – Lubet describes the legal harassment that was inflicted on two slave-catchers as including being 'subjected to daily arrests on trivial and trumped-up charges including smoking in the streets, slander, swearing and cursing, carrying concealed weapons, reckless driving, and failure to pay bridge tolls'.[36] In Boston, it could be impossible to bring to trial even someone who killed a federal officer in the course of a failed rescue; that city maintained its status as the cradle of liberty by carrying out a charmingly comprehensive course of retaliation against a commissioner who had sent an escaped slave down South – firing him from a post at Harvard Law School (oh no! cancel culture!) and then, by legislative action, from a post as probate judge.[37] A Republican sheriff in Ohio skipped town in order to avoid being served with a writ of *habeas corpus* and made to free some slave-catchers who were being held his jail for kidnapping.[38]

More official resistance came in the form of the use of the idea of federalism in defence of the freedom under law of Black Northerners. Thus, Northern states enacted 'personal liberty laws' to rein in the depredations of slave-catchers who crossed their territory, and the first cry of state's rights in the conflict over slavery came not from the South but the North.

Perhaps the ultimate antislavery deployment of states' rights was the case of *Ableman v Booth*.[39] The Wisconsin courts had granted a writ of *habeas corpus* against a federal marshal who was holding Sherman Booth, an abolitionist who

---

[34] Georgia Secession, 29 January 1861, via Avalon Project, avalon.law.yale.edu/19th_century/csa_geosec.asp.
[35] Baker (n 14) 1166–67.
[36] S Lubet, *Fugitive Justice: Runaways, Rescuers, and Slavery on Trial* (Belknap Press of Harvard University Press, 2010) 134.
[37] ibid 216–25.
[38] ibid 312.
[39] *Ableman v Booth* 62 US 506 (1859).

had participated in a jailbreak to free a fugitive slave. The Wisconsin Supreme Court, in the course of commanding the release of Mr Booth, not only declared the Fugitive Slave Act unconstitutional, but refused to even acknowledge the authority of the US Supreme Court – on the theory that it had the independent capacity to strike down a federal law without review. Unsurprisingly, the Supreme Court was having nothing of this idea, and reversed Wisconsin's decision in no uncertain terms on the basis of the Supremacy Clause.

What are we to make of all of this? I think it reveals a paradox at the heart of institutional defences of the rule of law. Any tool that can be used to resist the abuse of state power can also be used to resist the use of that power to protect individuals. Thus, although jury nullification has been used against government lawlessness, it can also be a danger to the rule of law. In the Jim Crow South, such efforts to prosecute lynchers as were undertaken could be thwarted by defendants appealing to white supremacist juries and calling for nullification, thus permitting the lawless reign of terror of whites to continue.[40] Likewise with direct action itself: Black Americans were forcibly taken out of law enforcement custody both by abolitionists in the fight against the Fugitive Slave Act[41] and by lynch mobs during Jim Crow.[42]

We can juxtapose *Ableman v Booth* to the transposition of the legal invocation of states' rights to the other foot a century later in *Cooper v Aaron*.[43] There, once again, the Supreme Court was called upon to insist on its own authority in the face of a recalcitrant state, although this time it was the Arkansas governor and legislature, who had declared that they were not obliged to obey the ruling in *Brown v Board of Education* – governor Orval Faubus went so far as to call out the National Guard – and refused to desegregate their schools. Once again, the Supreme Court thundered about obedience to the Constitution and insisted that a state recognise the supremacy of federal judicial authority.

We probably ought to evaluate the Wisconsin Supreme Court's decision, but not Orval Faubus's, as praiseworthy. After all, the slave whom Mr Booth had freed was held pursuant to a statute that made a mockery of the basic principles of legal order, and under the colour of a claim that he was subject to a status, slavery, that itself was wholly incompatible with the rule of law. There could at most be the power of brute force holding Booth, not law, and hence he was entitled to be freed. While the Wisconsin court's refusal to acknowledge that

---

[40] Waldrep, 'National Policing, Lynching, and Constitutional Change' (2008) 74 *The Journal of Southern History* 589, 620, gives examples. Moreover, there is some suggestion that jury nullification was used (and, from the perspective of the federalist framers, abused) in the states during the Articles of Confederation period to avoid lawful debts. R Lettow Lerner, 'The Troublesome Inheritance of Americans in Magna Carta and Trial by Jury' in R Hazell and J Melton (eds), *Magna Carta and its Modern Legacy* (Cambridge University Press, 2015) 89.

[41] eg, Campbell (n 22) 148 et. seq.

[42] eg, W White, *Rope & Faggot: A Biography of Judge Lynch* (Alfred A Knopf, 1929) 23, 31, 33, 36.

[43] *Cooper v Aaron* 358 US 1 (1958).

the US Supreme Court had a right to review its decisions might seem a bit spiteful, since the decision would be reviewed at any rate, one can interpret it as a form of justifiable civil disobedience. That interpretation, however, depends on the underlying substantive character of the case: the Wisconsin Supreme Court was right, and Orval Faubus wrong, because the one was deploying the writ of *habeas corpus* on behalf of a person who had rightly used force to protect a person from enslavement by a kangaroo court, while the other was insisting on the right to operate separate and unequal schools.

Similarly, with respect to jury nullification and even violence, I think that we ought to evaluate seizing Black people from jails when they were about to be returned to enslavers as different from seizing Black people from jails in order to lynch them. Those who are enslaved are thrust into a Hobbesian state of war with their enslavers, and are for that reason entitled to defend themselves by any means necessary. But, again, this is a judgment that ineluctably depends on the underling evaluation of slavery as itself lawless.[44]

I think the same is true more broadly of the kinds of structural constitutional protections that would occupy a more prominent place in a less critical book about the American rule of law. Are federalism and separation of powers protections against arbitrary government? Well, sure, I guess, for essentially the same reasons as the jury: because such organisational techniques give the people an opportunity to participate in governance by counterpoising the power of one group of political institutions against another.[45] But the institutional capacity for resistance is only pro-rule-of-law to the extent the status quo, toward which institutional resistance establishes a bias, is itself lawful. The capacity of 'sanctuary cities' to refuse to turn over undocumented immigrants to the federal government promotes the lawful treatment of those immigrants just because (as described at length at the end of this book), the United States treats those immigrants in a lawless fashion; it would not be a defence of the rule of law for cities to refuse to prosecute those who committed hate crimes to facilitate the oppression of subordinated minorities. Whether activity or stasis is more likely to promote lawful governance is not discoverable *a priori*.

---

[44] As noted in the previous chapter, one of the dominant theories of slavery's justification in the intellectual background of America's founding was as an outgrowth of war, according to which one might be enslaved as an alternative to being killed in combat, see discussions in W Uzgalis and N Zack, 'John Locke, Racism, Slavery, and Indian Lands', *The Oxford Handbook of Philosophy and Race* (Oxford University Press, 2017); DJ Schaub, 'Montesquieu on Slavery' (2005) 34 *Perspectives on Political Science* 70; B Hinshelwood, 'The Carolinian Context of John Locke's Theory of Slavery' (2013) 41 *Political Theory* 562. The Supreme Court endorsed this justification for slavery in *The Antelope* 23 US 66, 120 (1825) On that logic, it seems to me that slavery's constitution implicitly conceded the existence of a state of war.

[45] *cf* EA Young, 'Welcome to the Dark Side – Liberals Rediscover Federalism in the Wake of the War on Terror' (2004) 69 *Brooklyn Law Review* 1277; SF Kreimer, 'Federalism and Freedom' (2001) 574 *The ANNALS of the American Academy of Political and Social Science* 66; A Reed Amar, 'Of Sovereignty and Federalism' (1987) 96 *Yale Law Journal* 1425.

The Inevitability of the State of War

Charles Langston, standing in the dock to be sentenced for violating the Fugitive Slave Act by rescuing a kidnap victim in Ohio, explained that by abandoning even the pretence of permitting those who were alleged to be slaves any legal process even in the North, the Fugitive Slave Acts thrust all Black Americans into a state of nature and compelled them to resort to arms for their own defence:

> [I]f any man whatever were to claim me as his slave and seize me, and my brother, being a lawyer, should seek to get out a writ of *habeas corpus* to expose the falsity of the claim, he would be thrust into prison under one provision of the Fugitive Slave Law, for interfering with the man claiming to be in pursuit of a fugitive, and I, by the perjury of a solitary wretch, would, by another of its provisions, be helplessly doomed to life-long bondage [...] [I]f ever again a man is seized near me, and is about to be carried Southward as a slave, before any legal investigation has been had, I shall hold it to be my duty, as I held it that day, to secure for him, if possible, a legal inquiry into the character of the claim by which he is held. And I go farther; I say that if it is adjudged illegal to procure even such an investigation, then we are thrown back upon those last defenses of our rights, which cannot be taken from us, and which God gave us that we need not be slaves.[46]

And yet the Acts were themselves necessitated by the enforcement of the slave system in the first place. If we take the Southern claims to be simply trying to enforce their property rights against Northern resistance seriously, then the unwillingness of some Northern courts to enforce the law, and of Northern citizens to comply with it, necessitated substituting an arbitrary federal system for the courts of the free states. But this is only to be expected: a system of law which classifies some people as bearing no rights will inevitably provoke resistance, and that resistance will inevitably include at least *some* resistance from within the legal system, for – as EP Thompson famously argued in the abstract, and Ariela Gross illustrated with respect to real slave cases, respectively, the forms of the law and its claims to represent neutral justice impose an internal pressure on the participants to actually deliver such a thing; the efforts of the legal system to justify the difference in treatment between enslaved and free by representing the former as less than persons was belied by the fact that it needed to take their personhood into account in order to adjudicate cases in which they were involved.[47] In other words, the lawless nature of slavery generated the legal resistance of which the South complained, and which motivated the Fugitive Slave Act of 1850.

---

[46] JR Shipherd, *History of the Oberlin-Wellington Rescue* (John P Jewett and Company, 1859) 177.

[47] EP Thompson, *Whigs and Hunters: The Origin of the Black Act* (Allen Lane, 1975) 262; AJ Gross, *Double Character: Slavery and Mastery in the Antebellum Southern Courtroom* (Princeton University Press, 2000); *cf* J Cohen, 'The Arc of the Moral Universe' (1997) 26 *Philosophy & Public Affairs* 91.

Having substituted arbitrary adjudication for law – having done to the resisters of slavery what Parliament had first done to the resisters of taxes – it followed that the arbitrary system would sweep up some whom it (nominally) had not been intended to reach. As Martin Delany explained – writing about an 1848 ruling that a person need not know that an alleged fugitive was, in fact, a escaped slave before being subject to penalty under the 1793 Act for interfering with their kidnapping – the law effectively made slaves of every Black person, since it deprived them of assistance against kidnappers, and thus effectively presumed that any person subjected to a kidnapping was a slave.[48]

Delany, like David Walker, drew on the ideology of antityrannicism to capture the entwining of slave status and lawlessness and of Blackness and enslavement: 'I declare that every colored man in the nominally free states, under [the act], is reduced to abject slavery; because all slavery is but the arbitrary will of one person over another. This law is nothing more nor less.'[49] And like Langston, he recognised that in the absence of law all that was left to him was force.

---

[48] Letter from Martin Delany to Frederick Douglass, in *The North Star*, 28 July 1848, pp 2–3.
[49] ibid, p 2.

3

Reconstruction and the Black Liberation Rule of Law

ORTY ACRES AND a mule. It was a demand, a rallying cry, and a persistent legacy – even as far into the future as the Great Depression, elderly former slaves bitterly remembered the broken promise of forty acres.[1] At the end of the Civil War, property rights briefly appeared to be turning from a tool of oppression to a tool of liberation for Black Americans.

In January 1865, at the urging of a group of Black Georgians, General Sherman issued Special Field Order no 15, which set aside a substantial swathe of land along the coast from South Carolina to Florida for the use of freed slaves, allocated as 'not more than forty acres' to each family, and 'in the possession of which land the military authorities will afford them protection until such time as they can protect themselves or until Congress shall regulate their title'.[2]

On 3 March 1865, Congress enacted the Freedmen's Bureau Act, which provided that up to forty acres of confiscated land could be allocated to freed slaves, to be rented for the first three years and then sold at market rate.[3] Congress's intention to promote full participation by the freed in the market economy can also be seen in the fact that the very same day it also chartered a bank to take their deposits and make investments on their behalf.[4]

In these efforts there was more than a hint of the classical republican conception of citizenship. Among the Radical Republicans in Congress, the most vigorous land reformer was probably George W Julian, and in a speech of 1874,

---

[1] J Kerr-Ritchie, 'Forty Acres, or, An Act of Bad Faith' (2003) 5 *Souls* 8, 20.

[2] L Cox, 'The Promise of Land for the Freedmen' (1958) 45 *The Mississippi Valley Historical Review* 413, 429; P Finkelman (ed), *Milestone Documents in African American History: Exploring the Essential Primary Sources* (Schlager Group, 2010) 607.

[3] An Act to Establish a Bureau for the Relief of Freedmen and Refugees, 38 Cong ch 90, 13 Stat 507 (3 March 1865).

[4] An Act to incorporate the Freedman's Savings and Trust Company, 38 Cong ch 92, 13 Stat 510 (3 March 1865). Consistent with the longtime connection between property and responsible independent citizenship, General Rufus Saxton reported that an earlier bank for freed slaves which he had established by military command had received substantial deposits, and that this was to be taken as evidence that the freed were at least as capable of intelligent activity as the whites who had so long disdained them, quoted in WEB Du Bois, *Black Reconstruction: An Essay Toward a History of the Part Which Black Folk Played in the Attempt to Reconstruct Democracy in America, 1860–1880* (Harcourt, Brace & Co, 1935) 74.

Julian explicitly connected land reform to the idea of completing the work of the abolitionist movement via ensuring that freedpeople could achieve citizenship as independence:

> The abolition of negro slavery was a grand work, but it was the abolition of one form of servitude only. Others remain to be abolished. Among these is that system of agricultural serfdom which we call land monopoly. A government which allows the land to became the patrimony of the few can not be democratic, can not be free. Land monopoly is one form of slavery, and, indeed, the underlying foundation of all slavery, because freedom must have its roots in the soil. The fact will not be disputed that the land owners of every country are its masters, and I repeat what I have so often said, that under our popular form of government we must have small farms, thrifty tillage, compact communities, free schools, respect for honest labor, and equality of political rights. We may as reasonably attempt to make brick without straw as to build our free institutions on any narrower foundation. On the other hand, if we journey on as we have started towards the policy of large estates, widely-scattered settlements, slovenly agriculture, the decline of education and the arts, contempt for honest labor, and a pampered aristocracy lording it over the poor, then the epitaph of our vaunted free government may be written, for it can not stand.[5]

Land ownership was the key signifier of independent American citizenship. Northern abolitionists like Julian knew this as did freedpeople themselves. And they were right to be particularly concerned about landownership for the recently freed: in terms of economics alone, secure land ownership perhaps could have protected at least some of the freedpeople from their return to near slavery under the Black Codes, convict leasing, sharecropping, and other tools of economic oppression that were soon to be deployed against them.

The failure of the promise of forty acres amounted to a failure to confer on the freed the full status of American citizenship in its intertwined legal, political, economic, and social senses. Patricia Williams aptly summarised the resulting state of incomplete liberation:

> Blacks went from being owned by others, to having everything around them owned by others. In a civilization that values private property above all else, this effectuates a devaluation of humanity, a removal of blacks not just from the market, but from the pseudospiritual circle of psychic and civic communion.[6]

From the government's perspective, the failure of this programme can be summarised in one question: where was the land to come from? Congress had earlier passed a series of bills providing for the confiscation of rebel lands, but only for the life of the rebel.[7] There was a plausible constitutional basis for that

---

[5] GW Julian in G Julian Clarke (ed), *Later Speeches on Political Questions With Select Controversial Papers* (Carlon & Hollenbeck, 1889) 60.

[6] P Williams, 'Spirit-Murdering the Messenger: The Discourse of Fingerpointing as the Law's Response to Racism' (1987) 42 *University of Miami Law Review* 127, 148.

[7] Cox (n 2) 432–34; E Cary Royce, *The Origins of Southern Sharecropping* (Temple University Press, 1993) 88.

limitation: the Treason Clause provides that 'no Attainder of Treason shall work Corruption of Blood, or Forfeiture except during the Life of the Person attainted', and Lincoln was planning to veto any broader confiscation on that basis.[8] Such life estates would obviously not be sufficient to provide a secure economic footing for freed slaves.

The federal government had seized firmer title to some land under tax and abandoned property statutes, and a paltry 2,500 acres of it actually ended up in the hands of Black people in 1864.[9] Unfortunately, the bulk of the seized land, many thousands upon thousands of acres, was under the control of the Freedmen's Bureau only briefly: in May 1865, Andrew Johnson used the pardon power to return it all to its former owners.[10] Even those of the freed who had taken possession of the lands under General Sherman's order were evicted.[11]

In part, rule of law-related incentives participated in the resistance to land reform. Northern economic interests were reluctant to countenance land redistribution – there was an established economy of trade between North and South, and the plantation system was part of that economy; breaking up the plantations and replacing them with Black-owned subsistence farms would disrupt that arrangement and disrupt the investments Northerners had made in those plantations.[12] This is also the root of a familiar rule of law objection to property expropriation, appearing in contemporary law in the form of the Takings Clause doctrine according to which a regulation of land is more likely to be treated as expropriation, and hence as requiring compensation, if it upsets the 'investment-backed expectations' of the landowner.[13] Moreover, at least some opponents of distribution were heard to worry that it would promote more general land confiscations/land reform – even reaching people who had not forfeited their land in rebellion.[14] Julian's rhetoric about the dangers of 'large estates' illustrates where these fears could have come from.

---

[8] He prepared a veto message for an anticipated broader bill. Lincoln's Message to the House of Representatives of 17 July 1862, in *A compilation of the messages and papers of the presidents, prepared under the direction of the Joint Committee on Printing, of the House and Senate, pursuant to an act of the Fifty-second Congress of the United States* (with additions and encyclopedic index by private enterprise), vol VIII, Bureau of National Literature, 1817, pp 3286–88. CF Oubre, *Forty Acres and a Mule: The Freedman's Bureau and Black Land Ownership* (Louisiana State University Press, 1978) 3, has a discussion. See also DW Hamilton, *The Limits of Sovereignty: Property Confiscation in the Union and the Confederacy during the Civil War* (University of Chicago Press, 2014) 75–76, 154–55.

[9] Royce (n 7) 88–89.

[10] ibid 89–91.

[11] ibid 92–93; WEB Du Bois, *The Souls of Black Folk: Essays and Sketches*, 4th edn (AC McClurg & Co, 1904) 32.

[12] Royce (n 7) 94–99. As usual, Du Bois (n 4), was decades ahead of white scholars in seeing this: his entire analysis of the failure of Reconstruction centers around Northern industry switching sides after the war in order to prevent what he called a 'dictatorship of labor' – Du Bois was a Marxist, this was a term of praise – from arising from 'abolition democracy'.

[13] *Penn Central Transportation Co v New York City* 438 US 104, 124 (1978).

[14] Royce (n 7) 98.

The problem of the lands of enslavers and the ability to deliver what Du Bois called 'a sort of poetic justice' to the freed also reveals a fundamental challenge to the rule of law, one which was to reappear almost a century later at the Nuremberg Trials: what is a legal system to do when addressing the wrongs done by a system of lawlessness written into law itself?[15] The freed had an undoubted claim of justice to the lands of their enslavers. But at the same time, plantation owners did have vested, real, legal interests in their land. To divest them of those interests ran into two serious legal obstacles.[16] First, as noted above, the Constitution limited the forfeiture of lands for treason to the life of the traitor.[17] Secondly, the real underlying crime, namely, the enslavement of their fellow humans, wasn't actually a crime under the positive law of the period.

So how could the government more generally get at the property of the enslavers without retroactively making enslavement a crime? To some extent, this challenge could be raised against the Thirteenth Amendment itself,[18] but it seems to me to be perfectly reasonable to justify the Thirteenth Amendment from a rule of law standpoint by resting on the underlying constitutional theory articulated by Frederick Douglass, Lysander Spooner, Gerrit Smith, and others.[19] Such a theory would suggest that the ownership of property in persons had

---

[15] Poetic justice: Du Bois (n 11) 24.

[16] The government had some legal options. Some Civil War forfeitures were legal under Supreme Court rulings allowing the government to treat property seized during the active conflict as legally equivalent to prizes of an enemy sovereign at sea under the laws of war rather than the criminal punishment of domestic traitors. *Miller v United States* 78 US 268 (1870). For an extensive discussion of this theory, see Hamilton (n 8) 32–33, 51–53, 62–64, 150–54. It is not clear, however, just how much property would have been available under this theory had Johnson not given it all back. Such confiscations had happened during the Revolutionary War, and arguably they would be consistent with the broader republican conception of property that attached the rights of propertyholding to citizens, insofar as avowed Confederates denied just that citizenship.

[17] There's something deeply bizarre about this limitation in the contemporary world. Under the power of civil asset forfeiture, people's homes can be seized for minor drug crimes of which they aren't even individually guilty – for example, the seizure of the parents' home because the child sold 40 dollars worth of heroin. P Brown, 'Parents' House Seized After Son's Drug Bust' (*CNN Digital*, 8 September 2014) www.cnn.com/2014/09/03/us/philadelphia-drug-bust-house-seizure/index.html. And this vicarious liability attached to family members – what in the treason context might be called 'corruption of blood' – has been accepted in the civil asset forfeiture context: in the words of the Supreme Court, 'the innocence of the owner of property subject to forfeiture has almost uniformly been rejected as a defense'. *Calero-Toledo v Pearson Yacht Leasing Co* 416 US 663, 683 (1974)). Memo to small-time criminals: instead of selling weed, try betraying your country – your property will be safer. Formally speaking, the theory of contemporary forfeiture rests on the involvement of the property itself in crime, as opposed to the kind of general forfeiture of the guilty traditionally associated with treason. But aggressive lawyers could arguably have used the contemporary theory against Confederates too – did they permit troops to cross the land? Were the products of the land used to supply the traitor armies? Maybe even (most aggressively): were the treasonous acts committed to preserve the economic value of the land by securing enslaved labor for it?

[18] *cf* Hamilton (n 8) 9–11.

[19] See F Douglass, 'The Constitution of the United States: Is It Pro-Slavery or Anti-Slavery? 1' in P Sheldon Foner and Y Taylor (eds), *Frederick Douglass: Selected Speeches and Writings*, 1st edn (Lawrence Hill Books, 1999); L Spooner, *The Unconstitutionality of Slavery* (Burt Franklin, 1860); RE Barnett, 'Was Slavery Unconstitutional Before the Thirteenth Amendment?: Lysander Spooner's Theory of Interpretation' (1997) 28 *Pacific Law Journal* 977.

been void *ab initio* just because property interests in persons were inconsistent with the entire rest of the constitutional structure of the United States – with ideas such as the writ of habeas corpus and the protection of liberty in the Due Process Clause of the Fifth Amendment. Such an argument is more than sufficient to explain why emancipation could be conducted consistent with the rule of law without compensation. But holding a void property interest is not the same as committing a crime, and saying that some act is a crime – and hence warrants a broader forfeiture of land – even though it was sanctioned by nominal law is traditionally considered far more troubling from the standpoint of the rule of law. The Latin jargon for the principle is *nullum crimen sine lege*. Perhaps the United States could have pioneered the legal theory that ultimately only came into existence in the Nuremberg Trials, namely that some acts are so patently and obviously criminal that the principle of *nullum crimen sine lege* does not apply to them.[20]

Although the land was never delivered, the demand for forty acres can stand as one of the first goals of post-emancipation Black liberation. As the rest of the chapter details, the freed had many other demands, and their activism became the foundation of the rule of law for all Americans.

BLACK AUTHORSHIP OF THE RECONSTRUCTION AMENDMENTS

The primary act of Black constitutional authorship and the core of the American rule of law is the trifecta of Reconstruction Amendments. From the perspective of the freed, the Thirteenth Amendment ought to be seen as far more important – and many Black Americans were arguing that the condition of slavery was all that stood in the way of their enjoyment of the status of full citizens. But white resistance required that citizenship to be reconfirmed in the Fourteenth and the Fifteenth.

For present purposes, the Fourteenth Amendment is most important, because it is the core textual instantiation of foundational rule of law principles in the United States. Only with the Fourteenth Amendment did the United States have a written commitment to comply with the rule of law principle of general law, in its Equal Protection Clause. And only with the Fourteenth Amendment did the federal government commit to requiring states to comply with the rule of law obligations of procedural justice, through its application of the idea of due process to the states – a change that also promoted a flowering of the idea of due process on the federal level that permitted substantially greater doctrinal

---

[20] It might have been more difficult to apply that argument to enslavement than it was to Nazi genocide. Arguably, the Nuremberg trials avoided *nullum crimen sine lege* because genocide was clearly rejected by all other nations. See discussion in C Tomuschat, 'The Legacy of Nuremberg' (2006) 4 *Journal of International Criminal Justice* 830, 835–37. But slavery still existed in other places, such as Brazil and the Caribbean, when American slaves were liberated.

developments, for example, including the 'reverse incorporation' of the idea of equal protection into due process, and hence a prohibition on federal government discrimination, in *Bolling v Sharpe*.[21]

Of course, the claim that Black Americans authored the Reconstruction Amendments may be controversial. And I certainly do not claim that Black Americans authored those amendments alone – their actual text was written by white Radical Republicans, such as John Bingham (the primary author of the Fourteenth Amendment), and they were pushed through Congress by other white Radical Republicans. But Black Americans nonetheless deserve a substantial amount of the credit, and, for the reasons given in the introduction to this volume, that credit should be emphasised in order to pave the way toward correcting the racist history of misunderstandings of the Black constitutional role and the Black rule of law role.

The canonical American vision of the end of slavery and the rise of Reconstruction has long tended, with a handful of exceptions such as the hagiography of Frederick Douglass, to focus on white agency – on Northern Quakers, Radical Republicans in Congress, Lincoln, and so forth. Erased in that narrative are the many Black hands and Black minds that shaped first abolition, then the Civil War, then Reconstruction. As Manisha Sinha details at length, slave resistance and rebellion, as well as white encounters with free Black communities, fed the growth of the early white antislavery movement in the colonies. Northern emancipation was driven in part by self-assertion by the enslaved, including by the bringing of freedom suits that shaped the legal doctrines of Northern freedom.[22] Free Black leaders in Northern Masonic and religions communities came up with early versions of the constitutional case against slavery.[23] Unsurprisingly, Black women's leadership in the abolition movement has been even more neglected, even though they occupied many important leadership roles and challenged depoliticised conceptions of gender as well as the oppression of slavery.[24] And the enslaved continued to articulate their cause not merely with their words but also with their bodies, most famously in the great nautical revolts of the Amistad and the Creole, which helped radicalise the abolitionist movement and accelerate the crisis that ultimately led to war and liberation.[25]

As WEB Du Bois first recognised, the enslaved engaged in a project of self-liberation at the start of the Civil War, walking off the plantations and depriving the Confederacy of the labour needed to support their military enterprise.[26] A full 180,000 ended up serving in the Union Army, and hence deserve direct credit

---

[21] *Bolling v Sharpe* 347 US 497 (1954).
[22] M Sinha, *The Slave's Cause: A History of Abolition* (Yale University Press, 2017) 68–70.
[23] ibid 139.
[24] ibid 267–78.
[25] ibid 406–20.
[26] Du Bois (n 4) 55 et seq; S Hahn, *A Nation Under Our Feet: Black Political Struggles in the Rural South, From Slavery to the Great Migration* (Belknap Press of Harvard University Press, 2003) 67 et seq.

for their participation in the victory that led to their own freedom and thereby to the Reconstruction Amendments.[27] About 400,000 deprived the Confederacy of their labor by taking shelter behind union lines.[28] Others who remained in Confederate-controlled territory nonetheless took advantage of the shift in power to impose burdensome demands on their masters, and some gave valuable intelligence to the Union army.[29] We can also not ignore the propaganda effect in the North and the demoralising effect in the South of masters being abandoned by their slaves.[30]

Moreover, their military experience provided valuable education, social contacts among the Black community, and experience in organising – even at one point organising while still at arms to demand fairer pay from the Union army itself.[31] Before the Fourteenth Amendment even appeared on the horizon, Black Americans understood their military contributions as entitling them to the rights of citizens, including suffrage and equal legal status.[32]

Radical Republicans in Congress recruited Black voters in order to get the Fourteenth Amendment ratified: in the first Reconstruction Act, Congress placed the South under military rule and required that Southern states, to be readmitted to the Union, (a) hold constitutional conventions with an electorate for delegates that included freedmen; (b) adopt a new constitution guaranteeing suffrage to freedmen, and (c) ratify the Fourteenth Amendment.[33] Hahn argues that this transition from 'Presidential Reconstruction' to the military enforcement of 'Radical Reconstruction' was occasioned by Black agitation for land reform, and by the violent Southern response to that agitation.[34] And, of course, it was Black votes that provided the electoral weight that put the ratification over the top – before Radical Reconstruction every Southern state except Tennessee had refused to ratify the Amendment.[35] Nor was Black voting easy: there was, unsurprisingly, resistance to Black suffrage, and the freedmen overcame that resistance and showed up to the polls en masse, even adopting forms of military organisation to register and vote.[36]

Accordingly, we must count Black self-assertion in the demand for equal legal rights and full citizenship as instrumental in the enactment of the Fourteenth

---

[27] E Foner, 'Rights and the Constitution in Black Life During the Civil War and Reconstruction' (1987) 74 *The Journal of American History* 863, 864.

[28] Hahn (n 26) 82.

[29] ibid 84–89.

[30] J Oakes, 'The Political Significance of Slave Resistance' (1986) 22 *History Workshop Journal* 89.

[31] Foner (n 27) 864; Hahn (n 26) 95–96.

[32] Hahn (n 26) 106–09, 121–22; Foner (n 27) 864–65.

[33] An Act to provide for the more efficient Government of the Rebel States, 14 Stat 428-430 (1867), s 5.

[34] Hahn (n 26) 157–59.

[35] E Foner, *The Second Founding: How the Civil War and Reconstruction Remade the Constitution*, 1st edn (WW Norton & Company, 2019) 90–91.

[36] Hahn (n 26) 193–94, 204–05.

Amendment from start to finish – from well before the Civil War through ratification.

Moreover, even after the enactment of the Reconstruction Amendments, Black Americans have been leaders in the development of the ideas in those texts. There is a vast literature in disciplines such as political science and sociology on the role of Black liberation movements and Black agency in achieving the discrete outcomes of post-Reconstruction legal inclusion.[37] The most obvious example is the defeat of state-sponsored segregation in *Brown v Board of Education* – a clear victory for the principle that law must be general. *Brown* and other civil rights cases have been credited not to some kind of persuasion of whites as to the moral rightness of the cause, but as a remedy for Soviet cold-war propaganda which highlighted America's racial oppression.[38] But the reader should not be misled into thinking that this research questions the role of Black self-liberation movements in these victories. Quite the contrary, this line of scholarship recognises that the Soviet propaganda would not have been available had civil rights activists not made the plight of Black Americans salient, both domestically, by incorporating the international relations consequences of Jim Crow into their advocacy, and internationally, by seeking foreign attention for the oppression they suffered at home – up to the point of petitioning the United Nations for a remedy.[39] Equally importantly, the particular remedies achieved could not have been secured without the courage of those activists to demand them and (as with the bravery of the children who desegregated their schools) to put their bodies on the line in order to bring them to fruition – and of course, the litigation efforts of Thurgood Marshall and many less famous Black Americans.

---

[37] See eg, T Lee, *Mobilizing Public Opinion: Black Insurgency and Racial Attitudes in the Civil Rights Era* (University of Chicago Press, 2002); AD Morris, 'A Retrospective on the Civil Rights Movement: Political and Intellectual Landmarks' (1999) 25 *Annual Review of Sociology* 517; S Mazumder, 'The Persistent Effect of U.S. Civil Rights Protests on Political Attitudes' (2018) 62 *American Journal of Political Science* 922; KT Andrews, 'The Impacts of Social Movements on the Political Process: The Civil Rights Movement and Black Electoral Politics in Mississippi' (1997) 62 *American Sociological Review* 800; JW Button, *Blacks and Social Change.* (Princeton University Press, 1989); DQ Gillion, 'Protest and Congressional Behavior: Assessing Racial and Ethnic Minority Protests in the District' (2012) 74 *The Journal of Politics* 950; L Guinier and G Torres, 'Changing the Wind: Notes toward a Demosprudence of Law and Social Movements' (2014) 123 *Yale Law Journal* 2740; KT Andrews, 'Social Movements and Policy Implementation: The Mississippi Civil Rights Movement and the War on Poverty, 1965 to 1971' (2001) 66 *American Sociological Review* 71; M Biggs and KT Andrews, 'Protest Campaigns and Movement Success: Desegregating the U.S. South in the Early 1960s' (2015) 80 *American Sociological Review* 416; WA Santoro, 'The Civil Rights Movement's Struggle for Fair Employment: A 'Dramatic Events-Conventional Politics' Model' (2002) 81 *Social Forces* 177; J Chernega, 'Black Lives Matter: Racialised Policing in the United States' (2016) 14 *Comparative American Studies An International Journal* 234; O Wasow, 'Agenda Seeding: How 1960s Black Protests Moved Elites, Public Opinion and Voting' (2020) 114 *American Political Science Review* 638; RL Goluboff, 'The Thirteenth Amendment and the Lost Origins of Civil Rights' (2001) 50 *Duke Law Journal* 1609.

[38] ML Dudziak, *Cold War Civil Rights: Race and the Image of American Democracy* (Princeton University Press, 2011); DA Bell Jr, 'Brown v. Board of Education and the Interest-Convergence Dilemma' (1980) 93 *Harvard Law Review* 518, 524.

[39] Dudziak (n 38) 29, 43–45.

Martin Luther King Jr, Rule of Law Theorist

In describing the outcome of the general strike of the enslaved in the Civil War, Du Bois highlights the importance of achieving the protections of law and the rudiments of the rule of law by raising it to a level on the par with escaping the master's whip itself: 'Yet the Negroes had accomplished their first aim in those parts of the South dominated by the Federal army. They had largely escaped from plantation discipline, were receiving wages as free laborers, and had protection from violence and justice in some sort of court.'[40] Yet even as Black Americans fought for their inclusion in the protections of law, the invocation of rule of law values against Black liberation activists has been a persistent theme through American history. We've already seen the example during slavery, but the same was true during Reconstruction, when some Southern polemicists equated federal judicial efforts to protect Black citizens from redeemer terrorism to despotic show trials.[41] A century later, the literature of the Civil Rights Movement is replete with sanctimonious scolding of activists for doing things like sit-ins and unpermitted marches. Justice Black, for example, accused participants in a lunch counter sit-in of attempting to 'substitute rule by force for rule by law'.[42]

Perhaps the most important rule of law debate in the Civil Rights era came in conjunction with Martin Luther King Jr's decision to defy an injunction against his Birmingham Campaign. The Supreme Court upheld punishment of the protesters for that defiance, and, in doing so, declared that the rule of law and indeed the entire structure of constitutional government was on the line:

> The rule of law that Alabama followed in this case reflects a belief that in the fair administration of justice no man can be judge in his own case, however exalted his station, however righteous his motives, and irrespective of his race, color, politics, or religion. This Court cannot hold that the petitioners were constitutionally free to ignore all the procedures of the law and carry their battle to the streets. One may sympathize with the petitioners' impatient commitment to their cause. But respect for judicial process is a small price to pay for the civilizing hand of law, which alone can give abiding meaning to constitutional freedom.[43]

Martin Luther King Jr responded to this kind of critique in his letter from the Birmingham jail.[44] Much of that letter articulates an alternative conception of the rule of law bringing together two ideas. The first is a natural law theory

---

[40] Du Bois (n 4) 79.

[41] GC Rable, *But There Was No Peace: The Role of Violence in the Politics of Reconstruction* (University of Georgia Press, 2007) 107.

[42] *Bell v Maryland* 378 US 226, 346 (1964) (Black, J dissenting).

[43] *Walker v City of Birmingham* 388 US 307, 320–21 (1967). For an apt defenestration of this ruling and defence of civil disobedience, see D Luban, 'Difference Made Legal: The Court and Dr. King' (1989) 87 *Michigan Law Review* 2152, 2173–86.

[44] But not the Supreme Court's specific articulation of it: King wrote the letter before the ruling.

of civil disobedience, according to which 'an unjust law is no law at all', and hence obedience is not required (indeed, disobedience is positively demanded). The second is somewhat more interesting: where classical rule of law values come in, for King, is in the identification of those laws that are unjust and hence disobedience-apt.

King clearly recognises that he can't just say that segregation laws are unjust because they violate his naked moral judgment (although he certainly makes moral arguments as well), for that would leave him vulnerable to precisely the charge the Supreme Court ultimately levied of proposing to be a judge in his own case. Instead, he needs to articulate an agent-independent ground for identifying unjust and disobedience-apt laws. So he does: for those who disagree with his moral judgments, we can identify unjust laws with respect to their legal as well as democratic failures. The key two paragraphs of the letter:

> Let us consider a more concrete example of just and unjust laws. An unjust law is a code that a numerical or power majority group compels a minority group to obey but does not make binding on itself. This is *difference* made legal. By the same token, a just law is a code that a majority compels a minority to follow and that it is willing to follow itself. This is *sameness* made legal.
>
> Let me give another explanation. A law is unjust if it is inflicted on a minority that, as a result of being denied the right to vote, had no part in enacting or devising the law. Who can say that the legislature of Alabama which set up that state's segregation laws was democratically elected? Throughout Alabama all sorts of devious methods are used to prevent Negroes from becoming registered voters, and there are some counties in which, even though Negroes constitute a majority of the population, not a single Negro is registered. Can any law enacted under such circumstances be considered democratically structured?[45]

The first of those paragraphs articulates the self-application conception of the rule of law principle of general law – the principle that the rule of law requires the lawmakers to apply the laws to themselves. As discussed in chapter 1, such a principle was deeply rooted in American constitutional theory: it could have been ripped directly from the pages of Federalist 57 – and just like Madison, King ties the institutional instantiation of the self-application principle in the American rule of law to democracy. Recall that I read Madison to argue that Congress would be resistant to the temptation to exempt itself and its members' friends from its own laws because of the broader capacity of the form of government to resist faction: if no faction can capture Congress, then no faction can get laws passed which are so blatantly rigged in their favour.

Alas for Madison, the system was established with the ultimate factional division, namely that of race, built right into the machinery. And that takes us to King's second paragraph, which he importantly describes as 'another explanation' of the first: the persistence of that founding faction is the source of the

---

[45] Martin Luther King, *Why We Can't Wait*, Signet Classics edn (New American Library, 2000) 71.

lawlessness of the laws he broke. Because the redeemers seized political control of the South back for white supremacy after the fall of Reconstruction, Black Americans had been systematically disenfranchised; that disenfranchisement permitted Southern legislatures to enact discriminatory and oppressive laws, and hence to violate the rule of law requirement of generality. Therefore, the failure of democracy enabled the failure of the rule of law, and provided for an *objective* criterion by which we could identify disobedience-apt laws rather than merely relying on King's moral judgment. King brilliantly establishes that he could conduct civil disobedience against the laws of Jim Crow without in any way acting as judge in his own case.

DUE PROCESS AND EQUAL PROTECTION

With the enactment of the Fourteenth Amendment, and, in particular, its Equal Protection and Due Process clauses, the Constitution gained a textual memorialisation of both sides of the rule of law: its procedural side (which already appeared in the Fifth Amendment, but only for the federal government), as well as its demand for substantive equality. King and other civil rights leaders filled out its interpretation, but, to fully understand the context in which they worked, we must back up and consider the general approach of those two clauses and their history.

Due Process: The Protections of Judicial Procedure

The Due Process Clauses are derived from Chapter 39 of Magna Carta (29 in the 1297 version), traditionally given as:

> NO Freeman shall be taken or imprisoned, or be disseised of his Freehold, or Liberties, or free Customs, or be outlawed, or exiled, or any other wise destroyed; nor will We not pass upon him, nor condemn him, but by lawful judgment of his Peers, or by the Law of the Land. We will sell to no man, we will not deny or defer to any man either Justice or Right.[46]

The first use of the term 'due process' that I can find in English (although I am no historian, so there may be earlier) is from a statute from the 28th year of Edward III in 1354, which re-enacts Magna Carta, and which (in the modern English form) rephrases that chapter as 'That no Man of what Estate or Condition that he be, shall be put out of Land or Tenement, nor taken, nor imprisoned, nor disinherited, nor put to Death, without being brought in Answer by due Process

---

[46] This version as given in English by the British National Archives, www.legislation.gov.uk/aep/Edw1cc1929/25/9/section/XXIX.

of the Law.' And that idea captures the natural linguistic meaning of the Due Process Clauses: that the government will not impose punishments on people or take away their goods or liberty without first giving them legal process to defend themselves. In other words, the rule of law ideal of a right to access to the courts, and to the law, and the capacity to put on a defence – to not be subjected to irregular procedure or the sheer arbitrary use of power.

In contemporary American constitutional law, that implementation of the Due Process Clauses is called 'procedural due process', the area of law that encompasses the identification of those interests that count as 'property' or 'liberty', and then the identification of the procedural protections that a person must receive before being deprived of such interests by individualised government action, such as on the basis of an accusation of misconduct. And the currency of due procedural process is the stuff of standard judicial and quasi-judicial procedures: typical issues in procedural due process cases include, for example, whether or not the individual is entitled to a hearing before the interest in question (like welfare benefits) is taken, whether at that hearing they are entitled to compulsory process to subpoena witnesses, and so forth. As such, the doctrine of procedural due process represents a core principle in the American rule of law.

The Due Process Clause also draws on the other element of the core idea of the rule of law, the requirement that law be general. As Justice Oliver Wendell Holmes explained in the landmark *Bi-Metallic* case, in a decision 'in which all are equally concerned' (ie, a general enactment), what due process amounts to is the political process itself.[47] Because, in the case before the Court, there was merely 'a general determination dealing only with the principle upon which all the assessments in a county had been laid', the plaintiffs had no right to demand individualised process to resist the tax increase in question. Put differently, the American rule of law, as captured by our Due Process doctrine, bars the government from directly targeting individuals with arbitrary seizures of property, but does not prevent legislative change altering the general framework for property ownership, like the rate of taxation.[48]

Holmes's opinion in *Bi-Metallic* also indirectly reveals an idea that Chapman and McConnell defend at length on historical grounds as well – the relationship between procedural due process and separation of powers. By resting on a distinction between individualised deprivation of property or liberty and the enactment of general legislation, procedural due process also marks out the respective territory of legislatures and judges.[49] Acting on its own, a legislature can only act on

---

[47] *Bi-Metallic Investment Co v State Board of Equalization* 239 US 441 (1915).

[48] Takings Clause doctrine does, however, bar some legislative changes that the Supreme Court has interpreted as retroactive deprivations of property through overly restrictive land use rules, which go under the name 'regulatory takings'.

[49] NS Chapman and MW Mcconnell, 'Due Process as Separation of Powers' (2012) 121 *The Yale Law Journal* 1672.

the people in general, not on individuals (at least not to harm them – the tradition of private bills in a person's favour remains undented by this principle). In order to directly apply coercive force to individuals, the judiciary must be involved. This separation of powers principle is also captured in other constitutional provisions like the prohibition on ex post facto legislation and bills of attainder which reinforce the limitation of the legislative power to general law.

Abstractly, such a division of authority can be seen as directly restraining the arbitrary use of power by barring the legislature from lashing out at individuals and requiring the executive to go through a court to do so. This restrains the state's overall capacity to upset individuals' pre-existing legal expectations even if some judges are also motivated to act oppressively, insofar as the structural limitations on judicial power (such as the case or controversy requirement, which keeps judges from roaming the streets, gavel in hand, adjudicating at people) entail that any imprisonment or expropriation has to recruit the cooperation of both the executive to initiate a case and a judge to adjudicate it – and those officials may have different incentives.

Pushing the Bounds of What We Call 'Property'

For present purposes, the most interesting part of the doctrine of procedural due process is that its actual application rests on the contested terrain of what sorts of things count as 'property.' Recall that in chapter one, I described the republican side of the centrality of the property to the rule of law as focused on the idea of economic independence as critical to full citizenship. In the twentieth century, this ideal would be turned to the defence of those who specifically *lacked* independence. In the landmark case of *Goldberg v Kelly*, the Supreme Court recognised that welfare benefits and other government-provided entitlements were, in the words of a famous article by law professor Charles Reich, 'The New Property'.[50]

Reich directly invoked the republican conception of independence: the worry associated with not treating such benefits as property, and hence subjecting them to administrative discretion, was that it made individuals dependent on government and subjected their wills to those of bureaucrats. In that way, the relationship of property to the rule of law became almost completely inverted from the founding period: it was the propertyless and those who were dependent on the government who were to be protected by the law *in virtue of* that dependence, and as a way cure it, rather than being deprived of its protections for that reason. As the Court said in *Goldberg*:

> From its founding, the Nation's basic commitment has been to foster the dignity and wellbeing of all persons within its borders. We have come to recognize that forces not within the control of the poor contribute to their poverty. This perception, against

---

[50] CA Reich, 'The New Property' (1964) 73 *Yale Law Journal* 733.

the background of our traditions, has significantly influenced the development of the contemporary public assistance system. Welfare, by meeting the basic demands of subsistence, can help bring within the reach of the poor the same opportunities that are available to others to participate meaningfully in the life of the community.[51]

Clearly, the historical claim that starts that quotation was false: the nation had to get through slavery before it could use property to 'foster the dignity and wellbeing' of Black Americans. But historical fidelity isn't necessarily a virtue for lawyers (as Edward Coke teaches us): the Court *in Goldberg v Kelly* seems to be reappropriating the republican ideology of property to turn it toward greater inclusion and toward independence for all, much as Coke reappropriated Magna Carta for the sake of Parliamentary power. From a republican ideology in which the poor were viewed as dependent and for that reason denied a full civic status, Reich and the Supreme Court developed a theory according to which the poor were to be supported in order to permit them to be independent, and hence to fully exercise their civic role.

This development, too, cannot be cleanly separated from Black activism. Black civil rights organisations at least from the 1930s have had a welfare rights agenda that has focused on providing a universal social safety net. These efforts included an initially unsuccessful campaign to secure inclusion of household and agricultural workers (ie, most Black workers) in the social security system in the 1930's followed by successful inclusion in 1950; and federal control over the welfare system, to prevent state discriminatory administration, especially in the South.[52]

Of course, the welfare rights movement encompassed a much broader constituency than simply Black Americans. However, some of the distinctive rule of law wrongs associated with the welfare system were undoubtedly racialised. In particular, scholars have written extensively about the harms inflicted by broad executive discretion – probably the most well-understood rule of law problem – vested in state-level welfare officials, and how that discretion was used, for example, to police the reproductive choices of poor women, and exclude black women altogether, or provide lower benefits to Black families on the grounds that 'blacks needed less to live on than whites'.[53] The same is true of works programmes, which were administered in a discriminatory fashion by Employment Service offices.[54] When Martin Luther King Jr. gave his legendary 'I have a dream' speech, it was at the 'March on Washington for Jobs and Freedom', a march that heralded the demand not just for political rights but for

---

[51] *Goldberg v Kelly* 397 US 254, 264–5 (1970).

[52] D Cooper Hamilton and CV Hamilton, 'The Dual Agenda of African American Organizations Since the New Deal: Social Welfare Policies and Civil Rights' (1992) 107 *Political Science Quarterly* 435, 27–32, 87.

[53] E Roberts, 'Welfare and the Problem of Black Citizenship' (1996) 105 *Yale Law Journal* 1563, 1568–71; JS Quadagno, *The Color of Welfare: How Racism Undermined the War on Poverty* (Oxford University Press, 1996) 130.

[54] Quadagno (n 52) 32.

economic rights – a demand to which President Johnson responded with univer-salistic programmes in an attempt to take away administrative power, and hence administrative discretion, from the racist welfare agencies of the states, and divert them to the federal government as well as to neighbourhood-based agencies that hopefully could avoid the state racial hierarchies.[55] Hence, we ought to read the Due Process victories associated with the expanding conception of property and the federalisation of welfare – and hence the victories for legal process over discretionary process – as in significant part associated with Black activist movements.

The Problem of Substantive Due Process

Yet due process is also supposed to have a 'substantive' aspect. Recall that in chapter one I noted that that scholars and justices have supposed that the Taney Court applied such a notion of 'substantive due process' when it invalidated the Missouri Compromise. Substantive due process's first modern flowering was around the turn of the twentieth century when the Supreme Court used it to invalidate economic regulation in the infamous 'Lochner era'. Its second phase began with *Griswold v Connecticut*, when the Court began to use it to protect a variety of intimate and familial rights.[56] In either iteration, the doctrine prohibits both state and federal governments from infringing specific but unenumerated individual rights which are interpreted to be part of the 'liberty' protected by the Fifth and Fourteenth amendments. This is the constitutional source most prominently of today's right to choose abortion (unless by the time this book reaches print the Supreme Court removes it).

On some readings of the Constitution, substantive due process is just that set of doctrines that the Supreme Court has developed to address its negligent misreadings of other provisions of the Constitution. The Fourteenth Amendment's Privileges and Immunities Clause ought to be the textual source for the incorporation of the Bill of Rights against the states, but the Supreme Court mistakenly ruled to the contrary in the *Slaughter-House* cases, so when they realised their mistake, respect for stare decisis and a certain unwillingness to admit systematic judicial error drove them to find it in substantive due process.[57] Likewise, the constitutional protection of unenumerated rights could have been found in the Ninth Amendment, but, for inexplicable reasons, the Court chose to find it in the Fifth and Fourteenth.

On another reading, the origin of substantive due process can be traced back to procedural due process, and to the priority in American law of protection of property. According to Orth, the paradigm role for substantive due process at its

---

[55] ibid 40–52.
[56] *Griswold v Connecticut* 381 US 479 (1965).
[57] *The Slaughter-House Cases*, 83 US 36 (1873).

birth in the latter part of the nineteenth century was in finding a constitutional source for the principle that the legislature cannot rob Peter to pay Paul – that is, directly use legislative action to expropriate people.[58] On Orth's account, the subsequent industrialisation and commercialisation of the American economy and the resultant shift in economic emphasis from property law to contract law carried this substantive doctrine with it. That transition ushered in the Lochner era with the idea of extending to contractual rights the same status as property rights.

Yet, if Orth's story is right, this merely reemphasises that substantive due process is a mistake. Protection against expropriation seems like a poor fit for the notion of substantive due process for several reasons. First, and most plainly, the Fifth Amendment's Takings Clause (which would have been available for incorporation via the Fourteenth by the period Orth discusses) can easily be read to directly prohibit robbing Peter to pay Paul by imposing public use and just compensation requirements on any such legislative property transfer – no due process needed. But, perhaps more foundationally, once we understand that *procedural* due process in part demarcates the line between the legislative power to enact general laws and the judicial power to apply those general laws to individual cases, we can see why the prohibition on robbing Peter to pay Paul is inherent in the structural provisions of the Constitution, buttressed by ideas like procedural due process and the prohibition on bills of attainder and ex post facto laws – rather than requiring the discovery of a discrete unenumerated individual constitutional right.[59] Put differently, the courts could have easily interpreted procedural due process, as such, to require the judicial adjudication of individual rights *under a general law* before permitting Peter's property to be whisked away, and thus forbidden expropriation without inventing the notion of substantive due process.

This is a broader problem with the insistence on labelling core rule of law ideas like not expropriating property as the textually dubious 'substantive due process'. If we reduce 'procedural due process' to the simple idea expressed by *Matthews v Eldridge* that before striking at a person's legal interests, the government must provide them with sufficient procedural protection to avoid an unfair risk of error, then everything else that we might ascribe to 'due process' must be 'substantive'. But this is clearly incorrect. We draw on the broader idea of due process as basic legal justice all the time in our law.

---

[58] JV Orth, *Due Process of Law: A Brief History* (University Press of Kansas, 2003) 9–13.

[59] Here is another story about an initial judicial misreading leading to endless doctrinal complexities and compounding errors down the road, one in which the Court misreads the ex post facto clause to only apply to criminal law, ibid 45, and hence gets ultimately thrown into the lap of substantive due process. Incidentally, Orth's, ibid 44–50, general discussion of the alternative pathways to preventing expropriation is very useful; and as he, ibid 91–93, details, our judiciary eventually did manage to fit expropriation into the Takings Clause – although it only took about a century after cooking it up as a matter of substantive due process to get there.

For an important example, a criminal statute is 'void for vagueness' if the law does not give individuals sufficient guidance that they may obey it and avoid punishment. This, of course, is a classic rule of law principle – the key objections the Supreme Court has articulated to vague laws include the idea that 'ordinary people can understand what conduct is prohibited and in a manner that does not encourage arbitrary and discriminatory enforcement' – in other words, avoiding boundless law enforcement discretion.[60] This isn't the same thing as notice and opportunity to be heard, the sine qua non of what we traditionally call 'procedural due process', and it doesn't follow from the *Matthews* test. But it obviously isn't 'substantive due process': it hardly represents the kind of 'unenumerated fundamental right' like abortion, or the incorporation principle, to which 'substantive due process' typically refers.

Yet the void for vagueness doctrine is unquestionably due process – the Supreme Court always identifies the source of this principle as the Due Process Clauses. Moreover, history strongly suggests that the vagueness doctrine ought to be included: it's no coincidence that the law is so often used to strike down laws about things like 'vagrancy' or 'loitering', such laws that were pioneered in the postbellum Southern Black Codes as an excuse to subject Black workers to the control of the state, and, ultimately, back to the control of planters.[61] Of course the doctrine that struck those laws down should be seen as the core of the due process protected by the Fourteenth Amendment.

The ordinary linguistic meaning of 'due process of law' could easily encompass void for vagueness doctrine without making it into 'substance'. We could observe, for example, that a person charged with a vague crime is stymied by that vagueness in the effort to defend themselves in court. Or we could adopt a broad view of what 'process' means to include pre-judicial stages in interacting with the law, such as learning what the law is and conforming one's behaviour to it, so that laws that are not compatible with these steps in the organisation of the legal regulation of behaviour cannot support the subsequent deprivation of a person of life, liberty, or property.

Equal Protection and General Law

If the Due Process Clauses stand for rule of law requirements rooted in what we might call 'bare legality,' ie, the requirement that the state go through courts and public laws rather than through arbitrary commands enforced by goons when it wants to lock people up and take their stuff, the Equal Protection Clause corresponds to the broader egalitarian requirement that law be general. That is,

---

[60] *Kolender v Lawson* 461 US 352 (1983).
[61] E Foner, *Reconstruction: America's Unfinished Revolution, 1863–1877*, updated edn (Harper Perennial, 2014) 200–205.

the Supreme Court has interpreted the Equal Protection Clause to require that law – and government action in general – treat people equally. Equal protection scrutiny is triggered whenever the government treats people differently than one another. Typically (though not always), this will come in the form of a law or an executive practice that identifies, formally or informally, categorical divisions in the coverage or application of some law – for example, a law limiting voting to people over 18 (or to property-holders), or a police policy or informal practice of preferentially engaging in traffic stops against people of particular races.[62] Hence, the Equal Protection Clause is fundamentally an antidiscrimination rule.

Of course, some kinds of discrimination are permissible, even unavoidable. For example, a decent society probably ought to provide parking spaces that are reserved for people with mobility impairments. Hence, the courts must differentiate between those categorical distinctions that are pernicious, and those that are justified by legitimate public policy purposes. This is essentially the same problem that King faced in deciding which laws were disobedience-apt: how can we tell which laws are discriminatory in a non-general way, 'difference made legal?' From the judicial side, Equal Protection doctrine contains a two-step process of review, where the court first identifies the category along which legal distinctions have been drawn (disability, race, etc), and then, depending on how pernicious that category is seen as, demands a greater or lesser government reason to justify it – in the terms of other legal systems, a kind of proportionality review.

The Anti-Classification Response to the Problem of Generality

Constitutional law scholars have, for decades, seen two possible theoretical bases for the identification of Equal Protection violations. These theories are known as anti-subordination, according to which the government violates the Equal Protection Clause when it treats people differently in a way that creates or reinforces relationships of hierarchy and subordination; and anti-classification, according to which the government violates the Equal Protection Clause when it creates legal classifications that rest on particular pernicious categories of group difference (race, sex, etc), regardless of whether the particular government act in question advances or impairs social equality.[63] In most cases, these theories do not come apart, but there are socially important areas of law where they

---

[62] Equal Protection doctrine also covers nominally universal policies adopted for the purpose of targeting particular groups. For example, the Fourth Circuit in *NAACP v McCrory* 831 F3d 204 (4th Cir 2016), ruled that supposedly universal changes to voting rules, such as to the hours of voting, had actually been adopted for the purpose of reducing Black voting, and hence struck the changes down.

[63] RB Siegel, 'Equality Talk: Antisubordination and Anticlassification Values in Constitutional Struggles over Brown' (2004) 117 *Harvard Law Review* 1470, has a good summary of the fundamentals of the debate and its history. ML Barnes and E Chemerinsky, 'The Once and Future Equal Protection Doctrine' (2011) 43 *Connecticut Law Review* 1059, have a strong and concise critique of the anticlassification approach.

potentially lead to opposite results; the most prominent is in state-sponsored affirmative action. Under an anti-subordination theory, affirmative action to, for example, promote the hiring of public employees from subordinated racial groups would not provoke any particular constitutional alarm, since such an initiative would be oriented toward remedying racial hierarchy rather than rein-forcing it. By contrast, on an anti-classification theory, the mere fact that such a law requires government to treat people with different racial ascriptions differ-ently vests it with a presumption of constitutional impermissibility, represented doctrinally in the idea of 'strict scrutiny' which requires any such government action to be carried out in pursuit of a 'compelling government interest' and to be 'narrowly tailored', ie, based as little on race as possible to achieve that compelling interest.

Formally speaking, US constitutional law has adopted an anti-classification theory (though not in those explicit terms): government affirmative action is in fact subject to strict scrutiny like any other use of race. The core rationale for this doctrine seems to rest on some scepticism about the reliability either of the government's efforts to correctly determine which race-based acts are actually counter-hierarchical, or of the court to evaluate such acts after the fact. Would an anti-subordination theory merely care about the government's intent (itself notoriously hard to measure, especially in multimember legislative contexts where there may be no coherent intent), even if that intent leads to unintended consequences? Would it merely care about the effect of a government action? Would the expressive meaning of a government action be inquired into? In the context of affirmative action in particular, a number of critics have argued that it actually exacerbates stigmas attached to subordinated racial groups by lead-ing others to believe that employees or students of colour are not qualified for the permissions they occupy.[64]

Yet read that way it's not obvious that the normative foundations of anti-classification and anti-subordination theory are fundamentally different. If the anti-classification approach is justifiable, it is justifiable only for anti-subordination reasons, in other words, based on the claim that certain kinds of classifications by the government are likely to be pernicious whether or not they are so intended, and that the pursuit of anti-subordination is likely to be systematically unreliable.

Understood from the rule of law perspective, we can see the anti-classification approach as a way of responding to a technical difficulty in achieving the regulation of citizens by general law. As I have argued, the fundamental problem

---

[64] See eg Justice Thomas's concurrence in *Fisher v Texas* (*Fisher I*) 570 US 297, 328 (2013) where he claimed that 'the University's [affirmative action] program is instead based on the benighted notion that it is possible to tell when discrimination helps, rather than hurts, racial minorities', which he equated to '[s]laveholders argu[ing] that slavery was a "positive good"' and claimed 'taints the accomplishments of all those who are admitted as a result of racial discrimination'.

with the idea of general law is that the identification of which laws are general and which laws are not, which is most plausibly captured within contemporary theory in the idea of 'treating like cases alike', requires some more-than-merely-formal relevance criterion for identifying which cases are alike – and such a criterion can only be defined with respect to the values underling the requirement of general law itself.[65] In other words, the criteria along which the benefits and the burdens of a given law or other government act are allocated must in some sense be relevant to the underlying policy consideration – race is not relevant to the amount of taxes one ought to pay, while income clearly is – but that relevance judgment is ineluctably normative.[66] In that earlier article I suggested, but did not develop in detail, the idea that the American doctrine of suspect classifications and levels of scrutiny serves the function of resolving the problem of generality in the distinctive American historical context.[67]

To fill in the idea somewhat: no court can substitute its overall policy judgment for that of a legislature while carrying out its judicial review functions. But an unbounded application of a kind of general law relevance test – in which every distinction between persons written into law is reviewed for the extent to which that distinction is relevant to the underlying legitimate policy goals of the enactment – would capture something like a coherent idea of general law, but only at the expense of subjecting every act of legislation to an overall proportionality review incompatible with a strong judicial review system such as the one in the US.

Almost all laws make fairly basic distinctions between persons – there is a certain age at which one is permitted to get a driver's licence; one's property tax rate and the school to which one's children are assigned depends on the location of one's residence; we can proliferate examples endlessly. Moreover, some behavioural rules can safely be treated as de facto legal categorisations; consider, for example, the position of a poor person who is told that there is an unaffordable fee for access to the courts, an example of which the Supreme Court struck down as early as 1956 on the grounds that it effectively excluded the poor from appellate review of their cases.[68] So, are all of these things to be subjected to an unbounded proportionality review by a federal court with the power to strike down a law if it thinks that the distinction is not justified by the legislative purpose? If, for example, a litigant can show that there is no strong statistical difference between 17 year old drivers and 18 year old drivers, may they

---

[65] P Gowder, 'Equal Law in an Unequal World' (2014) 99 *Iowa Law Review* 1021, 1031–32.

[66] The Supreme Court endorsed such an idea as early as 1921: 'Classification is the most inveterate of our reasoning processes. We can scarcely think or speak without consciously or unconsciously exercising it. It must therefore obtain in and determine legislation, but it must regard real resemblances and real differences between things and persons, and class them in accordance with their pertinence to the purpose in hand.' *Truax v Corrigan* 257 US 312, 337–38 (1921).

[67] Gowder (n 64) 1046, 1049, 1079.

[68] *Griffin v Illinois* 351 US 12 (1956).

have a federal court strike down a legislative judgment that the drivers' licences of those under 18 come with additional restrictions? To permit that would be, most Americans would probably think, wildly undemocratic – it would amount to substituting judicial policy judgments about minutiae such as drivers' licences for the judgments of elected officials.

To resolve this dilemma, given America's distinctive history with some particularly pernicious forms of discrimination – and especially with race discrimination – it appears to have seemed natural to the Court to adopt a system of categorical review. In rule of law terms, this amounts to a kind of presumption of irrelevance for certain categories of legal distinction: if the government distinguishes among people by race, or a handful of other 'suspect classifications' such as religion, it is assumed by the courts that the distinction is not relevant to some legitimate policy outcome. Hence, a heavy burden is imposed on the government to come forward with evidence that the distinction is relevant. By contrast distinctions with a less tainted history like age are presumed to be relevant, and hence a challenger typically must meet a heavy judicial burden in order to prove that a legislature had no rational reason to treat people of different ages differently. Such a system represents a reasonable heuristic that balances the importance of judicial scrutiny of potentially non-general laws with the need to preserve the policy autonomy of democratically elected officials. It also represents an acknowledgment of the historical fact that the core purpose of the Reconstruction Amendments was to wipe out the stain of slavery and regularise the legal status of Black Americans – and thus state-sponsored race discrimination stands as a distinctive wrong which ought to be treated differently from other forms of legal discrimination.

Once a categorical approach is adopted, however, there's a kind of practical pressure toward taking an anti-classification approach rather than an anti-subordination approach toward reviewing acts within a given classification. Having decided that state-sponsored race discrimination, for example, is particularly unlikely to be relevant to any legitimate state purpose, to say that race-based legislation loses its presumption of impermissibility depending on which racial groups are 'advantaged' or 'disadvantaged' has a kind of feeling of inconsistency to it.

However, anti-subordination purposes could be accommodated within the anti-classification framework. Consider affirmative action again: under current law, educational diversity is a compelling interest; hence, if a public university can prove that its 'race discrimination' (by which we mean putting a slight thumb on the scale in the aggregate in favour of admitting subordinated minorities) is necessary to achieve a diverse educational environment, a policy can stand. But the Supreme Court could rule that remedying the effects of underlying social and economic race discrimination or even underlying significant racial inequality is a compelling interest too.

In the context of affirmative action qua private employment 'discrimination' the Court has in effect done as much, ruling that affirmative action is permissible under Title VII of the Civil Rights Act to 'eliminate manifest racial imbalances in traditionally segregated job categories' in *United Steelworkers v Weber*.[69] It isn't a much larger step to recognise that the same policy – to remedy broader economic exclusion – could be a compelling interest in public education, especially when we consider that the Black framers of the Fourteenth Amendment were also demanding broader economic inclusion at the time of enactment.

Process and Protection Together: The Path Not Taken

One major problem that freedpeople faced during Reconstruction was that Southern courts typically were unwilling to entertain testimony from Black witnesses. Intuitively, this refusal offends against core rule of law ideals, for it rendered Black victims of crime, fraud, and dispossession unprotected by the law. In response to this problem, the Freedmen's Bureau attempted to set up its own system of adjudication to supply what were, effectively, military tribunals to provide basic legal justice to the freed in place of the ordinary courts.[70]

The refusal to entertain Black testimony, particularly as victims in prosecutions or civil suits against private persons who attacked them, also poses a challenge for our conventional interpretations of the Due Process and Equal Protection clauses of the Fourteenth Amendment. Supposing that the testimonial bar had continued after the enactment of that Amendment, what would it violate? One naturally has the urge to say 'the Due Process Clause', for due process is the traditional site of our demands to things like access to the courts and the resolution of disputes by law rather than by force. But it's somewhat awkward to fit this particular legal abuse under the formulaic mode of modern conventional procedural due process doctrine, (although much easier under the reinterpretation of doctrines like void for vagueness which I articulated above), in which we must first identify some discrete 'life, liberty, or property' interest of which the government is depriving a person – unless testifying itself is the liberty interest, it would seem like the actual deprivation was carried out by the Klan or similar private oppressor. Even if testifying itself is the liberty interest, how could it also be the 'process that is due?' It doesn't quite work, at least not without resorting to the much-maligned concept of 'substantive due process'.

A more obvious route under contemporary doctrine is to focus not on the substance of the wrong but on its discriminatory allocation. Under the law as it

---

[69] *United Steelworkers v Weber* 443 US 193 (1979). There is, however, some reason to think that precedent is in danger. DC Malamud, 'The Strange Persistence of Affirmative Action Under Title VII' (2015) 118 *West Virginia Law Review* 1.

[70] DG Nieman, *To Set the Law in Motion: The Freedmen's Bureau and the Legal Rights of Blacks, 1865–1868* (KTO Press, 1979); BB Donald and PJ Davis, 'To This Tribunal the Freedman Has Turned: The Freedmen's Bureau's Judicial Powers and the Origins of the Fourteenth Amendment' (2018) 79 *Louisiana Law Review* 1.

stands today, this is how such a case would most easily be disposed: it's a facial race classification, and there isn't a compelling government interest to justify it, so it must be struck down. Yet this really seems to miss the point: while the refusal to entertain Black testimony in court certainly is wrong in the same way that things like segregated schools are wrong, it also seems to be wrong in an additional and distinct way in virtue of its utter exclusion of a class of persons from access to the judicial process, and a simple race discrimination theory fails to capture that.

There's a way to read the Due Process and Equal Protection clauses together that seems to more closely track the problem, however, and one that also provides a little bit more linguistic respect to that word 'protection' in the latter clause.[71] One can imagine an alternative history in which the notion of protection, interpreted as something like protection from violence and predation, and in particular against the susceptibility to private arbitrary violence that went along with slavery, became the core of the doctrine surrounding the Equal Protection Clause. In that counterfactual legal history, the Due Process Clause works hand in hand with the Equal Protection Clause to identify that a primary (although not exclusive) mechanism through which protection is to be delivered is through guaranteeing access to the courts. Such a view has a distinctive historical fidelity: as Robin West has aptly explained, if we understand slavery as the creation of a kind of 'dual sovereignty' in which the slave is under the rule not just of the state (and its laws) but also of the master – the latter enforced by arbitrary violence – then the 'protection' of the Fourteenth Amendment can be seen as continuing the abolitionist work of the Thirteenth by committing the government to tearing down not just the juridical face of slavery in the form of the chattel principle but also its factual face in the form of the capacity of some to engage in untrammelled violence against others.[72]

In such a world, it is not obvious that Black Americans would be worse off than today. While that parallel universe Equal Protection Clause would not have been available as a legal tool to end *de jure* segregation starting with *Brown v Board of Education*, Black activists may have been able to use it to force the states to prevent the racist mob violence that scourged the nation from the end of Reconstruction to the Civil Rights Movement. If the Equal Protection

---

[71] Evan Bernick has a wonderful working paper called 'Antisubjugation and the Equal Protection of the Laws' (currently available at papers.ssrn.com/sol3/papers.cfm?abstract_id=3664925) which captures a compelling version of this idea. This paper, incidentally, also serves as a sterling example of what originalism can be when it takes Black Americans seriously as constitutional authors. Other important discussions of the idea of Equal Protection as protection include R West, 'Toward an Abolitionist Interpretation of the Fourteenth Amendment' (1991) 94 *West Virginia Law Review* 111; SJ Heyman, 'The First Duty of Government: Protection, Liberty and the Fourteenth Amendment' (1991) 41 *Duke Law Journal* 507; CR Green, 'The Original Sense of the (Equal) Protection Clause: Pre-Enacting History' (2008) 19 *George Mason University Civil Rights Law Journal* 1, among many others (Green and Bernick combined cite most of the literature).

[72] West (n 70) 129–32.

Clause had been interpreted to entitle Black Americans to protection from racist violence in the first instance, and if the clause had actually been enforced, we may not have needed *Brown v Board of Education*: as discussed in the next chapter, it was lawless violence that stole political power away from freed slaves in the South; genuinely politically empowered Black citizens might have been able to secure things like equal access to education without the intervention of the Warren Court and many decades beforehand. And as Derrick Bell suggested, real political power may have achieved educational equality for Black schoolchildren much more reliably than court-ordered integration.[73]

Moreover, the notion of *actual protection* could, at least in principle, be deployed to combat the cruel dilemma that so many Black communities face today. Scholars have long observed that Black Americans are simultaneously underprotected from crime but overpoliced in a dehumanising and intimidating fashion.[74] Perhaps a constitutional right to real protection on the terms extended to whites – not merely *by* police but also *from* police – could also have been used as leverage to promote the development of solutions to crime that do not merely add oppression.

This interpretation made an important appearance in the middle of the twentieth century. In *Monroe v Pape*, the Supreme Court dusted off 42 USC 1983, originally enacted as part of the Civil Rights Act of 1871 (17 Stat 13), better known as the 'Ku Klux Klan Act' because of its purpose to suppress that organisation.[75] In explaining the origins of this act, the Court first observed that part of its purpose was to provide access to the federal courts for Black Americans who had been deprived of the right to testify in state courts in the South:

> it provided a remedy where state law was inadequate. That aspect of the legislation was summed up as follows by Senator Sherman of Ohio: '... it is said the reason is that any offense may be committed upon a negro by a white man, and a negro cannot testify in any case against a white man, so that the only way by which any conviction can be had in Kentucky in those cases is in the United States courts, because the United States courts enforce the United States laws by which negroes may testify.'[76]

---

[73] D Bell, *And We Are Not Saved: The Elusive Quest for Racial Justice* (Basic Books, 1989) 111–13.

[74] R Kennedy, *Race, Crime, and the Law*, 1st Vintage Books edn (Vintage Books, 1998); see also J Forman, *Locking Up Our Own: Crime and Punishment in Black America*, 1st edn (Farrar, Straus and Giroux, 2017); G Prowse, VM Weaver and TL Meares, 'The State from Below: Distorted Responsiveness in Policed Communities' (2019) 56 *Urban Affairs Review* 1423.

[75] Again, credit allocation is important. Manifestly, much of the motivation for Republican legislators to enact this bill was a desire to prevent the Klan from suppressing enough Black voters in the South to forcibly elect Democrats – ie, to protect their partisan interests. AW Trelease, *White Terror: The Ku Klux Klan Conspiracy and Southern Reconstruction*, Louisiana paperback edn (Louisiana State University Press, 1995) 388–89. But, of course, those interests in turn depended on protecting the suffrage of Black voters, and it was the suffrage of Black voters and the motivation of Black voters to use that suffrage in defence of their liberty which provoked the Klan terrorism in the first place. More immediately, Black petitioners helped persuade Congress to actually act to enforce the Fourteenth Amendment. Foner (n 35) 116–19.

[76] *Monroe v Pape* 365 US 167, 173–74 (1961).

The Court goes on to explain the broader purposes of the Act in fulfilling the duty to secure Equal Protection to Black Americans:

> Mr. Beatty of Ohio summarized in the House the case for the bill when he said: 'certain States have denied to persons within their jurisdiction the equal protection of the laws. The proof on this point is voluminous and unquestionable. ... Men were murdered, houses were burned, women were outraged, men were scourged, and officers of the law shot down, and the State made no successful effort to bring the guilty to punishment or afford protection or redress to the outraged and innocent. The State, from lack of power or inclination, practically denied the equal protection of the law to these persons.'[77]

The deployment of section 1983 to permit civil suits against police on the basis of a statute enacted in part to make up for the Southern failure to use their law enforcement apparatus to protect Black Americans from private terrorism illustrates that the protection conception of Equal Protection maintained its salience well into the twentieth century and could licence the demand both for protection by police and protection from police, just as I argue.

Still, that conception of Equal Protection is almost entirely unused today. The protection interpretation of Equal Protection would have, were it more firmly embedded into our doctrine, borne a complex relationship to the idea of rule of law. Had the clause been consistently read that way, we might fairly have said that it represented a kind of peace and order conception of the rule of law, one in which law is widely obeyed and creates a kind of social as well as merely governmental fixed point through which private lives may be organised. Ironically, in contemporary American discourse, such a conception of the rule of law seems to be most prominent in anti-egalitarian movements, paired with calls for more vigorous policing against protesters who call for legal reform.[78]

This challenge – how to actually deliver legal protection to Black Americans – turned out to frame the entire post-Reconstruction period, for, as we shall see, whites immediately resorted to terrorist violence to overturn the result of the Civil War. That violence largely succeeded for many decades, in part because the law found itself unsuited to protect the freed. As it turned out, Black Americans had to protect themselves, and ultimately to force the courts and the political system to do their jobs.

[77] ibid 175.

[78] For example, conservative commentator D French, 'Anti-Cop Rioters Don't Care about 'Justice'' (*National Review*, 21 September 2016) www.nationalreview.com/2016/09/black-lives-matter-rioters-rule-law-under-attack/) claimed that Black Lives Matter protests (including, to be fair, protests that on his account turned violent) have 'moved from attacking the police, to attacking the rule of law itself' and 'represent an oppressor criminal class rising against the rule of law and against the very value of human life'.

4

Turning the Constitution Around: Black Liberation and the Rule of Law in the Last Century

T HE FALL OF Reconstruction was also the fall of the rule of law in the South. After the 1877 deal that put Rutherford B Hayes in the White House and ended active executive branch involvement in Reconstruction, white terrorist 'Redeemers' seized and maintained political control of the South by using violence to keep Black citizens away from the voting booth and then, having taken control of the governments, building blatantly unfair institutions such as poll taxes and literacy tests in order to keep them out and keeping lynchers on hand to ensure that none of their victims resisted too vigorously. This ushered in the long darkness of Jim Crow.

There's a plausible (albeit contestable) interpretation of the Redemption period that directly lays the blame at the feet of the judiciary. Southern white terror began before the election of 1876, and the Supreme Court directly impeded the federal government's efforts under President Grant to prevent it. The deed was done in *United States v Cruikshank*, which, in Foner's words, 'gave a green light to acts of terror where local officials either could not or would not enforce the law'.[1] The immediate licence was granted not by the Supreme Court's opinion, but the earlier ruling of a single justice, sitting in at the circuit level, two years beforehand: Justice Bradley's opinion letting the terrorists off scot-free was widely publicised, and was immediately taken by white paramilitaries as declaring open season and leading to numerous violent assaults on Black officeholders across the South.[2] Thereafter the Supreme Court's opinion resonated through the generations to undermine the use of the Reconstruction Amendments to actually secure the rule of law.

---

[1] E Foner, *Reconstruction: America's Unfinished Revolution, 1863–1877*, updated edn (Harper Perennial, 2014) 531. *United States v Cruikshank* 92 US 542 (1876).

[2] J Gray Pope, 'Snubbed Landmark: Why United States v. Cruikshank (1876) Belongs at the Heart of the American Constitutional Canon' (2014) 49 *Harvard Civil Rights-Civil Liberties Law Review* 385, 412–15; GC Rable, *But There Was No Peace: The Role of Violence in the Politics of Reconstruction* (University of Georgia Press, 2007) 129. Justice Bradley's opinion was *United States v Cruikshank* 1 Woods 308, 13 Am Law Reg (NS) 630, 25 FCas 707 (Circuit Ct, D LA, 1874).

Arguably, *Cruikshank* directly set off the fall of Reconstruction by facilitating the violent suppression of Black votes in the election of 1876. Here's how such an attribution could be defended. After the votes were cast, Republican electoral boards in the South refused to certify the election results based on the (eminently plausible) claim that Southern white terrorists had violently impeded Black electoral participation, and the (perhaps less plausible) claim that the terrorism swung the election in Tilden's favour.[3] This was the dispute which was resolved in the compromise in which Hayes agreed to end federal involvement in Reconstruction. If the federal government been permitted back in 1874 to punish some terrorists, it may have been able to protect Black voters; accordingly, the election might have come out decisively in Hayes's favour, and Reconstruction might have continued. That being said, any such hypothesis is more than a little speculative, and we should remember that there were many political forces pushing against the use of federal troops to protect Black voters as well – thanks to an economic collapse, the Republicans had been badly hurt even in the North in the 1874 elections, and there was a widespread uproar against General Sheridan's proposal to have the white terrorists declared 'banditti' and put down by military commission; as a whole the political tide in the North seemed to be turning against Reconstruction.[4] So it may be that the Republicans would have lost even without the terrorist suppression of Black votes, or that the federal government would have failed to protect Black voters even in the absence of *Cruikshank*, or that Hayes would have put a stop to Reconstruction even without the deal to resolve the election. We cannot know. Still, *Cruikshank* did not help matters, and could have been the precipitating factor.

Cruikshank's factual background should have signalled to the Court that it needed to defend federal power to secure the bare minimum of lawful governance in the South. The case came out of the infamous Colfax massacre, in which Grant Parish, Louisiana was taken over by an armed coup led by the white sheriff (or at least the white Democrat who claimed to be sheriff and ended up in control of the office at the end of the bloodshed) against the Black Republicans who had won control of the rest of the government of the parish.[5] The Supreme Court refused to permit the government to convict the perpetrators under a section of Enforcement Act of 1870 which the Court quoted as follows:

> That if two or more persons shall band or conspire together, or go in disguise upon the public highway, or upon the premises of another, with intent to violate any provision

---

[3] Foner (n 1) 574–76.

[4] ibid 523–28, 554–55; N Lemann, *Redemption: The Last Battle of the Civil War*, 1st edn (Farrar, Straus and Giroux, 2006) 79, 93–94; D Kato, *Liberalizing Lynching: Building a New Racialized State* (Oxford University Press, 2016) 45–46.

[5] Lemann (n 4) 3–26, describes the massacre. For some of the political background in terms of disputes over the rightful government of Louisiana, see Rable (n 2) ch 8. A 'parish' is Louisiana's version of a county.

of this act, or to injure, oppress, threaten, or intimidate any citizen, with intent to prevent or hinder his free exercise and enjoyment of any right or privilege granted or secured to him by the Constitution or laws of the United States, or because of his having exercised the same, such persons shall be held guilty of felony, and, on conviction thereof, shall be fined or imprisoned, or both, at the discretion of the court – the fine not to exceed $5,000, and the imprisonment not to exceed ten years – and shall, moreover, be thereafter ineligible to, and disabled from holding, any office or place of honor, profit, or trust created by the Constitution or laws of the United States.[6]

Part of the problem came from indictments which the Court read narrowly – and perhaps the government could have avoided some of the case's worst implications by more carefully drafting them. But doctrinally the important part of *Cruikshank* for the crippling of the federal government's efforts to stop the Redeemers was its interpretation of the Fourteenth Amendment, which the court claimed did not grant Congress the power to punish 'private' murders within a state.[7] As Pope cogently argues, *Cruikshank* pioneered a number of important (and bad) doctrines in the course of its dismissal of the indictment against participants in the white coup: not only the 'state action doctrine' just mentioned, but also the exemption of the Fourteenth Amendment from the broad freedom of choice given Congress to choose the means necessary to effectuate the rest of its enumerated powers, and the narrow interpretation of what kinds of acts would constitute constitutionally cognizable race discrimination; in particular, to limit that interpretation to provably *intentional* acts.[8]

The narrow interpretation of the Fourteenth Amendment (and the strict reading of the indictments under the statute) seems to rest on an unwillingness to admit that the acts of the murderers were, in fact, forms of state action, as they manifestly were. How else ought we to characterise the actions of people who claim that they're the lawful government of a jurisdiction, seize the reins of that government by force, and then, having seized the government, kill those who resisted them? If that isn't state action, nothing is. Attending to those basic facts would have reaffirmed rather than undermined the federal government's power to deter similar coups in other Southern jurisdictions. And *Cruikshank's* legacy of federal abandonment echoed throughout the centuries: even as late as the civil rights movement, federal officials appealed to the idea that it wasn't their job to prevent local violence to justify their refusal to prevent attacks on Freedom Riders and other activists that were patently carried out by or in collaboration with the state.[9]

In view of the plain purpose of the Reconstruction Amendments to raise Black Americans to full citizenship, and, indeed, the specific history of the

---

[6] *United States v Cruikshank* 92 US 542, 548 (1875).

[7] The variety of holdings on the 16 counts of the indictment the Court considered can be somewhat confusing; WR Huhn, 'The Legacy of Slaughterhouse, Bradwell, and Cruikshank in Constitutional Interpretation' (2009) 42 *Akron Law Review* 1051, 1071–74, gives a very helpful explanation.

[8] Pope (n 2) 388–89.

[9] H Zinn, *SNCC: The New Abolitionists* (Haymarket Books, 2013) 197–98.

enactment of the Fourteenth Amendment through Black suffrage which was established via military force, it required a kind of wilful blindness to suppose that Congress could not rectify a state's failure to protect its Black citizens in that right under the enforcement provisions of the three Reconstruction Amendments.[10]

More fundamentally, the idea of the state action doctrine doesn't really work in the context of the white supremacist politics of the period, because that politics radically undermined the boundaries between private and public action. Mobs of redeemers had clear political purposes for their violence, and their victories achieved political, indeed, governmental, ends. Perhaps the best analogy is to a contemporary failed state that dissolves into the battles of competing warlords: at a certain point, those warlords are all the state there is, and the law ought to attend to that fact.

The state action doctrine and the requirement that race discrimination under the Fourteenth Amendment be intentional work together in contemporary doctrine. Their joint operation shields from constitutional control private persons who use tools provided by the state to engage in race discrimination, except insofar as someone within the state can be proven to have intended that those tools be used that way. The conjoining of those two *Cruikshank* doctrines even today vexes efforts to pursue racial legal equality by ignoring the merger between state and private agency, most importantly by serving as an impediment to efforts to remedy the effects of residential racial segregation through practices like affirmative school integration plans.

Consider *Milliken v Bradley*, a case in which the Supreme Court reversed a school desegregation order covering the entire Detroit metropolitan area on the grounds that the district court had ordered students bused across school district lines despite the (alleged) absence of any evidence that the suburban school districts had intentionally done anything to bring about the existing segregation.[11] Of course, we know the reality of the relationship between state action, municipal boundaries, and school segregation is far more complicated: municipal boundaries may encourage private action, for example, by creating districts to which 'white flight' may occur; and the creation of municipal boundaries may also be motivated by the desire to avoid school integration.[12]

---

[10] There might also be a case to be made that Congress had the power to do so under the Guarantee Clause.

[11] *Milliken v Bradley* 418 US 717 (1974).

[12] eg, GR Weiher, 'Public Policy and Patterns of Residential Segregation' (1989) 42 *Western Political Quarterly* 651, 672, argues that legal developments, including *Milliken* itself, 'have increased the salience of political boundaries for racially motivated settlers', ie, themselves facilitating white flight. N Burns, *The Formation of American Local Governments: Private Values in Public Institutions* (Oxford University Press, 1994), has traced out the conjunction of economic and racial motivations in the creation of new municipal governments for the purposes of hoarding resources. Justice Marshall, at least, could recognise state-sponsored residential racial segregation when he saw it, as in his opinion in *Memphis v Greene* 451 US 100 (1981), a case in which a local government shut

Nonetheless, the Court turned a blind eye to the complex intermixture of public and private action that led to allegedly de facto school segregation – a blind eye exemplified by the concurring opinion of Justice Stuart, who dismissed the underlying residential segregation that led to the school segregation as 'caused by unknown and perhaps unknowable factors such as in-migration, birth rates, economic changes, or cumulative acts of private racial fears'. Such blithe dismissals of reality are only possible within the framework of a strict state action doctrine according to which a federal court may remedy public racial injustice only if it can identify a specific individual with a government employee ID card who provably intended to create that racial injustice – an idea whose origins trace right back to *Cruikshank*.

Further reinforcing the core theses of this book, the most important case in which the state action doctrine gave way was *Shelley v Kraemer*, a case prohibiting the judicial enforcement of private racially restrictive covenants in real estate sales – yet again illustrating the way in which the protections of America's rule of law become much stronger when property rights, and especially property rights in land, are involved.[13] As I have been arguing throughout this volume, the American conception of the rule of law is centred around the protection of such property interests, so it should be unsurprising that Black Americans could win the protections of law for their exercise of rights associated with real estate ownership long before even more basic protections such as the protection against being lynched would take hold.[14]

Actually, property rights took the driver's seat in an even earlier case: in 1917, the Supreme Court struck down an ordinance prohibiting the sale of land in a designated area to Black people – not on the grounds that race discrimination was unconstitutional as such – but because that the law unjustifiably barred the alienability of property.[15] The Court explicitly disclaimed the ambition to remedy race discrimination, saying: 'The case presented does not deal with an attempt to prohibit the amalgamation of the races. The right which the ordinance annulled was the civil right of a white man to dispose of his property if he saw fit to do so to a person of color and of a colored person to make such disposition to a white person.' Other than, however, the rare case where the Supreme Court is willing to recognise the intertwined nature of private and state action to protect property interests, we to this day labour under the legacy of

---

down a street between the Black and the white neighbourhoods to bar 'undesirable traffic'. But, alas, Justice Marshall's opinion was a dissent. For further discussion of the racial character of municipal boundaries see P Gowder, 'Racial Classification and Ascriptive Injury' (2015) 92 *Washington University Law Review* 325, 373–90.

[13] *Shelley v Kraemer* 334 US 1 (1948). To be fair, the Court also permitted the state action doctrine to be compromised in the case of political parties that held 'white primaries' and were effectively merged with the state in the same period. See, eg, *Smith v Allwright* 321 US 649 (1944).

[14] RD Godsil, 'Race Nuisance: The Politics of Law in the Jim Crow Era' (2006) 105 *Michigan Law Review* 505, describes another iteration of the same property bias: the surprising tendency of courts to reject the abuse of nuisance laws to chase out Black landowners.

[15] *Buchanan v Warley* 245 US 60 (1917).

Redemption jurisprudence – the core way that the court in *Cruikshank* operated the Fourteenth Amendment is, alas, still good law.[16]

Yet paradoxically, property rights and republicanism contributed to the loss of Reconstruction's promise. Heather Cox Richardson attributes the fall of Reconstruction to a growing northern perception that freedpeople's political empowerment was not consistent with the dominant 'free labour' ideology of the time. The free labour ideology understood regional, national, and individual progress to revolve around workers who, through productivity and thrift, rose to become small-scale capitalists (much like republicanism's yeoman farmers); the idea was that the freedpeople would advance themselves through the unlocking of their capacity to benefit from their own work, and in doing so promote economic development in the South.[17]

But free labour had an internal tension: it was a view inconsistent with land monopolisation, since land monopolisation meant there was no path to upward mobility for workers; Radical Republicans deployed free labour ideology to challenge plantation aristocrats. But when freedpeople acquired political power in the South and began to actually challenge those monopolies themselves, by increasing taxes on concentrated land and by creating avenues to easier land ownership for the freed, this allowed Democrats to invoke the ideology of property rights to turn free labour ideals – and rule of law ideals – around, and portray the Republicans and freedpeople as interested in 'corrupt' expropriation (especially after the terrifying spectre of the Paris Commune in 1871). Richardson convincingly argues that this contributed to the electoral defeat of the Republicans in 1874 and to Northern unwillingness to fight the violent assaults on Black suffrage and officeholding.

JUDGE LYNCH'S AFFRONT TO THE RULE OF LAW

After the redeemer coup, the white racists of the South continued to resort to terror to maintain their hold on power. Jim Crow was enforced not merely by laws such as poll taxes, literacy tests, segregation statutes combined with

---

[16] The property theme might also be discernible in Justice Bradley's early intervention in *Cruikshank*. Pope (n 2) 410–11, helpfully draws our attention to the fact that the circuit opinion hinted at yet another hypocritical assertion of rule of law interests as a reason to not protect Black people: that it would amount to class legislation in favour of Black Americans. Moreover, according to Pope, ibid 418–22, Bradley's motivations for writing the circuit opinion that led to the violence and to the errors inflicted on the law by the full Court later were all about the protection of property holders as a class – Bradley had supported the 'property' interests of planters before the Civil War on the basis of what Pope calls 'the commonality of interest and outlook among all businessmen, slave owners and employers of wage labor alike' – and his circuit ruling reflected the belief that the labouring classes – which in the South meant Black people – were appropriately under the rule of the owners of property (even if they were entitled to a vote to pick among those who were qualified to be their rulers).

[17] H Cox Richardson, *The Death of Reconstruction: Race, Labor, and Politics in the Post-Civil War North, 1865–1901* (Harvard University Press, 2001).

inferior public services (like schools), and the like, but also by Judge Lynch.[18] As Ida B Wells-Barnett, the mother of the antilynching movement, explained, 'The real purpose of these savage demonstrations is to teach the Negro that in the South he has no rights that the law will enforce.'[19] Because the state routinely turned away from lynch mobs with a nod and a wink, the message that Wells-Barnett described was delivered quite clearly.[20]

Other civil rights activists explicitly invoked the concept of the rule of law to capture the demand that the government act to prevent this terror. For example, Hayword Burns published an essay in *Commentary* with the title 'The Rule of Law in the South', which described organised efforts to impede Black enfranchisement as a 'reign of violence and lawlessness' and called for the deployment of federal force to 'enforce law and foster a new atmosphere of public law and order'.[21]

Wells-Barnett and Burns realised that, contra *Cruikshank*, lynch mobs *were* the state. After the redeemers used terrorism to seize the state, their heirs used terrorism to hold onto it; just as the state de jure authorised the 'private' arbitrary violence of masters over slaves, it also de facto authorised the 'private' violence of lynchers over their victims. Lynchers knew that the arm of the state would not be extended to prevent or punish their behaviour, so long as they confined their violence to Black victims. Indeed, sometimes lynch mobs included members of the police or other state officials. And the state worked hand in hand with private mobs late into the civil rights era; in an infamous example, Bull Connor once agreed to hold the police back for 15 minutes to permit the Klan some unrestrained time to beat Freedom Riders before restoring order.[22]

Black Americans first tried to solve this problem in Congress: they repeatedly asked it to use its Fourteenth Amendment powers (those powers denied by the Court in *Cruikshank*) to end lynching. But anti-lynching laws went down to defeat in Congress. Racist members of Congress didn't bother to conceal the reasons: they opposed those laws to permit the violent private enforcement of the existing social hierarchy, and to prevent 'social equality' between the races, a term that at least partially seemed to be code for Black men being allowed to

---

[18] To use the language of W White, *Rope & Faggot: A Biography of Judge Lynch* (Alfred A Knopf, 1929).

[19] IB Wells-Barnett, *Lynch Law in Georgia* (Chicago Colored Citizens, 1899) 1.

[20] P Gowder, 'Resisting the Rule of Men' (2018) 62 *Saint Louis University Law Journal* 333, 347–48; P Gowder, *The Rule of Law in the Real World* (Cambridge University Press, 2016) 54–55; D Kato, 'Strengthening the Weak State: Politicizing the American State's "Weakness" on Racial Violence' (2012) 9 *Du Bois Review: Social Science Research on Race* 457.

[21] H Burns, 'The Rule of Law in the South' (1965) 40 *Commentary* 80.

[22] C Deitle Leonardatos, 'California's Attempts to Disarm the Black Panthers' (1999) 36 *San Diego Law Review* 947, 951; P Magnusson, 'FBI Knew Policeman Was Leak to Klan on Freedom Riders' (*Washington Post*, 20 August 1978), www.washingtonpost.com/archive/politics/1978/08/20/fbi-knew-policeman-was-leak-to-klan-on-freedom-riders/b7c9511b-8805-4ff6-a4dd-3da31a05f1af/.

date white women, but also seemed to refer to a broader upsetting of the racial hierarchy in the South.[23]

The speechmaking was remarkably blatant. The following words (which I have excerpted to highlight the open racial hatred) were uttered by a Representative from Georgia by the name of Brand, in opposition to a bill which would have criminalised lynching, on the floor of Congress in 1922:

> The truth is, this proposed legislation is partisan and political. It is a blow at the white people of the South – nothing more and nothing less. The bill was introduced and is being prosecuted in order to promote the welfare of many of the Republicans in this House. It was introduced and is being prosecuted at the instance of their Negro constituents, among others, and the Negro societies in the North, who are not so much interested in preventing lynching of Negroes for assaults upon our white women as they are for establishing social and political equality with the white people. This is the fruitage which they hope and pray may grow out of the agitation of the Negro question and be the result of the pending legislation. Human villany has sounded no lower depths than is here fathomed in this political effort to bring about such an infamous heritage. [...] Social equality may come to pass in the territory north of the Mason and Dixon Line, but the stars will cease to shine and the heavens will be rolled up as a scroll before this state of affairs will ever exist among white people of the South.[24]

A Representative named Sisson from Mississippi said made matters even more explicit: what lynching really was about was interracial marriage:

> Now, I know that there is not a man on this floor who has among the Negroes acquainted with him more friends than I have. I work them on a little plantation which I own. All these Negroes are my friends. But I will tell you what I do not want; I will tell you what I am not going to have; I will tell you what every good white man on this earth will not have-I do not want him as a son-in-law and I do not want her as a daughter-in-law.[25]

A bit later in his diatribe, Sisson forgets his admission that he's really worried about his daughters having consensual relationships with Black men, and pretends that he's worried about rape; but in doing so he also manages to provide a backhanded faux-reluctant endorsement of the practice of lynching from the floor of Congress:

> This problem has heretofore been looked upon as the problem of the South, and here fifty-odd years after the Civil War, when you have the power, you have not presented to us any measure to help us solve the problem, but are making it harder for us. The man who says lynching will be stopped by virtue of this law does not know the instincts of the Anglo-Saxon blood. Do you know when, the crime of lynching is

---

[23] B Holden-Smith, 'Lynching, Federalism, and the Intersection of Race and Gender in the Progressive Era' (1996) 8 *Yale Journal of Law and Feminism* 31, 58.
[24] 62 Cong Rec 1703 (1922).
[25] 62 Cong Rec 1718 (1922).

going to stop in my country? It is going to stop when the beast shall cease to outrage white girls in the South, and thank God it will never stop until then. [...]

No good man in the South believes in lynching as a method of enforcing law. But as long as rape continues, lynching will continue. For this crime, and this crime alone, the South has not hesitated to administer swift and certain punishment. We have about broken up lynching in the South, and we are going to break it up, so help us God. We are going to protect our girls and womenfolk from these black brutes. When these black fiends keep their hands off the throats of the women of the South then lynching will stop, and it is never going to stop until that crime stops. [...]

Before God and high heaven this is the sacred truth. I would rather the whole black race of this world were lynched than for one of the fair daughters of the South to be ravished and torn by one of these black brutes. Now, if this be treason, make the most of it.[26]

At the most homicidal parts of this speech, the Congressional Record reports that Sisson's open bloodlust was punctuated by '[Applause]'. And one need not wonder very long how, precisely, it was supposed to be the case that passing a federal law against mob homicides would lead to poor Mr. Sisson having to deal with the horrors of having the Black Americans whom he 'worked' (!!) on his plantation (no less) marrying his precious daughters: the arbitrary violence of the white mobs was deemed necessary in order to maintain the social condition of subordination between the races in the South. When this bill fell to a filibuster in the Senate, the federal government effectively chose to preserve that state of affairs.[27] Hence, we can easily see the reign of lynch terror as a deliberate choice about how to use the power of the government at both the state and the federal levels; as a choice that subjected all Black Americans to the terror of arbitrary violence, it, like slavery, was an unquestionable offence against the rule of law.

THE SECOND LIBERATION MOVEMENT:
FROM ANTI-LYNCHING TO CRIMINAL JUSTICE

Unsurprisingly, a core concern of the twentieth century civil rights movement from the start was to bring an end to lynching. Recent work has emphasised, however, that the anti-lynching movement led to some of the great legal victories of the twentieth century. Political historian Megan Ming Francis has described how the early NAACP's work to end lynching shifted from Congress, where it achieved no real success – which should be utterly unsurprising, given the language just quoted – to the courts.[28] As a result of this effort, the development of procedural protections in the criminal justice system, including protections

---

[26] 62 Cong Rec 1720–21 (1922).
[27] Holden-Smith (n 23) 58.
[28] M Ming Francis, *Civil Rights and the Making of the Modern American State* (Cambridge University Press, 2014).

that represent the basic demands of the rule of law, can be traced directly to Black activism.

Francis identifies *Moore v Dempsey* as a key historical turning point in the development of American legal protections.[29] *Moore* was a case involving another of the main features of Lynch Law: it also corrupted the judicial process in the south by ensuring that Black defendants would be subject to rigged trials and brutal punishments, while whites who killed Black citizens would be able to get off scot-free. Judicial railroading of Black defendants was seen in the South not as an alternative to a fair trial but as an alternative to no trial at all and to death by lynching.[30] This is, of course, another example of how legal caste leads to procedural injustice: if Black Southerners were to receive fair trials for the crimes of which they were accused, they might sometimes be acquitted – their alleged victims might sometimes be revealed as liars – they might sometimes even get to stand tall in a courtroom and cross-examine whites and demand to be treated as free citizens under law. The racial hierarchy in Jim Crow could not permit such a thing, and so it could not offer fair trials.

Moore concerned the legal aftermath of mob violence in Arkansas, in which white residents, in cahoots with local law enforcement, massacred a number of Black citizens who were seeking to organise to oppose exploitative sharecropping practices; after the killing was done, the whites rubbed salt in the wound by charging and convicting several Black citizens of murder and putting them on death row.

The Supreme Court described the facts surrounding these convictions:

> A Committee of Seven was appointed by the Governor in regard to what the committee called the 'insurrection' in the county. The newspapers daily published inflammatory articles. On the 7th, a statement by one of the committee was made public to the effect that the present trouble was 'a deliberately planned insurrection of the negroes against the whites, directed by an organization known as the 'Progressive Farmers' and Household Union of America' established for the purpose of banding negroes together for the killing of white people.' According to the statement, the organization was started by a swindler to get money from the blacks.

> Shortly after the arrest of the petitioners, a mob marched to the jail for the purpose of lynching them, but were prevented by the presence of United States troops and the promise of some of the Committee of Seven and other leading officials that, if the mob would refrain, as the petition puts it, they would execute those found guilty in the form of law. The Committee's own statement was that the reason that the people refrained from mob violence was 'that this Committee gave our citizens their solemn promise that the law would be carried out.' According to affidavits of two white men and the colored witnesses on whose testimony the petitioners were convicted, produced by the petitioners since the last decision of the Supreme Court hereafter

---

[29] *Moore v Dempsey* 261 US 86 (1923).

[30] MJ Klarman, 'The Racial Origins of Modern Criminal Procedure' (2000) 99 *Michigan Law Review* 48, 56–57.

mentioned, the Committee made good their promise by calling colored witnesses and having them whipped and tortured until they would say what was wanted, among them being the two relied on to prove the petitioners' guilt. However this may be, a grand jury of white men was organized on October 27 with one of the Committee of Seven and, it is alleged, with many of a posse organized to fight the blacks upon it, and, on the morning of the 29th, the indictment was returned. On November 3, the petitioners were brought into Court, informed that a certain lawyer was appointed their counsel, and were placed on trial before a white jury – blacks being systematically excluded from both grand and petit juries. The Court and neighborhood were thronged with an adverse crowd that threatened the most dangerous consequences to anyone interfering with the desired result. The counsel did not venture to demand delay or a change of venue, to challenge a juryman or to ask for separate trials. He had had no preliminary consultation with the accused, called no witnesses for the defence, although they could have been produced, and did not put the defendants on the stand. The trial lasted about three-quarters of an hour, and in less than five minutes, the jury brought in a verdict of guilty of murder in the first degree. According to the allegations and affidavits, there never was a chance for the petitioners to be acquitted; no juryman could have voted for an acquittal and continued to live in Phillips County, and if any prisoner by any chance had been acquitted by a jury, he could not have escaped the mob.[31]

But even this brutal background did not guarantee that the Supreme Court would save the prisoners: the Court had recent precedent suggesting that it would not intervene in mob-dominated state criminal proceedings; it took the deliberate strategic advocacy of the NAACP to nonetheless bring the case before the Court, and to win new precedent that would lead to decades of further Court-directed reforms in American criminal procedure.[32]

Michael Klarman traces out some of the repercussions of this civil rights effort for the later innovations of constitutional criminal procedure.[33] While the most famous decisions, such as *Miranda v Arizona* (coerced confessions), *Gideon v Wainwright* (right to counsel), and *Mapp v Ohio* (exclusionary rule) would not occur until the 1960s, it was the interwar period which saw the first steps by the Supreme Court to intervene in state criminal trials. As Klarman argues, these interventions were only possible – in the face of a baseline ideology of strong federalism which would have traditionally forbidden federal judicial interference in state prosecutions – because the prosecutions which got to the Court were so egregiously illegal. And the reason they were so egregiously illegal and provoked enough public outrage (at least in the North) to provide political support for the Supreme Court's interventions was because they were racist prosecutions by formerly Confederate states at the height of Jim Crow.

For example, *Powell v Alabama* arose from the infamous 'Scottsboro Boys' events, where a number of Black teenagers were accused of raping a white

---

[31] *Moore v Dempsey* 261 US 86, 87–89 (1923) (internal paragraph breaks modified).
[32] Francis (n 28) 6, 128–29.
[33] Klarman (n 30).

woman.[34] The teenagers were held in jail under military guard to protect them from the lynch mob that had formed and were not given access to counsel until the morning of trial. Even at trial, there was some ambiguity about the relationship between the lawyers and the defendants; the Court quoted a bizarre rambling conversation between counsel and the court where a lawyer hemmed and hawed about whether he was actually going to represent the defendants. The Court reversed several death penalty sentences and held that when the defendant in a capital case was unable to acquire a lawyer, the state was under an obligation to appoint one.

In *Brown v Mississippi*, another of Klarman's examples, the Court reversed an even more outrageous conviction. The Black defendants were sentenced to death for allegedly murdering their landlord; the sole evidence on the basis of which they were convicted was their confessions. These confessions were procured by extreme torture perpetrated by a deputy sheriff in combination with a mob of white private citizens. The Court quotes a description by a dissenting state judge which describes how one defendant was partially hanged (and the rope scars were still visible on his neck at trial) then carried out of state and whipped until he confessed; two others were beaten with 'a leather strap with buckles on it', 'and in this manner the defendants confessed the crime, and as the whippings progressed and were repeated, they changed or adjusted their confession in all particulars of detail so as to conform to the demands of their torturers'.[35] Moreover, the deputy who perpetrated these acts was called as a witness by the state and casually admitted that he had beaten one of the defendants 'not too much for a negro; not as much as I would have done if it were left to me'.

These cases were doctrinal predecessors for the 1960s Warren Court innovations. *Gideon* cited and depended on *Powell v Alabama*; while the Court does not rely on it, *Brown v Mississippi* is a clear predecessor for *Miranda*. These gains, of course, rebounded to the benefit of all of American society. Many of the rules of constitutional criminal procedure on which the current generation of criminal defendants depends arose as judicially crafted remedies for systematic police abuses, often though not exclusively against Black Americans, and in response in substantial part to an entire campaign of Black-led organising and litigation to achieve the rule of law against the depredations of Judge Lynch.

The claims of Black Americans, and racial injustice more generally, were also at the forefront in the Warren Court's reforms of criminal procedure. Thus, *Mapp v Ohio* involved the abusive search of a black woman's home by white police officers.[36] *Miranda* involved a Latino victim of police misconduct.[37]

[34] *Powell v Alabama* 287 US 45 (1932).
[35] *Brown v Mississippi* 297 US 278, 281–82 (1936).
[36] B Capers, 'Rethinking the Fourth Amendment: Race, Citizenship, and the Equality Principle' (2011) 46 *Harvard Civil Rights-Civil Liberties Law Review* 1, 7.
[37] ibid.

Duncan v Louisiana, involving the right to a jury trial, was another case infected with Southern racism, and directly involved criminal charges of a young Black man arising out of racial conflict.[38] Other cases where Black criminal defendants led the charge to successfully get the Warren court to continue its trend of ratcheting up federal scrutiny of the constitutionality of the misconduct of state law enforcement officials include *Thompson v City of Louisville*, striking down the conviction, on the basis of zero evidence whatsoever, of a Black man for 'loitering' and *Monroe v Pape*, permitting a civil rights claim for damages against police officers who conducted a blatantly illegal raid against a Black family; former ACLU lawyer Burt Neuborne describes these cases as evidence of a 'gravitational pull' of race on the Court.[39]

Should you meet a veteran of the Civil Rights Movement, you may want to consider thanking them for helping protect you from coerced confessions, retaliatory searches, and rigged criminal trials.

From the Black Panthers to the Movement for Black Lives

The most famous, or perhaps notorious, of the Black organisations of the Civil Rights era is the Black Panther Party. To be more accurate, they ought to be called by their full name, the Black Panther Party for Self-Defense, for the key proposition for which they were and continue to be known was their advocacy for armed self-defence by Black Americans. Images of the Black Panthers universally show them carrying very large guns, and their continuing image in American culture revolves around perceptions of violent resistance to authority.

Yet from a different perspective we can understand the Panthers as a rule of law organisation, oriented around demanding that the police follow the law – even if, as Papke argued, that demand was in part 'cynical'.[40] The Black Panther Party began primarily as a movement against police brutality, spending the bulk of its early efforts patrolling Black neighbourhoods in Oakland to deter police misconduct – and carrying not just their famous guns but also (unspecified) lawbooks to use to remonstrate with the police.[41] Indeed, the

---

[38] ibid 7–9.

[39] B Neuborne, 'The Gravitational Pull of Race on the Warren Court' (2011) 2010 *The Supreme Court Review* 59; see also HL Packer, 'The Courts, the Police, and the Rest of Us' (1966) 57 *The Journal of Criminal Law, Criminology, and Police Science* 238, 240. This may not have all been to the good: S Ossei-Owusu, 'The Sixth Amendment Facade: The Racial Evolution of the Right to Counsel' (2019) 167 *University of Pennsylvania Law Review* 1161, 1192–1202, thoughtfully argues that race actually 'impeded the development of indigent defense' because the egregious race cases allowed the Court to spend decades focusing on the distinctive vulnerability of the Black victims of Jim Crow justice rather than the broader right to counsel.

[40] D Ray Papke, 'The Black Panther Party's Narratives of Resistance' (1994) 18 *Vermont Law Review* 645, 662–71.

[41] JA Courtright, 'Rhetoric of the Gun: An Analysis of the Rhetorical Modifications of the Black Panther Party' (1974) 4 *Journal of Black Studies* 249, 253.

material of the Party was replete with references to the Constitution and the Declaration of Independence, and its core message was that Black Americans, even in the course of engaging in armed self-defence against the police, would merely be resorting to arms in order to secure the legal rights which they were being denied by racist police.[42]

In their famous Ten-Point Program, issued in 1967, there was only one mention of carrying arms, and it came accompanied directly with an appeal to law:

> We believe we can end police brutality in our Black community by organizing Black self defense groups that are dedicated to defending our Black community from racist police oppression and brutality. The Second Amendment of the Constitution of the United States gives us a right to bear arms. We therefore believe that all Black people should arm themselves for self defense.[43]

Other elements of the Ten-Point Program included demands focused on core rule of law issues of criminal procedure: the Panthers demanded the release of Black men from jail 'because they have not received a fair and impartial trial', for example. In other material the Party directly invoked the rule of law and its traditional contrast to the rule of men to capture the treatment of Black Americans by the police, complaining of 'rule of man over man instead of the rule of the laws of Human Rights and Justice'.[44] Their demands for institutional changes to remedy police brutality and discrimination were aimed to subject the police to more direct control from those over whom they used force.[45]

Perhaps most interestingly, the Program articulated an alternative conception of what it might mean to offer a person a fair jury trial – one connected to the idea of a legal community of equals:

> We want all black people when brought to trial to be tried in a court by a jury of their peer group or people from their black communities, as defined by the Constitution of the United States. We believe that the courts should follow the United States Constitution so that black people will receive fair trials. The Fourteenth Amendment of the U.S. Constitution gives a man the right to be tried by his peer group. A peer is a person from a similar economic, social, religious, geographical, environmental, historical and racial background. To do this the court will be forced to select a jury from the black community from which the black defendant came. We have been, and are being, tried by all-white juries that have no understanding of the 'average reasoning man' of the black community.[46]

---

[42] M Roman, 'The Black Panther Party and the Struggle for Human Rights' (2016) 5 *Spectrum: A Journal on Black Men* 7, 14–15.
[43] 'What We Want Now! What We Believe', reprinted in J Bloom and WE Martin, Jr, *Black Against Empire: The History and Politics of the Black Panther Party*, 2nd edn (University of California Press, 2016) 72.
[44] Roman (n 42) 14.
[45] ibid 22.
[46] Bloom and Martin, Jr (n 43) 72.

The proposition that a jury of one's peers requires a kind of social identification between the defendant and the members of the jury is somewhat unfamiliar to contemporary American law (and 'peers' does not appear in the Constitution – it comes from the Magna Carta). Nonetheless, the demand had some important historical fidelity. At least sometimes in the period between the Magna Carta and the nineteenth century, the notion of a jury of one's peers was taken seriously in both England and America. Efforts to assure a jury of one's peers to ethnic and national minorities included the notion of a 'mixed jury', in which efforts were made to ensure representation from the defendant's social group.[47] At least one Black defendant in Jim Crow had unsuccessfully tried to demand a jury *de medietate linguae* – containing representation from his own group – in 1887 in North Carolina.[48] And in the context of the framing-era idea that a jury could serve as a democratic guardian of the government's legal fidelity – as well as the Federalist 57 idea that democratic inclusion would be instrumental in achieving general law – the demand makes perfect sense.

The Black Panthers were also notable for directly challenging the property-oriented conception of the American rule of law. Much like contemporary Black Lives Matter activists argue that focusing on property destruction at protests rather than the killings by police that occasion the protests represents the placing of property rights over rights to live, the Panthers articulated a conception of the hated 'pig' as a police officer or other authority who valued property rights above human rights.[49]

To be sure, the Black Panthers also produced rhetoric replete with calls for violent revolution, to 'off the pigs', and the like.[50] But I do not aim to offer a general defence of the Black Panther Party; rather, I offer it as an example of how we can find rule of law ideas embedded even in the most 'radical' of Black liberation organisations.

Indeed, the use of the law and the values captured by the law as a tool both of internal solidarity and of external solidarity – to appeal to shared values and simultaneously reveal the hypocrisy and corruption of the powerful – can be vividly seen

---

[47] C Davies and C Edwards, '"A Jury of Peers": A Comparative Analysis' (2004) 68 *The Journal of Criminal Law* 150, 151–53; M Constable, *The Law of the Other: The Mixed Jury and Changing Conceptions of Citizenship, Law, and Knowledge* (University of Chicago Press, 1994); DA Ramirez, 'The Mixed Jury and the Ancient Custom of Trial by Jury De Medietate Linguae: A History and Proposal for Change' (1994) 74 *Boston University Law Review* 777.

[48] Ramirez (n 47) 795.

[49] Roman (n 42) 12–13.

[50] No organisation is a monolith. Different members and sub-groups had different orientations toward the law and to violence. Indeed, there was a violent schism within the Party in 1971 precisely over this issue; later, individual leaders began to abandon the principles they advocated earlier and engage in outright criminal behaviour. DJ Garrow, 'Picking up the Books: The New Historiography of the Black Panther Party' (2007) 35 *Reviews in American History* 650, 657–59). But this does not change the character of the message embedded in their legal system advocacy.

in Bobby Seale's story of the Party. As he described it, Huey Newton drew on the law because of its capacity to be a basis for collective solidarity and action:

> Huey used to teach the brothers on that; he wouldn't let them get around it, because Huey understood that the brothers had no guidelines about how to deal with the pigs. So Huey went off in the area of law and he found out the brothers respected law. Huey knew something about law, and he could use it to make it serve him. That's all he was doing, he was bringing them basic things in everyday life about law.[51]

That passage comes from a description of an exchange in which the police stopped a heavily-armed Huey Newton in front of the Black Panther headquarters.[52] Newton stubbornly stood on his rights and refused to provide the police with any information or permission to search his car or inspect his weapons – simply handing over his driver's licence and invoking his Fifth, Fourth, and Second Amendment rights.[53]

The police officer's exclamations of frustration come out in the repeated statement that Newton is 'turning the Constitution around' – an utterance that I can only interpret as reflecting the experience of an unsettled hierarchy. Seale quotes him: '"You, you, you ..." the pig was mad. "You're just turning the Constitution around."'[54] Evidently, in the officer's mind, the Constitution is supposed to be a tool for him and people like him, and the patriotic foundation of their authority – and he's clearly horrified by the upset status hierarchy, on Seale's telling, when he realises that it can be 'turned around' against him. In fact, Newton's provocation forces the police to reveal that they specifically associated the right to appeal to the Constitution with hierarchical status:

> They were blabbing and oinking to each other about who in the hell we thought we were and, 'Constitution, my ass. They're just turning it around.' Then a pig said to Huey, 'Who in hell you think you are?'[55]

When Seale recounts this story, he also recounts the way that a crowd of people formed to watch the police be humiliated by the pairing of law and arms, and that the incident provided a notable boost to their recruiting – because others in the community also wanted to stand up to the police by 'turning the Constitution around'. Such are the tactics of the radical demand for the rule of law in the face of oppression.

Radical Black movements in the period drew on the resources of the law in other ways as well. Another important tactic in challenging police behaviour was to draw directly on the fact that trials were public – a fact whose traditional

---

[51] B Seale, *Seize the Time: The Story of the Black Panther Party* (Black Classic Press, 1991) 86.
[52] ibid 85–93.
[53] Of course, being the Black Panthers, these assertions of legal right were also paired with threats to shoot back if the police escalated the situation to violence – but how different is that from the Lockean right to revolution and broader classical liberal right to self-defence that inspired the Framers?
[54] ibid 90.
[55] ibid 89.

rule of law signification is that it permits the public to monitor the conduct of their officials – to highlight the lawless conduct of officials for the public and articulate oppositional accounts of legality. For example, Felber describes how the Nation of Islam combined highly-disciplined street-protest tactics with courtroom trials to demonstrate their organisational solidarity and build both legal and political credibility for the claim that police were simultaneously violating their property rights and their religious liberties.[56] As Felber characterises the tactic, the Nation 'sought to shift the discourse of the trial through political theatre and community organising around a united platform against police brutality'.[57] Such techniques are both challenges to and affirmations of traditional conceptions of the rule of law – challenges because they refuse to permit the court to operate under normal order and deny that the issue of justice for an oppressed people can be conducted with the same de-politicised processes that we might use to adjudicate a dispute over a stock swap – thus, the Nation upset the conventional context of the courtroom by, for example, demanding that their religious beliefs be respected by seating Muslim women in a separate section and at one point even patrolling the hallways and denying white spectators admittance under the colour of the claim that the trial was not 'public' – yet affirmations in that they actually used the publicity of the trials to draw attention to their claims and invite the broader democratic community to judge the behaviour of the police, replicating the republican conception of the function of the jury in the public at large.[58]

We can see the contemporary Movement for Black Lives as a continuation of the overall focus of Black liberation activists on fair criminal justice in the twentieth century, whether of the liberal and within-the-system orientation of the NAACP, or the radical and subversive orientation of the Black Panther Party and the Nation of Islam.[59] While Black activism was instrumental in challenging the worst policing abuses of the twentieth century, the struggle continues to this day.

The very first newsletter put out by the Black Panther Party, on 25 April 1967, accused the police of murdering Denzil Dowell, an unarmed Black man who was shot six times.[60] The same number of bullets struck Michael Brown, an unarmed Black man in Ferguson, Missouri in August 2014.[61] During the late nineteenth

---

[56] G Felber, *Those Who Know Don't Say The Nation of Islam, the Black Freedom Movement, and the Carceral State* (2020) 99–103.

[57] ibid 124.

[58] ibid 100, 123.

[59] It is important not to stereotype the tactics either of civil-rights-era Black liberation activists or their contemporary heirs. As Hooker has argued, Americans tend to hold a harmfully romanticised image of the Civil Rights Movement and a pernicious tendency to use that romanticised image as an impossible ideal against which to criticise contemporary activists. J Hooker, 'Black Lives Matter and the Paradoxes of U.S. Black Politics: From Democratic Sacrifice to Democratic Repair' (2016) 44 *Political Theory* 448.

[60] Bloom and Martin, Jr (n 43) 162.

[61] J Hafner, *Police Killings of Black Men in the U.S. and What Happened to the Officers*, (USA Today, 29 March 2018) www.usatoday.com/story/news/nation-now/2018/03/29/police-killings-black-men-us-and-what-happened-officers/469467002/.

and early twentieth century, Black Americans were financially exploited when they were brought into the criminal system, particularly through the infamous practice of 'convict leasing', where prisoners were rented out, effectively replicating slavery through the legal process.[62] In Ferguson, the Department of Justice disclosed a pattern of abuses that amounted to a racially discriminatory police and court system being effectively run as a for-profit operation, extracting revenue from citizens with fines and fees.[63] Of course, Ferguson is not convict leasing, but the overall corruption of the criminal justice system, in which it is used not as a method for securing socially responsible behaviour from all citizens but for expropriating Black citizens, is similar between the two cases.[64] And the US continues to use extensive prison labour.[65]

Much like the Nation of Islam, contemporary activists associated with the Movement for Black Lives have articulated important counterpublic challenges to the dominant conceptions of what the rule of law could be. Keeanga-Yamahtta Taylor's analysis of the movement emphasises that the Black women who have been its most important leaders have framed it in terms of an account of what sort of things constitute 'state violence'. This framing demands that we focus on the *state* as the agent rather than individual violent police officers, and hence calls the state itself to account for the failure to use its power consistent with the liberty and equality of Black Americans – precisely the analytic move that the Supreme Court missed in *Cruikshank*, and Wells-Barnett made in interpreting lynching. It also demands that we see the violent character of a broader array of racist and unequal state practices, such as mass incarceration, hierarchies of citizenship and lawful presence, and gender-based, sexuality-based, and disability-based discrimination – all of which are rooted in coercion which in turn is backed by the threat of violence.[66]

To that contemporary identification of the rule of law failures at the heart of police violence against Black Americans, I would add that policing, in particular, also raises that other foundational concern of rule of law activists: the control of executive power. To this, the next chapter turns.

---

[62] MJ Mancini, 'Race, Economics, and The Abandonment of Convict Leasing' (1978) 63 *The Journal of Negro History* 339.

[63] Department of Justice, Investigation of the Ferguson Police Department (4 March 2015), www.justice.gov/sites/default/files/opa/press-releases/attachments/2015/03/04/ferguson_police_department_report.pdf. For a useful discussion of the historical thread from convict leasing to Ferguson, see D Murch, '*Paying for Punishment*' (*Boston Review*, 1 August 2016) bostonreview.net/editors-picks-us/donna-murch-paying-punishment.

[64] Contemporary activists recognise the continuity of the movement across time. For example, a leading Chicago movement focused on police abuse of youth adopted the name We Charge Genocide, in a conscious reference to the landmark 1951 petition in which the Civil Rights Congress called upon the United Nations to act against police abuse as well as lynching.

[65] eg, P Goodman, 'Hero and Inmate: Work, Prisons, and Punishment in California's Fire Camps' (2012) 15 *WorkingUSA* 353.

[66] K-Y Taylor, *From #BlackLivesMatter to Black Liberation* (Haymarket Books, 2016) 166–67.

5

Security and Discretion: The Problem of Executive Power

THE CONTROL OF executive power is probably the quintessential rule of law problem. The executive in any government is, by definition, the branch with the most immediate control over the state's monopoly over violence; as all conceptions of the rule of law at a minimum require that this violence be used against members of a political community only pursuant to law, the subjection of the executive to law is the first goal of every rule of law state. Moreover, executive power is typically the site for the application of that perennial *bête noire* of the rule of law, discretion. And the executive is the traditional governmental site for the state's interaction with the outsider, the Schmittian enemy – to exclude someone from the political and legal community is often to turn them over to the tender mercies of the executive to be addressed with pure force. Thus, it shouldn't be surprising that major controversies over the rule of law have often centred around bringing under control entities that directly wield executive power, such as monarchs, and, of course, the American President.

The problem of controlling executive power in the American context has a kind of disjointed character. On the one hand, libertarian scholars such as Richard Epstein and Philip Hamburger have articulated a prominent rule of law critique of American administrative law and the way that it seems to confer arbitrary power on executive branch officials.[1] While that critique is important, it is also almost entirely an elite phenomenon: its participants are academics at US law schools and senior judges; its object of concern is heavily focused on companies and commercial activity – on the idea that administrative processes such as Securities and Exchange Commission enforcement actions and Environmental Protection Agency rulemakings are subject to bias and to lack of fair notice

---

[1] eg RA Epstein, 'The Perilous Position of the Rule of Law and the Administrative State' (2013) 36 *Harvard Journal of Law & Public Policy* 5; P Hamburger, *Is Administrative Law Unlawful?* (University of Chicago Press, 2014). I have discussed the warped character of the rule of law debate over American administrative law at length in P Gowder, '(Untitled) Review of Cass Sunstein and Adrian Vermeule, Law and Leviathan: Redeeming the Administrative State' (2021) 31 *Law and Politics Book Review* 12, available at www.lpbr.net/2021/01/law-and-leviathan-redeeming.html.

in ways that undermine the economic activities and perhaps even the property interests of firms. From the normative standpoint, one might fairly consider the problem identified by this literature to be somewhat low priority: regulated industries also tend to have substantial resources with which to defend themselves in administrative processes, to the point that there is an entire alternative literature on the phenomenon known as 'regulatory capture'. Those who are supposedly subject to arbitrary power may on the whole benefit from or even control the administrative processes that apply to them. This is not to deny that this literature raises a real problem – in particular, it may suggest secondary rule of law concerns with respect to the capacity of dominant regulated entities to deploy government power in an arbitrary fashion to deter potential market entrants or to abuse consumers. But the force of the critique seems to me to be overstated by the scholars who focus on it.

However, there is a second critique of executive power which draws from but is not limited to the critique of administration – a critique which is centred on, and often advanced by, the most vulnerable. For the awesome power of the US President is not limited to, or even primarily about, industrial regulation – rather, the US President commands the most powerful military and law enforcement apparatus in the world, and those forces of violence are routinely turned on vulnerable individuals without full legal process. Most infamous in this respect is the conduct of the post-9/11/2001 'War on Terror', featuring uses of executive power including torture, the holding of individuals without trial in offshore military bases, and the extrajudicial assassination of US citizens with missiles from the sky. Equally important, however, is the combination of the logics of national security and of administration in US immigration law – delved into at depth in the next chapter – in which administrative agencies apply executive power not with licence revocations and fines to multibillion dollar corporations but with guns and cages to some of the most vulnerable people in the world – like stateless refugees from war and oppression – and in which even ordinary administrative law protections, such as the existence of Administrative Law Judges with some degree of independence from the agencies whose cases they adjudicate, are absent.

Moreover, the President is not the only person who wields executive power in the United States. Rule of law worries surrounding executive power have also been applied to subordinate executive officials and to state-level officials. However, the conversation about those officials is typically – and, I contend, inappropriately – separated from the conversation about executive power more broadly. One example is the welfare rights movement discussed in chapter three: the victory represented by treating welfare as a property right rather than a mere boon to be granted or withheld at the government's discretion was substantially a victory for the control of executive power – to protect individuals from having intrusive discretionary control over their lives exercised by the bureaucrat who could decide at will whether they would receive the cheque necessary to meet their basic needs that week.[2]

Yet executive discretion at levels beneath the President continues today and frames the extent to which vulnerable individuals in their real lives experience the United States as a government of laws or as one of the arbitrary power of individuals. Consider prosecution. American criminal laws notoriously tend to come attached to vastly stiffer penalties than other liberal democracies and tend to be used more aggressively.[3] Those penalties give prosecutors with charging discretion an immense bargaining chip with which to coerce plea bargains: a criminal defendant can take a prosecutor's deal and accept a sentence after which it might be possible to rebuild a life – or they can take the risk of a trial, and the risk of receiving a sentence, almost regardless of how minor the crime is, of years or decades of imprisonment.[4] With that kind of a negotiating position, many defendants lack the genuine option of a jury trial even if they are innocent of the crime with which they are charged. Some scholars have suggested that America's extreme over-incarceration – and the extreme racial injustice embedded in that incarceration – is largely due to the power and incentives of prosecutors.[5]

According to a 2011 Department of Justice report, an estimated 90–95 per cent of criminal cases in the United States are resolved by plea bargaining.[6] In addition to the lawless harms this prosecutorial strategy inflicts on individual defendants, it sets up a kind of conflict of interest between individual defendants and the community at large: if we suppose, with scholars like Appleman, that part of the function of the jury is to preserve the power of the People at large to both directly monitor and directly control the criminal process, then plea bargaining

---

[2] For an example and further discussion, see P Gowder, 'Equal Law in an Unequal World' (2014) 99 *Iowa Law Review* 1021, 1074–76.

[3] J Travis, B Western and S Redburn (eds), *The Growth of Incarceration in the United States: Exploring Causes and Consequences* (The National Academies Press, 2014) 36–37; JQ Whitman, *Harsh Justice: Criminal Punishment and the Widening Divide Between America and Europe* (1 issued as paperback, Oxford University Press, 2005).

[4] Human Rights Watch, 'An Offer You Can't Refuse: How US Federal Prosecutors Force Drug Defendants to Plead Guilty' (5 December 2013) www.hrw.org/report/2013/12/05/offer-you-cant-refuse/how-us-federal-prosecutors-force-drug-defendants-plead; DA Dripps, 'Guilt, Innocence, and Due Process of Plea Bargaining' (2016) 57 *William & Mary Law Review* 1343; GM Gilchrist, 'Plea Bargains, Convictions and Legitimacy' (2011) 48 *American Criminal Law Review* 143; WJ Stuntz, 'Plea Bargaining and Criminal Law's Disappearing Shadow' (2004) 117 *Harvard Law Review* 2548; A Manuel Crespo, 'The Hidden Law of Plea Bargaining' (2018) 118 *Columbia Law Review* 1303; M Langer, 'Rethinking Plea Bargaining: The Practice and Reform of Prosecutorial Adjudication in American Criminal Procedure' (2006) 33 *American Journal of Criminal Law* 223; TL Meares, 'Rewards for Good Behavior: Influencing Prosecutorial Discretion and Conduct with Financial Incentives' (1995) 64 *Fordham Law Review* 851.

[5] J Pfaff, *Locked In: The True Causes of Mass Incarceration-and How to Achieve Real Reform* (Basic Books, 2017).

[6] L Devers, 'Plea and Charge Bargaining Research Summary', Department of Justice, Bureau of Justice Assistance 24 January 2011, p 1, bja.ojp.gov/sites/g/files/xyckuh186/files/media/document/PleaBargainingResearchSummary.pdf.

offers to individual defendants a way to escape the risks of trial but only at the expense of sacrificing a major tool for the public at large to rein in overbearing prosecutors.[7] And yet so many of the American scholars who write about the rule of law and wring their hands about securities and environmental regulation have little or nothing to say about the proliferation of executive officials who have the *de facto* power to lock up the potentially innocent at will.

The United States also contains vast armies of executive officials who exercise the most consequential discretion of all – the too-often unchecked power to shoot and kill their fellow citizens. The Movement for Black Lives has in recent years brought into vivid relief that the complaints of the Black Panthers continue today. While, according to racial justice advocates, the criminal justice system in its entirety falls hardest on Black and Brown Americans in numerous respects, from the initial encounters with law enforcement, mired in racial profiling, all the way through sentencing, it all begins – and too often ends in the most permanent sense – with an encounter between a police officer and an individual on the street.[8] Much like Jim Crow, the hyper-policing of Black communities is traced back to the fall of Reconstruction, and, with it, the

---

[7] LI Appleman, 'The Plea Jury' (2010) 85 *Indiana Law Journal* 731, 756–59.

[8] The literature on racial disparities in criminal justice is immense, but some examples that seem worth noting to me (either because of their importance in the literature or simply because I think they summarise matters well) include M Alexander, *The New Jim Crow: Mass Incarceration in the Age of Colorblindness* (The New Press, 2012); J Forman, *Locking Up Our Own: Crime and Punishment in Black America*, 1st edn (Farrar, Straus and Giroux, 2017); D Cole, *No Equal Justice: Race and Class in the American Criminal Justice System* (New Press 1999); R Kennedy, *Race, Crime, and the Law*, 1st Vintage Books edn (Vintage Books, 1998); IF Haney López, 'Post-Racial Racism: Racial Stratification and Mass Incarceration in the Age of Obama' (2010) 98 *California Law Review* 1023; KR Johnson, 'How Racial Profiling in America Became the Law of the Land: United States v. Brignoni-Ponce and Whren v. United States and the Need for Truly Rebellious Lawyering' (2010) 98 *Georgetown Law Journal* 1005; DE Roberts, 'The Social and Moral Cost of Mass Incarceration in African American Communities' (2004) 56 *Stanford Law Review* 1271; B Pettit and B Western, 'Mass Imprisonment and the Life Course: Race and Class Inequality in U.S. Incarceration' (2004) 69 *American Sociological Review* 151; L Wacquant, 'From Slavery to Mass Incarceration' (2002) 13 *New Left Review* 41; AJ Davis, 'Racial Fairness in the Criminal Justice System: The Role of the Prosecutor' (2007) 39 *Columbia Human Rights Law Review* 202; J Soss and V Weaver, 'Police Are Our Government: Politics, Political Science, and the Policing of Race–Class Subjugated Communities' (2017) 20 *Annual Review of Political Science* 565; G Prowse, VM Weaver and TL Meares, 'The State from Below: Distorted Responsiveness in Policed Communities' (2019) 56 *Urban Affairs Review* 1423; MC Bell, 'Police Reform and the Dismantling of Legal Estrangement' (2017) 126 *Yale Law Journal* 2054; MD Holmes and BW Smith, 'Intergroup Dynamics of Extra-Legal Police Aggression: An Integrated Theory of Race and Place' (2012) 17 *Aggression and Violent Behavior* 344. There is also currently a heated debate within the empirical literature about the measurement of street-level police bias, which is a notably difficult task due to: (1) the numerous potential confounding variables associated with race and police contact, and (2) the fact that available data is itself derived from police contact, and hence reflects a substantial selection bias. D Knox, W Lowe and J Mummolo, 'Administrative Records Mask Racially Biased Policing' (2020) 114 *American Political Science Review* 619; D Knox and J Mummolo, 'Toward a General Causal Framework for the Study of Racial Bias in Policing' (2020) 1 *Journal of Political Institutions and Political Economy* 341; SB Starr, 'Testing Racial Profiling: Empirical Assessment of Disparate Treatment by Police' (2016) 2016 *University of Chicago Legal Forum* 485.

enactment of the Black Codes that set the precedent for the representation of Black populations as inconvenient people to be managed by law enforcement, as well as the use of convict leasing to achieve effective reenslavement under the guise of criminal law.[9] Yet it goes through executive power in the purest sense: the discretionary decision of an individual with a gun and a badge to stop a private citizen, to interrogate them, to commit acts of violence against them, and to arrest them. As such, it poses a core rule of law question. And while some earlier American scholars of administrative law and discretion – most prominently Kenneth Culp Davis – recognised the relationship between policing and administrative discretion, and thereby the rule of law; today the administrative law conversations and the policing conversations are largely distinct from one another.[10]

Policing also bears a complex relationship to the rule of law in its face as the protection of property rights. Black scholars since Du Bois have long identified that white identity itself can have, or substitute for, economic value. Contemporary critical race scholars have often followed Cheryl Harris in conceptualising whiteness itself as a form of property.[11] And that property interest can be projected onto both social relations and on space – thus, the private violence of both lynch mobs and of modern racial bias killings like George Zimmerman's killing of Trayvon Martin can be interpreted as defences of both white-property-as-status as well as white-property as white space, that is, as the defence of spaces that gain economic and social value from being identified as white and occupied primarily by whites and by those who claim white identity.[12] Policing too has been conceptualised as the defence of white space, as police enforce 'de facto' spatial segregation by, among other prominent examples, treating non-white Americans as suspicious when they are found 'out of place' and perpetuating relative stigma of non-white spaces; in that way facilitating both the economic advantage ('property values') and the status advantage of white spaces.[13]

For those reasons, this chapter starts with a closer examination of policing – the area that seems to me to be the most consequential site of unconstrained executive power, both in virtue of the sheer number of people who find their freedom even to occupy public space undermined by out-of-control policing and in virtue of the connection between contemporary policing and the ongoing Black liberation quest for the benefits of the rule of law. I then turn to

---

[9] K-Y Taylor, *From #BlackLivesMatter to Black Liberation* (Haymarket Books, 2016) 108–12.

[10] For a discussion of Davis's transition from administrative law to police discretion and the failure of the rest of the legal academy to listen, see RM Levin, 'The Administrative Law Legacy of Kenneth Culp Davis' (2005) 42 *San Diego Law Review* 315, 331–35.

[11] CI Harris, 'Whiteness as Property' (1993) 106 *Harvard Law Review* 1707.

[12] A Onwuachi-Willig, 'Policing the Boundaries of Whiteness: The Tragedy of Being out of Place from Emmett Till to Trayvon Martin' (2017) 102 *Iowa Law Review* 1113.

[13] For a general discussion, see MC Bell, 'Anti-Segregation Policing' (2020) 95 *New York University Law Review* 650.

presidential power in national security (and in doing so, briefly leave behind the property-oriented themes of this book), but with an emphasis on the connections between security, race, and discretion. Those concepts then lead to the discussion in the next chapter of immigration; an area of American law(lessness) that brings together national security, law enforcement, administration, and the heritage of settler ideology and racialised property through a kind of Schmittian site of sovereignty at the literal as well as figurative boundaries of American law.

POLICE AS EXECUTIVES: THE PROBLEM OF DISCRETION IN STREET-LEVEL CRIMINAL JUSTICE

The Movement for Black Lives and #BlackLivesMatter began, approximately, between the 2012 killing of Trayvon Martin by private citizen George Zimmerman and the summer of 2014, which saw the police killings in short succession of Michael Brown in Ferguson, MO, and Eric Garner in New York City, although the complaints of racist police violence and the epidemic of killings of Black Americans by police, frequently when those who are killed are unarmed and even children, has been salient and been the object of Black activism for much longer. Some of the most egregious of the many cases in which police have killed Black Americans since the summer of 2014 include Tamir Rice, a 12-year old boy who was killed for his toy gun; Freddie Gray, who died from neck injuries after police placed him in the back of a police van shackled but without a seatbelt – alleged to be a deliberate 'rough ride' meant to punish him for his conduct during the arrest; Breonna Taylor, who was killed in her own home in the course of a surprise midnight raid in which the police attempted to execute a search warrant to find drugs allegedly dealt by an ex-boyfriend; Botham Jean, who was killed inside his own apartment by an off-duty police officer who entered it, believing that it was her own unit, and shot him as a burglar; Atatiana Jefferson, whom police shot through the window of her own house following a 'welfare check' police call from the neighbour; and George Floyd, who suffocated after being held face-down, while handcuffed, on the ground, with a police officer's knee on his neck, for more than seven minutes – after repeatedly telling the police that he was struggling to breathe (the police officers who killed Mr Jean and Mr Floyd were eventually convicted of murder).

The bare fact of repeated police killings of Black Americans, especially when the victims are innocent of any crime and/or the police receive no consequences for the killing, is itself a challenge to the US's self-conception as a rule of law state, and we can interpret the Movement for Black Lives' challenges to the racial disparity in such killings and the lack of accountability for them as core rule of law demands on their own strength. However, we can also go a little bit deeper: exploring some of the causal factors plausibly contributing to police killings of Black Americans can draw out some underlying tensions and weaknesses in the American conception of the rule of law.

In particular, among the contributors to the police killing crisis that scholars have identified include: (a) widespread underlying police enforcement discretion, (b) legal doctrines which shield police from consequences from illegal acts, hence conferring a kind of *ex post* discretion on police, and (c) the effects of physical segregation on policing, which in turn are attributable in part to a number of underlying conditions in how the United States has managed and partly continues to manage property rights.[14]

I will take up each in turn.

Ex Ante Police Discretion: Street-Level Arbitrary Power

The statute books are replete with a set of background offences and authorisations which allow police a substantial amount of day-to-day enforcement discretion by licensing some kind of coercive official law enforcement response against most or potentially even all persons whom the police might encounter on the street. For example, loitering, vagrancy, and disorderly conduct laws, traffic and public transit infractions that authorise arrest rather than merely citation, laws against obstructing public rights of way (ie, being on them and being perceived to be in the way), and laws against disobeying the commands of police in the abstract may confer on police the authorisation to arrest individuals in a vast array of situations.[15] Moreover, current doctrines in constitutional criminal procedure permit the police to bring themselves in contact with a vast

---

[14] See especially DW Carbado, 'Blue-on-Black Violence: A Provisional Model of Some of the Causes' (2016) 104 *Georgetown Law Journal* 1479; DW Carbado, 'From Stopping Black People to Killing Black People: The Fourth Amendment Pathways to Police Violence' (2017) 105 *California Law Review* 125; D Roithmayr, 'The Dynamics of Excessive Force' (2016) 2016 *University of Chicago Legal Forum* 407.

[15] Disorderly conduct laws, for example, permit the police to enforce conceptions of appropriate public behaviour even though those conceptions are not only open-ended, but replete with background assumptions about class, race, and disability, among others: J Morgan, 'Rethinking Disorderly Conduct' [Forthcoming] *California Law Review*. Unsurprisingly, vagrancy laws and the like were a prominent feature of the post-civil-war Black Code system in the South, which was an effort to force freed people back onto the plantations. WEB Du Bois, *Black Reconstruction: An Essay Toward a History of the Part Which Black Folk Played in the Attempt to Reconstruct Democracy in America, 1860-1880* (Harcourt, Brace & Co, 1935) 166–79; E Foner, *Reconstruction: America's Unfinished Revolution, 1863–1877*, updated edn (Harper Perennial, 2014) 198–205. While some of these broad types of laws are occasionally struck down on Due Process vagueness grounds, eg, *Chicago v Morales*, 527 US 41 (1999); *Papachristou v Jacksonville*, 405 US 156 (1972); *Kolender v Lawson* 461 US 352 (1983), they still appear to be in sufficiently common use that we, alas, cannot safely characterise them all as unconstitutional on the basis of the discretion they confer. For an important history of the fight against vagrancy laws in particular, which recognises that the fall of those laws was at least in part replaced by other discretion-conferring police strategies, see RL Goluboff, *Vagrant Nation: Police Power, Constitutional Change, and the Making of the 1960s* (Oxford University Press, 2016). For analytic purposes, it may be helpful to subdivide discretion-conferring laws into three rough categories: 'vague' laws, such as the laws struck down by the Supreme Court cases just noted, which fail to give people notice of the conduct that constitutes an offence, see generally TJ Boutrous Jr and BH Evanson, 'The Enduring and Universal

array of people, either by 'stopping and frisking' them in the absence of any strong reason to believe they're engaged in crime or 'pretextual' stops in which they stop citizens for things like broken taillights, but with the real purpose of engaging in a dragnet for more serious crimes.[16]

The rule of law case against such laws is that they effectively subject individuals to the arbitrary authority of the police. If everyone is committing a crime all the time, then the police may inflict state violence on whomever they want. And such power translates into the capacity to deliver commands that organise the environment in legally unauthorised ways: the police may, for example, order a person hanging out on the corner with their friends to leave the street, even though they have the perfect legal right to be there, in view of the fact that the police may come up with some charge that can stick on them to punish them for disobedience or for 'contempt of cop'.[17] And, of course, such authorisations are more likely to be deployed against persons and communities that lack the political power to control the police, and in favour of those who hold the political power to use the police to control stigmatised and stereotyped communities – that is, along the lines of race and class. Finally, because police contact is risky, and especially risky for the stigmatised, when the police have the power to impose their interactions on private persons at will, they inherently have the power to impose the risk of an escalation to violence on those private persons.

Consider, as an example, the laws that led up to the killing of Michael Brown. My best guess for the ordinance that originally justified the police in stopping him for walking down the road was the following:

Manner of walking along roadway.

(a)   Where sidewalks are provided, it shall be unlawful for any pedestrian to walk along and upon an adjacent roadway.

Principal of Fair Notice' (2013) 86 *Southern California Law Review* 193; 'broad' laws as to which the conduct that violates it is perfectly clear, but so much conduct is covered that merely existing in public tends to constitute an offence, see generally K Brennan-Marquez, 'Extremely Broad Laws' (2019) 61 *Arizona Law Review* 641; and 'trivial' laws that punish behaviour so minor that even though the offence is narrow and clear, the collection of trivial laws *taken together* are likely to give police substantial discretion to arrest, and individual trivial laws are likely to be frequently violated just because nobody other than a police officer would seriously imagine that such a thing constitutes a crime. For an example of the last category, consider the fact that, in 2011, the New York police arrested some 1,600 people for violating laws regulating the manner of sitting on a subway seat, such as putting their feet up or taking up multiple seats, see J Goldstein and C Haughney, 'Relax, If You Want, but Don't Put Your Feet Up' (*The New York Times*, 6 January 2012) www.nytimes.com/2012/01/07/nyregion/minor-offense-on-ny-subway-can-bring-ticket-or-handcuffs.html.   More generally, on the proliferation of criminal laws, see SH Kadish, 'The Crisis of Overcriminalization' (1967) 374 *The ANNALS of the American Academy of Political and Social Science* 157; DN Husak, *Overcriminalization: The Limits of the Criminal Law* (Oxford University Press, 2008); E Luna, 'The Overcriminalization Phenomenon' (2005) 54 *American University Law Review* 703.

[16] *Terry v Ohio* 392 US 1 (1968); *Whren v United States* 517 US 806 (1996). Both *Terry* and *Whren* have been widely criticised for facilitating racial profiling. eg RL Jones, 'Terry v. Ohio: Its Failure, Immoral Progeny, and Racial Profiling' (2018) 54 *Idaho Law Review* 511; Johnson (n 8).

[17] CE Lopez, 'Disorderly (Mis)Conduct: The Problem with Contempt of Cop Arrests' (2010) 4 *Advance* 71.

(b) Where sidewalks are not provided, any pedestrian walking along and upon a highway shall, when practicable, walk only on the left side of the roadway or its shoulder facing traffic which may approach from the opposite direction.[18]

That ordinance was repealed in 2016 – perhaps due to the scandal over Mr Brown's death. But Ferguson's municipal code still contains another ordinance sufficiently broad to justify exactly the same interaction:

A person commits the offense of loitering if he obstructs or encumbers the passage of persons or vehicles upon, through or into any street, street corner, depot, building entrance or other public place and then refuses to move on when requested to do so by any police officer of the city.[19]

Observe that such a statute contains no standard for what constitutes an encumbrance or an obstruction. By its terms it would apply to sidewalks, city plazas, and just about anywhere outside a person's private home or office. Further observe the scope of probable cause for a permissible arrest (and hence the capacity to inflict the collateral consequences of an arrest, such as time in jail and possibly lost jobs, evictions, and other serious harms)[20] is broader than the scope of conviction, such that even if a court ultimately concludes that a person arrested under this ordinance was not encumbering the passage of others, it's quite unlikely that a police officer who arrests someone for violating this ordinance will be punished for the arrest.

Hence, a Darren Wilson today could stop, and potentially lose control of the situation or his own emotions and shoot, another Michael Brown today, in Ferguson, in essentially any public place where they might happen to meet, on the basis of the ordinance quoted above.[21] Such absolute police discretion is the anthesis of the rule of law.

---

[18] Former Ferguson Municipal Code Sec 44-344. This section was repealed in 2016. For the aid of future researchers: Ferguson distributes its municipal code, and historical versions thereof, via the third-party provider 'municode.com'. See City of Ferguson, www.fergusoncity.com/56/Government (linking to 'www.municode.com/library/MO/Ferguson' to provide the code of ordinances for the city). This ordinance can be viewed in a historical view of the city ordinances, at Municipal Code Sec 44-344, at library.municode.com/mo/ferguson/codes/code_of_ordinances/239430?nodeId=P TIICOOR_CH44TRMOVE_ARTVIIPE_S44-344MAWAALRO which I have archived at perma. cc/W8EN-NA57. The current municipal code notes that this section was repealed on 26 April 2016, by ordinance number 2016-3617. See library.municode.com/mo/ferguson/codes/code_of_ ordinances?nodeId=PTIICOOR_CH44TRMOVE_ARTVIIPE_S44-344RE&showChanges which I have archived at perma.cc/55QQ-PNLJ.

[19] Ferguson, Mo Municipal Code Sec 29-89. According to the Department of Justice report of the investigation into Mr Brown's death, the police officer who killed Brown claimed that 'cars [were] trying to pass' Mr Brown and his friend. Department of Justice Report Regarding the Criminal Investigation into the Shooting Death of Michael Brown by Ferguson, Missouri Police Officer Darren Wilson, (4 March 2015) www.justice.gov/sites/default/files/opa/press-releases/attach-ments/2015/03/04/doj_report_on_shooting_of_michael_brown_1.pdf, pp 12–13.

[20] R Harmon, 'Why Arrest?' (2016) 115 *Michigan Law Review* 307, 313–20.

[21] Bell (n 8) 2101–02, n 172, describes the commonality between Ferguson and Baltimore in the use of walking-in-the-street and similar ordinances to punish Black Americans for occupying public space.

The unbounded authority conferred by the numerous ordinances like Ferguson's across the United States effectively authorise a police officer to order anyone whom they want out of public space. And they are used that way. In Los Angeles, for example, researchers have observed these kinds of laws being used to target the homeless or to identify ostensible drug users for profiling. People who were unable to get through intersections at skid row at a normal walking speed – for example, because of a physical disability – were subject to police harassment on the basis of jaywalking laws.[22] Such harassment has concrete consequences on the lives of those whom police choose to supervise. Stuart gives as an example the experience of 'Tex', a homeless individual who was cited for 'obstructing the sidewalk' for momentarily setting his bags down on the street – an offence that spiralled into hundreds of dollars of fines and threats from a judge who apparently perceived Tex as a recidivist merely for existing.[23]

Sociologists and criminologists have gone so far as to equate the very function of policing with arbitrary discretion. For example, a famous definition of policing by Allan Silver in 1967 is that:

A policed society is unique in that central power exercises potentially violent supervision over the population by bureaucratic means widely diffused throughout civil society in small and discretionary operations that are capable of rapid concentration.[24]

Nor is this view just the province of left-wing academics. Part of the intellectual foundation for the 'broken windows' or 'order-maintenance' policing movement that took over many US cities, most famously Rudy Giuliani's New York, in the 1990s was an *Atlantic Monthly* article by George Kelling and James Wilson.[25] That article, which the New York police commissioner cited as a key influence on his policing strategy, openly applauded the lawless use of boundless police discretion.[26] Here's how Kelling and Wilson describe the conduct of a police officer in Newark whom they offer as a model to be admired:

The people on the street were primarily black; the officer who walked the street was white. The people were made up of 'regulars' and 'strangers.' Regulars included both 'decent folk' and some drunks and derelicts who were always there but who 'knew their place.' Strangers were, well, strangers, and viewed suspiciously, sometimes

[22] F Stuart, 'Becoming "Copwise": Policing, Culture, and the Collateral Consequences of Street-Level Criminalization' (2016) 50 *Law & Society Review* 279, 289–90.

[23] ibid 290–91.

[24] A Silver, 'The Demand for Order in Civil Society: A Review of Some Themes in the History of Urban Crime, Police, and Riot' in DJ Bourda (ed), *The Police: Six Sociological Essays* (Wiley, 1967) 8.

[25] GL Kelling and JQ Wilson, 'Broken Windows: The Police and Neighborhood Safety' (*The Atlantic*, March 1982) www.theatlantic.com/magazine/archive/1982/03/broken-windows/304465/.

[26] WJ Bratton, 'The New York City Police Department's Civil Enforcement of Quality-of-Life Crimes' (1995) 3 *Journal of Law and Policy* 447, 448.

apprehensively. The officer–call him Kelly–knew who the regulars were, and they knew him. As he saw his job, he was to keep an eye on strangers, and make certain that the disreputable regulars observed some informal but widely understood rules. Drunks and addicts could sit on the stoops, but could not lie down. People could drink on side streets, but not at the main intersection. Bottles had to be in paper bags. Talking to, bothering, or begging from people waiting at the bus stop was strictly forbidden. If a dispute erupted between a businessman and a customer, the business-man was assumed to be right, especially if the customer was a stranger. If a stranger loitered, Kelly would ask him if he had any means of support and what his business was; if he gave unsatisfactory answers, he was sent on his way. Persons who broke the informal rules, especially those who bothered people waiting at bus stops, were arrested for vagrancy. Noisy teenagers were told to keep quiet.

These rules were defined and enforced in collaboration with the 'regulars' on the street. Another neighborhood might have different rules, but these, everybody under-stood, were the rules for this neighborhood. If someone violated them, the regulars not only turned to Kelly for help but also ridiculed the violator. Sometimes what Kelly did could be described as 'enforcing the law,' but just as often it involved taking informal or extralegal steps to help protect what the neighborhood had decided was the appropriate level of public order. Some of the things he did probably would not withstand a legal challenge.[27]

Whatever else this model of policing might be, it isn't the rule of law – not when police take it as their responsibility to enforce 'informal' rules that bear no relationship to the law as enacted by some legislature or applied by some court; maintain a running list of 'regulars' and 'strangers' who have different rights; order people to leave public spaces on the basis of their 'unsatisfactory' answers to intrusive questions about their wealth and their plans; and single-handedly adjudicate disputes between businesspeople and consumers not on the basis of the facts of their conduct and the correspondence of that conduct to law but on the basis of the hierarchical identity of the parties. And it should surprise nobody that those who were regulated were 'primarily black' while the one doing the regulating was white. Of course, perceptions of disorder them-selves are often racialised.[28]

It might be imagined that police could carry out such an 'order-maintenance' role simply by using persuasion, rather than by directly deploying state violence. But they cannot, and Kelling and Wilson openly admit as much too:

> Though the police can obviously make arrests whenever a gang member breaks the law, a gang can form, recruit, and congregate without breaking the law. And only a tiny fraction of gang-related crimes can be solved by an arrest; thus, if an arrest is the only recourse for the police, the residents' fears will go unassuaged. The police will soon feel helpless, and the residents will again believe that the police 'do nothing.'

---

[27] Kelling and Wilson (n 25).

[28] DE Roberts, 'Race, Vagueness, and the Social Meaning of Order-Maintenance Policing' (1999) 89 *Journal of Criminal Law and Criminology* 775.

What the police in fact do is to chase known gang members out of the project. In the words of one officer, 'We kick ass.'[29]

Needless to say, using the state's monopoly over violence to 'kick the asses' of those who have admittedly violated no law is consistent with no conception of the rule of law whatsoever. Elsewhere in the Kelling and Wilson article, they observe that '[n]one of this is easily reconciled with any conception of due process or fair treatment'. That's something of an understatement. But for present purposes, what we should notice is that the capacity of the police to engage in such behaviour is contingent on the underlying legal tools with which they may operate – only if they can avoid sanction for 'kicking ass' and have a sufficient set of tools – like those vagrancy, disorderly conduct, loitering, and disturbing the peace laws – to actually enforce their wills over any person whom they meet may they rule a community on a day-to-day basis with arbitrary commands in the way that Kelling and Wilson advocate and that New York and other American cities implemented.[30]

Ex Post Police Discretion: The Qualified Immunity Doctrine

One of the reasons that Kelling and Wilson's Officer Kelly could engage in the lawless behaviour that they describe is that the American legal system lacks the

---

[29] Kelling and Wilson (n 25).

[30] There are many other ways in which the American police run afoul of the basic idea of the rule of law. My emphasis on discretion is not meant to suggest that we disregard, for example, the evidence of widespread 'dropsy' (planting of evidence and 'testilying' (perjured police testimony), S Zeidman, 'From Dropsy to Testilying: Prosecutorial Apathy, Ennui, or Complicity?' (2019) 16 *Ohio State Journal of Criminal Law* 423; the militarisation of police personnel, who now routinely parade around the streets with tanks and machine guns intimidating citizens and destroying their property; R Balko, *Rise of the Warrior Cop: The Militarization of America's Police Forces*, pbk edn (Public Affairs, 2014); and even police departments that maintain off the books 'black sites' where victims are secretly tortured, as in Chicago's infamous Homan Square facility; S Ackerman, 'Homan Square Detainee: I Was Sexually Abused by Police at Chicago "Black Site"' (*The Guardian*, 14 May 2015) www.theguardian.com/us-news/2015/may/14/homan-square-detainee-police-abuse; S Ackerman, 'Chicago's Homan Square "Black Site": Surveillance, Military-Style Vehicles and a Metal Cage' (*The Guardian*, 24 February 2015) www.theguardian.com/us-news/2015/feb/24/chicago-homan-square-black-site; BE Patterson, 'Chicago's "Black Site" Police Scandal Is About to Explode Again' (*Mother Jones*, 8 December 2015) www.motherjones.com/politics/2015/12/rahm-emanuel-chicago-police-homan-square-scandal/. Indeed, a torturer at the Guantanamo Bay military black hole apparently built up his resume torturing prisoners in Chicago first. S Ackerman, 'Bad Lieutenant: American Police Brutality, Exported from Chicago to Guantánamo' (*The Guardian*, 18 February 2015) www.theguardian.com/us-news/2015/feb/18/american-police-brutality-chicago-guantanamo; S Ackerman, 'How Chicago Police Condemned the Innocent: A Trail of Coerced Confessions' (*The Guardian*, 19 February 2015) www.theguardian.com/us-news/2015/feb/19/chicago-police-richard-zuley-abuse-innocent-man; S Ackerman, 'Guantánamo Torturer Led Brutal Chicago Police Regime of Shackling and Confession' (*The Guardian*, 18 February 2015) www.theguardian.com/us-news/2015/feb/18/guantanamo-torture-chicago-police-brutality; L Ralph, 'The Making of Richard Zuley: The Ignored Linkages Between the US Criminal In/Justice System and the International Security State' (2020) 122 *American Anthropologist* 133.

means to effectively sanction officers who ride roughshod over individual legal rights. Bureaucratic discipline within police departments is likely a nonstarter because of the internal solidarity of police departments which tend to view the world in an us-vs-them kind of way, plus the pernicious effects of powerful police unions which insulate their officers from discipline.[31]

An aggrieved citizen might look for a remedy in the courts. Such a remedy would be well within the Anglo-American tradition. AV Dicey's classic English conception of the rule of law revolved around the proposition that government officials were subject to ordinary law in ordinary courts – if a police officer beat one up, one would simply sue them for battery and receive a remedy, just as against an ordinary person.[32] At least in some contexts, the same principle held in the early United States – there is reason to believe that an early use of the warrant requirement for police searches was as a defence to an ordinary common law trespass action.[33]

But today in the US these classic torts have largely been supplanted by the 'constitutional torts', primarily the federal civil rights remedy of 42 USC 1983 brought back to life in *Monroe v Pape*.[34] Unfortunately, the Supreme Court has read a 'good faith' immunity into that statute as the qualified immunity doctrine.[35] This doctrine shields police and other officials from lawsuits for money damages for civil rights violations – such as unlawful stops, searches, arrests, and uses of force – unless the officer's violation of law was 'clearly established' at the time of the action. Worse, 'clearly established' is interpreted so narrowly that it effectively amounts to conferring on police impunity for violations of individual legal rights.[36]

---

[31] C Fisk and S Richardson, 'Police Unions' (2017) 85 *George Washington Law Review* 712; WG Skogan, 'Why Reforms Fail' (2008) 18 *Policing and Society* 23; JR Silver and others, 'Traditional Police Culture, Use of Force, and Procedural Justice: Investigating Individual, Organizational, and Contextual Factors' (2017) 34 *Justice Quarterly* 1272, 1274–75; J Van Maanen, 'Observations on the Making of Policemen' (1973) 32 *Human Organization* 407, 414–16.

[32] AV Dicey, *Introduction to the Study of the Law of the Constitution* (Liberty Fund, 1982) 114–15, 120–21.

[33] See discussion in D Dripps, 'Akhil Amar on Criminal Procedure and Constitutional Law: Here I Go Down That Wrong Road Again' (1996) 74 *North Carolina Law Review* 1559, 1600–03.

[34] The common law claims remain available, but may not be effective to bring practical relief to individuals subject to police abuses. One practical reason for the relative predominance of 1983 claims: lawyers who bring civil rights cases need to eat too, and federal civil rights cases come with statutory attorney's fees under 42 USC § 1988. Of course, access to federal rather than state courts is another motivation. Finally, state law immunity doctrines may immunise police misconduct from state common law tort claims, leaving the federal civil rights claim as the only remedy. See, eg, *Phillips v Hanse* 281 Ga 133 (2006) (under Georgia law, a police officer was immune from negligence liability for conducting a high-speed chase that killed the plaintiff in the absence of malice); *Brown v Town of Chapel Hill* 233 NC App. 257 (2014) (under North Carolina law, police officer was immune for false imprisonment liability for arresting plaintiff without reason then detaining him for an hour on the basis of mistaken identity).

[35] W Baude, 'Is Qualified Immunity Unlawful' (2018) 106 *California Law Review* 45, 52–61, argues that the supposed origins of this immunity in the common law are apocryphal.

[36] Carbado, 'Blue-on-Black Violence' (n 14) 1519–22; LC Feldman, 'Police Violence and the Legal Temporalities of Immunity' (2017) 20 *Theory & Event* 329.

Qualified immunity is subject to severe criticism from the standpoint of the rule of law to the extent it encourages the arbitrary use of government coercion. I characterise qualified immunity as *ex post* police discretion in virtue of the fact that, in practical effect, it expands the array of behavioural choices of police in interacting with citizens: even in situations where a use of force or an arrest is not legally justifiable, the qualified immunity doctrine adds it to the police menu by making it dramatically less likely that they will face sanctions for doing so.[37]

Segregation and Policing: How Property Rights and Local Quasi-Federalism Can Undermine the Rule of Law

The attentive reader will notice that the features of policing just described are, at least superficially, race-neutral, although they can be applied by racially motivated or unconsciously biased officers in a racialised way. Critical race scholars, however, have identified that there are not merely two ways that racial injustice can appear in a legal system (ie, conscious and unconscious bias), but also a third, which often goes under the name 'structural racism' or 'institutional racism'. To my mind, the relationship between segregation and policing stands both as a quintessential example of structural racism and as an important complication in this book's exploration of the relationship between property rights, especially in land, and the rule of law.

Note at the beginning that I speak of what is typically called de facto segregation, that is, segregation that is not caused by recent intentional government action – although past government action may be a contributing factor – with the quintessential example being suburban 'white flight'. Note also that it is well established that segregation is strongly associated with concentrated poverty.[38] With respect to such segregation, I make the following three observations about policing and residential segregation, which will be lightly sketched (rather than fully defended) below:

(1) Residential racial segregation facilitates the delivery of policing in a way that is racially biased in the aggregate (ie, falling with unjust harshness on subordinated racial groups, on average).

(2) Policing that is racially biased in the aggregate reinforces residential racial segregation.

---

[37] Even if the officer does something egregious enough for a court to refuse to apply qualified immunity, chances are that their government will indemnify them for the judgment, further insulating them from individual consequences for lawless uses of power. Carbado, 'Blue-on-Black Violence' (n 14) 1522–24.

[38] L Quillian, 'Segregation and Poverty Concentration: The Role of Three Segregations' (2012) 77 *American Sociological Review* 354.

(3)   Residential racial segregation and racially biased policing are also driven by the economic interests of white landholders in preserving property values, and those interests are sometimes translated into crime-control interests that invoke order-oriented conceptions of the rule of law.

A defence of claims (1) and (2) can be derived from the important recent work of Monica Bell, who has carefully elucidated the bidirectional relationship between policing and segregation, and Daria Roithmayr, who has given important network theory accounts of both police violence and segregation.[39]

Key ways in which policing reinforces already-existing segregation include *boundary-enforcement* by which Black and Brown Americans are subjected to police attention when they are found 'out of place', ie, in predominantly white neighbourhoods; and *capital destruction*, by which the consequences of hyper-policing in segregated and subordinated communities reduce the economic resources available to community members, thus making those communities both worse places to live and harder places to escape. Mechanisms of capital destruction include, for example, the incarceration of parents, thus reducing the resources available to their children; the infliction of criminal records and consequent job market consequences of same on community members; and the disruption of social networks and civic life through official behaviour such as anti-gang injunctions and the aggressive enforcement of quality-of-life laws like those described above to drive people out of public spaces.

On the other side of the vicious cycle, segregation contributes to aggregate racial bias in policing by mechanisms that include *neighbourhood stigma*, in which segregated and subordinated areas are perceived (either inaccurately, or accurately because of economic disadvantage) as high-crime and hence in need of more aggressive policing; and *organisational divergence*, in which police organisations adopt different strategies in subordinated and superordinated

---

[39] Bell (n 13); D Roithmayr, 'Locked in Segregation' (2004) 12 *Virginia Journal of Social Policy & the Law* 197; Roithmayr (n 14); see also S Bass, 'Policing Space, Policing Race: Social Control Imperatives and Police Discretionary Decisions' (2001) 28 *Social Justice* 156; RJ Sampson and SW Raudenbush, 'Neighborhood Stigma and the Perception of Disorder' (2005) 24 *Focus* 7; N Jones, '"The Regular Routine": Proactive Policing and Adolescent Development Among Young, Poor Black Men' (2014) 2014 *New Directions for Child and Adolescent Development* 33; D Pager, *Marked: Race, Crime, and Finding Work in an Era of Mass Incarceration*, pbk edn (University of Chicago Press, 2009); AJ Meehan and MC Ponder, 'Race and Place: The Ecology of Racial Profiling African American Motorists' (2002) 19 *Justice Quarterly* 399; B Capers, 'Policing, Place, and Race' (2009) 44 *Harvard Civil Rights – Civil Liberties Law Review* 43; LJ Krivo, RD Peterson and DC Kuhl, 'Segregation, Racial Structure, and Neighborhood Violent Crime' (2009) 114 *American Journal of Sociology* 1765; N Lacey and D Soskice, 'Crime, Punishment and Segregation in the United States: The Paradox of Local Democracy' (2015) 17 *Punishment & Society* 454; EA Stewart and others, 'Neighborhood Racial Context and Perceptions of Police-Based Racial Discrimination Among Black Youth' (2009) 47 *Criminology* 847; S Gaston and RK Brunson, 'Reasonable Suspicion in the Eye of the Beholder: Routine Policing in Racially Different Disadvantaged Neighborhoods' (2020) 56 *Urban Affairs Review* 188.

territories.[40] Organisational divergence is also a consequence of a number of factors, such as differences in political power and hence the capacity to control police misconduct; differences in municipal finance and hence in the capacity to support public services that provide an alternative to police contact as well as in the use of policing as a revenue source; organisational learning in which police pick up harsher strategies from one another in departments 'serving' segregated communities; and the vicious cycle destruction of police-community relationships in which harsh policing leads to non-cooperation and oppositional behaviour from community members, which in turn leads to more harsh policing, and so forth.[41]

Unsurprisingly, we see police compromising legal fidelity in other nations with segregated and disadvantaged communities. Of particular importance is the French *brigade anti-criminalité*, the special 'anti-crime' unit that patrols segregated immigrant *banlieues*. Didier Fassin's ethnographic study of the *brigade* revealed a pattern of behaviour that is barely distinguishable from the complaints about American police in Black neighbourhoods, including pervasive stop-and-frisk harassment, evident police endorsement of racial stereotypes about the criminal character of those whom they were policing, and swift violent escalation paired with a reputation for violence.[42] These are the sort of consequences that follow from the enterprise of policing a subordinated and segregated community.

As for my point (3) above: there is an obvious connection between the protection of property interests (and property values) in the advantaged and white flight and: (a) the creation of new municipalities, (b) entry restrictions in existing municipalities (such as zoning rules restricting multiple-occupancy units and the manipulation of transit networks), (c) the demand for boundary-enforcement policing, and (d) the demand for harsher policing strategies against groups of people and neighbourhoods stereotyped as dangerous and sources of crime. Charles Tilly has characterised many of these broader dynamics as 'opportunity hoarding'.[43] Wealthier people who also enjoy racial

---

[40] There's a grim cruelty to neighbourhood stigma: many Black leaders originally sought additional police presence in their neighbourhoods to combat the criminogenic consequences of poverty – but that only made matters worse. Forman (n 8).

[41] The fatal consequences of Ferguson's revenue-oriented policing are well known and worth particular note. Generally, on revenue-depleted cities resorting to lawless enforcement tactics and other challenges to legal order, see B Atuahene, 'Predatory Cities' (2020) 108 *California Law Review* 107; DW Carbado, 'Predatory Policing' (2017) 85 *UMKC Law Review* 545; Taylor (n 9) 126–29; Jy Fagan and E Ash, 'New Policing, New Segregation: From Ferguson to New York' (2017) 106 *Georgetown Law Journal Online* 33; MW Sances and H Young You, 'Who Pays for Government? Descriptive Representation and Exploitative Revenue Sources' (2017) 79 *The Journal of Politics* 1090.

[42] D Fassin, *Enforcing Order: An Ethnography of Urban Policing* (Wiley, 2013).

[43] C Tilly, *Durable Inequality* (University of California Press, 1999); see also E Anderson, *The Imperative of Integration* (Princeton University Press, 2010).

privilege have strong financial incentives, even if they do not personally have racially biased beliefs or preferences, to self-isolate, for example, to avoid having to financially subsidise their poorer neighbours, and hence to achieve benefits like more well-resourced schools with lower taxes.[44] Similarly, our public discourse is replete with demands for aggressive policing in response to threats to property; for vivid recent examples, there were demands for aggressive police responses to the summer 2020 Black Lives Matter protests in response to property damage that some people claiming affiliation with such protests committed. Then-President Donald Trump even took to Twitter to threaten military action in response to property damage, declaring 'when the looting starts, the shooting starts'.[45]

This seems to me to represent our recurrent paradox of property rights: while property rights are the core of the American rule of law, they also motivate lawless behaviour in their defence (recall the Fugitive Slave Acts). Financial motivations drive those who experience racial privilege and economic advantage to protect their wealth by physical isolation – and by supporting harsh and capital-destroying police practices which they will not personally experience. By excluding those residents in segregated communities from the benefits of regional wealth – wealth which also permits a dominance of political life – the advantaged have the capacity both to structure the delivery of policing (and other public services) in ways that differ across geographic and municipal lines, and to generate the demand for harsh policing in places where they, themselves, are not directly affected. Hence, some have the capacity to make rules that apply to others but not to themselves – with the predictable oppressive consequences. Thanks to inequality, the argument of Federalist 57 failed in 1788, and it fails today.

From Policing to National Security

The supposedly domestic problem of policing is also not separate from the regime of national security to which I will turn in a moment. Scholars and journalists have traced the connections between the militarisation of the police and the tactics and tools deployed in international theatres of conflict, including, inter alia, via the movement of personnel between domestic policing and foreign military action; the transfer of equipment from military forces to police

---

[44] See generally N Burns, *The Formation of American Local Governments: Private Values in Public Institutions* (Oxford University Press, 1994); Atuahene (n 41). For a revealing case study of wealth and race segregation in Los Angeles, see L Redford, 'The Intertwined History of Class and Race Segregation in Los Angeles' (2017) 16 *Journal of Planning History* 305.

[45] DJ Trump, (Twitter, 28 May 2020) twitter.com/realDonaldTrump/status/1266231100780744704. This is no longer available on Twitter due to its suspension of Trump's account, but is visible on the Internet Archive at web.archive.org/web/20210108042810/https://twitter.com/realDonaldTrump/status/1266231100780744704.

departments (such as the infamous 1033 program); and the development of technologies for international conflict that are then deployed domestically.[46]

Thus, in considering the killing of Breonna Taylor for example, we must ask: how did it come about that it seemed normal or acceptable to some police officers to assault a private residence after midnight with a battering ram in order to execute a surprise search warrant for some drugs allegedly associated with a person that didn't even live there?[47] Such a shock-and-awe midnight raid for a minor crime sounds like the antics of a secret police in a dictatorship, the KGB or the Gestapo, not a liberal democracy.

There's a kind of grim irony to the killing of Ms Taylor in particular, for the already-violent police assault may have escalated into deadly gunplay because her boyfriend took America's claims to the rule of law too seriously. As far as can be determined as of this writing, when the midnight banging on the door began, her boyfriend appears to have assumed that the people trying to break in were criminals, and that he was entitled to defend her home by firing a shot at the burglars.[48] It was this shot which led the police to respond with the hail of bullets that killed Taylor.

Ms Taylor's boyfriend's assumptions weren't unreasonable in the context of a political and legal culture that purports to control executives and respect private property. Such assumptions could never have been made in the Soviet Union, where the right of the police to kick down doors and snatch people in the middle of the night was clearly established. But in the United States, that alleged paragon of the rule of law, a person's home is supposedly their castle and they're supposedly entitled to defend it; more to the point, they're also supposedly entitled to assume that the police do not carry out home invasions, and hence that they need not make their decisions about what to do – in response to the sudden sounds of an attacker while they are sleeping – in the shadow of the possibility that their own state may be treating their home like an urban combat zone. Unfortunately, due to the infiltration of the logic of international military action and national security into domestic policing, these classical rule of law assumptions appear to no longer be sustainable. And with that, we move to an examination of the rule of law in the national security context.

PRESIDENTIAL POWER IN THE NATIONAL SECURITY STATE

In 1861, the army arrested John Merryman of Maryland for attempting to impede the passage of federal troops. When served with a writ of *habeas*

[46] CJ Coyne and AR Hall, *Tyranny Comes Home: The Domestic Fate of U.S. Militarism* (Stanford University Press, 2018); Balko (n 30).
[47] 'Breonna Taylor: What Happened on the Night of Her Death?' (*BBC News*, 8 October 2020) www.bbc.com/news/world-us-canada-54210448.
[48] ibid.

corpus, the military refused to produce Merryman before the court. Instead, the general commanding the fortress in which Merryman was held declared that Lincoln had authorised him to suspend the writ.[49] Chief Justice Taney held Cadwalader in contempt and sent a marshal to enforce his order. The marshal was not admitted to the fortress.[50]

Taney's outraged response wields the language of the rule of law in the severest tones:

> The constitution provides, as I have before said, that 'no person shall be deprived of life, liberty or property, without due process of law.' It declares that 'the right of the people to be secure in their persons, houses, papers and effects, against unreasonable searches and seizures, shall not be violated; and no warrant shall issue, but upon probable cause, supported by oath or affirmation, and particularly describing the place to be searched, and the persons or things to be seized.' It provides that the party accused shall be entitled to a speedy trial in a court of justice.
>
> These great and fundamental laws, which congress itself could not suspend, have been disregarded and suspended, like the writ of habeas corpus, by a military order, supported by force of arms. Such is the case now before me, and I can only say that if the authority which the constitution has confided to the judiciary department and judicial officers, may thus, upon any pretext or under any circumstances, be usurped by the military power, at its discretion, the people of the United States are no longer living under a government of laws, but every citizen holds life, liberty and property at the will and pleasure of the army officer in whose military district he may happen to be found.[51]

A second controversy arose around Lincoln's use of military tribunals to try Confederate sympathisers. In 1863, Congress passed the Habeas Corpus Act, which lent its authority to the withdrawal of *habeas corpus*, but provided for indictment by grand jury or release for those arrested under its authority.[52] In *Ex Parte Vallandigham*, the Court refused, on grounds of lack of jurisdiction, to hear the petition for release of a former Ohio Congressman who had advocated resistance against the Union.[53] After the crisis of immediate warfare had passed, however, the Court was evidently more comfortable handing the President – and the Reconstruction Congress – a defeat in this domain. In *Ex Parte Milligan*, the Court considered the case of an Indiana Democrat ordered arrested in 1864 by

---

[49] J Yoo, 'Merryman and Milligan (and McCardle)' (2009) 34 *Journal of Supreme Court History* 243, 247.

[50] There is some disagreement about the extent to which Cadwalader outright defied any binding court orders, as well as the extent to which any such defiance was directly authorised by Lincoln. S Barrett Tillman, 'Ex Parte Merryman: Myth, History and Scholarship' (2016) 224 *Military Law Review* 481; nonetheless, Taney certainly perceived it as defiance.

[51] *Ex parte Merryman* 17 F Cas 144, 152 (1861).

[52] JG Gambone, 'Ex Parte Milligan: The Restoration of Judicial Prestige?' (1970) 16 *Civil War History* 246, 251; Yoo (n 49).

[53] *Ex Parte Vallandigham* 68 US 243 (1863). For discussion, see Gambone (n 52) 251–52.

the governor of that state.[54] The Court ruled that military tribunals could not exercise jurisdiction over a noncombatant in a northern state.[55]

The precedents set during the Civil War have continued to impact the powers of presidents in other military conflicts. In *Ex Parte Quirin*, the Supreme Court ruled that President Roosevelt had the power to try eight Nazi saboteurs, two of whom were American citizens, by military commission on the basis of a claim that such a procedure was authorised by Congress – and distinguished *Milligan* on the grounds that *Milligan* was a non-belligerent charged with an ordinary crime, which was not triable except by a jury.[56] *Quirin*, in turn, served as an important precedent in the series of cases surrounding the Bush Administration's use of military detention and military commissions in the 'War on Terror'.

Today, presidential power to directly use force on private persons without the trappings of law remains a highly contested domain for the rule of law. The most alarming contemporary example of unconstrained executive power in the national security and emergency domain is the practice of targeted killing. In recent years, the executive branch has claimed – and exercised – the authority to assassinate US citizens found abroad, on the basis of their alleged connections to terrorism, on the basis of a unilateral presidential command and without any process or scrutiny outside the executive branch whatsoever. On this basis, US citizens Anwar al-Awlaki, Samir Khan, and sixteen-year-old Abdulrahman al-Awlaki were killed by US drone strikes in Yemen.

The purported legal justification for these actions – as stated in an executive branch internal memorandum attached (in redacted form) to the Second Circuit's opinion in Freedom of Information Act litigation compelling its disclosure – supposes that when, in the unilateral judgment of high-ranking intelligence officials and/or the President, a person abroad 'pose[s] a 'continued and imminent threat of violence' or death to US persons ... and a capture operation would be infeasible', and if 'the CIA and DoD "continue to monitor whether changed circumstances would permit such an alternative"', then the President is not obliged to offer a person any legal process whatsoever or seek the imprimatur of any other branch of government before ordering an assassination.[57] Arguably, the reasoning in the memorandum also depends on the victim's being in a combat zone – but while it is hard to deny that the US military might shoot back at a US citizen firing on its forces on a battlefield, the memorandum, to the extent its reasoning can be discerned through the redactions, seems to focus more on the role of citizens like al-Awlaki's in planning

---

[54] *Ex Parte Milligan* 71 US 2 (1866). See Yoo (n 49) 252.

[55] For an extended discussion of military tribunals of the period, including the trial of Lincoln's assassin, see MS Lederman, 'The Law (?) Of the Lincoln Assassination' (2018) 118 *Columbia Law Review* 323.

[56] *Ex Parte Quirin* 317 US 1 (1942). For helpful background, see J Goldsmith and CR Sunstein, 'Military Tribunals and Legal Culture: What a Difference Sixty Years Makes' (2002) 19 *Constitutional Commentary* 261.

[57] *New York Times v Department of Justice* 756 F3d 100 (2nd Cir 2014).

attacks against the United States – not their presence in live firefights (and who gets to say what counts as a 'combat zone' or how large that zone is?).

Consider also the irregular imprisonment and military pseudo-trial of accused terrorists in sites outside the ordinary territory of the United States, such as the Guantanamo Bay military base in Cuba. The practice of using military commissions in the cases of accused terrorists has come before the courts numerous times, but an abbreviated version goes along the following lines.[58] In 2004, the Supreme Court held, in a split opinion in *Hamdi v Rumsfeld*, that an American citizen alleged to be part of the Taliban and held by the military in a naval brig in Charleston, South Carolina, was entitled to some opportunity to contest his imprisonment.[59] In 2006, the Court decided *Hamdan v Rumsfeld*, which ruled that trying a Yemeni citizen held at Guantanamo Bay by military commission was beyond the executive power.[60] The Court distinguished *Quirin* on the ground that *Quirin* considered a crime (violation of the laws of war) for which Congress and the Constitution authorised the use of military commissions.

In response, Congress enacted the Military Commissions Act, which stripped the courts of *habeas corpus* jurisdiction and specifically provided for trial of noncitizens accused of terrorism by military commissions with weak procedural protections, although it permitted them to appeal to the District of Columbia Circuit. The Supreme Court, in *Boumediene v Bush*, struck down the Military Commissions Act, in part, on the grounds that Congress had not 'formally' suspended the writ, but merely limited it, and when Congress limits the writ of *habeas corpus* it must provide some 'adequate' alternative procedures to permit a detainee to challenge his or her confinement. In particular, the Court objected to the facts that:

> [T]he detainee has limited means to find or present evidence to challenge the Government's case against him. He does not have the assistance of counsel and may not be aware of the most critical allegations that the Government relied upon to order his detention. The detainee can confront witnesses that testify during the CSRT proceedings. But given that there are in effect no limits on the admission of hearsay evidence – the only requirement is that the tribunal deem the evidence 'relevant and helpful,' the detainee's opportunity to question witnesses is likely to be more theoretical than real.[61]

---

[58] For a fuller picture, see R Alford, *Permanent State of Emergency: Unchecked Executive Power and the Demise of the Rule of Law* (McGill University Press, 2017); CA Bradley and JL Goldsmith, 'Obama's AUMF Legacy' (2016) 110 *American Journal of International Law* 628; P Blenz, 'Hamad v. Gates and the Continuing Interpretation of Boumediene: A Note on 732 F.3d 990 (9th Cir. 2013)' (2015) 35 *Journal of the National Association of Administrative Law Judiciary* 443.

[59] *Hamdi v Rumsfeld* 542 US 507 (2004).

[60] *Hamdan v Rumsfeld* 548 US 557 (2006).

[61] *Boumediene v Bush* 553 US 723, 783–84 (2008) (internal citations omitted). This decision should be of particular interest to rule of law scholars, as its interpretation of the Military Commissions Act to not fully suspend the writ of *habeas corpus* is reminiscent of the classic common-law strategy of narrowly interpreting legislative enactments that threaten the rule of law, even when those

Yet despite this decision, irregular detention and trial by military commission has continued. And the lower courts do not appear to have taken *Boumediene* seriously; nor has the Supreme Court forced them to do so. Thus, the District of Columbia Circuit Court of Appeals held, in *Latif v Obama*, that district courts are required to presume that intelligence reports accurately recount the information provided to the government.[62] The same court upheld a military commission conviction for conspiracy against the argument that conspiracy was a common law crime, not a crime under the laws of war triable by military commission.[63] In general, the DC Circuit has shown a distinct hostility to *habeas* petitions from detainees.[64] Accordingly, it is unclear how much real-world impact the Supreme Court's holding that there must be adequate procedures to permit detainees to challenge their incarceration has had.[65]

To be sure, the military commissions aren't exactly producing a flood of convictions.[66] Yet there are still prisoners incarcerated at Guantanamo, for whom there are no options but military commission trial; it seems that the commissions are ineffective both to secure convictions and to secure releases – arguably, their primary real-world function is to provide a procedural gloss on the continuing lawless detention of prisoners at Guantanamo.

Efforts to subject the executive to legal control in the area of national security have also been stymied by self-inflicted limitations on the power of the courts. Most troubling is the existence of national-security-related limitations on private litigation even when egregious executive criminality is alleged. The federal courts have created a 'state secrets privilege' to bar litigation by the victims of truly extreme executive branch misconduct when that litigation would require the executive branch to reveal secret national security information, even *in camera* to a court. This privilege has been used, for example, to procure the dismissal of litigation by plaintiffs who allege that they were kidnapped by US intelligence agents and subjected to torture as part of the 'war on terror'.

Consider the Khaled El-Masri case.[67] El-Masri, a German citizen, alleged that he was kidnapped in Macedonia at the behest of the CIA, tortured, carried

---

enactments are concededly within the power of the legislature, in order to require that if the legislature seriously means to strip persons of fundamental rights, it must say so with absolute clarity. eg, D Dyzenhaus, *The Constitution of Law: Legality in a Time of Emergency* (Cambridge University Press, 2012) 102–17.

[62] *Latif v Obama* 677 F3d 1175 (2012).

[63] *Al Bahlul v United States* 840 F3d 757 (2016).

[64] SI Vladeck, 'The D.C. Circuit After Boumediene' (2011) 41 *Seton Hall Law Review* 1451.

[65] J Hafetz, 'Calling the Government to Account: Habeas Corpus in the Aftermath of Boumediene' (2011) 57 *Wayne Law Review* 99.

[66] As of 2019, '[i]n 13 years under the Military Commissions Act regime, and 17 years total, the commissions have produced a grand total of eight convictions [and] [s]ix of those eight convictions were obtained via plea bargain'. SI Vladeck, 'It's Time to Admit That the Military Commissions Have Failed' (*Lawfare*, 16 April 2019) www.lawfareblog.com/its-time-admit-military-commissions-have-failed.

[67] Full disclosure: I was briefly a very minor member of the plaintiff's legal team in this case. R M Chesney, 'State Secrets and the Limits of National Security Litigation' (2007) 75 *George Washington Law Review* 1249, gives another description.

to Afghanistan and imprisoned for five months, and then dropped off on the side of the road in Albania, even though for a substantial part of the period of his imprisonment the CIA knew that he had no affiliation with any terrorist organisation. The District Court dismissed his lawsuit against his kidnappers on the strength of the government's assertion that litigating it would require the revelation of secret national security information. Upholding the dismissal, the Court of Appeals expressed a standard so generous to the executive that it poses the risk of completely shielding even bad-faith executive branch assertions of a state secrets privilege from any judicial scrutiny:

> A court considering the Executive's assertion of the state secrets privilege, however, must take care not to force a disclosure of the very thing the privilege is designed to protect by demanding more information than is necessary. Frequently, the explanation of the department head who has lodged the formal privilege claim, provided in an affidavit or personal declaration, is sufficient to carry the Executive's burden. [...] Indeed, in certain circumstances a court may conclude that an explanation by the Executive of why a question cannot be answered would itself create an unacceptable danger of injurious disclosure. In such a situation, a court is obliged to accept the executive branch's claim of privilege without further demand.[68]

The combination of the state secrets privilege and the broad authority claimed by the executive to use military force against American citizens arguably amounts to a kind of national security impunity for agencies such as the CIA and the Pentagon. It is difficult indeed to imagine any argument capable of reconciling such powers to a serious conception of the rule of law. Rather, it seems to be a direct instantiation of a Schmittian state of exception, in which the executive can put on the crown of the Sovereign and declare the law not to apply.

The Schmittian Dilemma

Running through the problem of executive power is what we might call the 'Schmittian dilemma' – executive authority is particularly well-suited to addressing exceptional, emergent situations unanticipated in detail by existing law; but the delegation of emergency powers in that law to address it is inherently impossible or at least highly difficult to control, and hence subject to immense potential abuses unless surrounded by extremely strong political rather than legal controls.[69]

It should not be surprising that the domain of warfare and national security has been the source of some of the most shocking stories of American

---

[68] *El-Masri v United States* 479 F3d 296, 305-06 (4th Cir 2007) (internal quotes and citations omitted).
[69] EA Posner and A Vermeule, *The Executive Unbound: After the Madisonian Republic* (Oxford University Press, 2010).

lawlessness, for war has been the perennial source of emergencies and the scourge of efforts to control executives throughout political history. It has, alas, been universally accepted that military leadership by committee doesn't work; but it has also been universally recognised that handing over all the troops to one person poses dire risks of abuse. Sometimes this danger has manifested itself in the old-fashioned coup, as when Caesar crossed the Rubicon. Madison's famous fears of a standing army seem to have been directed at this end, as in his argument, in Federalist 46, about the capacity of the states and the public to fend off a hypothetical federal 'military force for the projects of ambition'.

Often the danger has been more subtle and complex. For example, the exigencies of military affairs have frequently led to a demand for money to support warfare which other elements in the government or society at large refuse; this was a particularly important aspect of the conflict between Crown and Parliament in the seventeenth century which precipitated lawless executive power grabs like ship money and forced loans as an alternative to receiving funds from Parliament – and which in turn contributed to the conflict that lead to Charles I losing his head, and informed the American framers' conceptions of what limited government should look like. The framing generation also had some direct experience in the area (albeit associated with Parliament as well as Crown), insofar as the taxes imposed on the colonies which set the whole revolution off had been occasioned by the need to pay for the Seven Years War. Likewise, some of the more egregious acts of colonial lawlessness (in particular the use of the vice-admiralty court – see chapter two) were in turn occasioned by the need to collect the taxes.

The Schmittian dilemma in its fundraising aspect is also clearly visible in Donald Trump's claim of authority to build a southern border wall based on an emergency statute allowing the diversion of funds appropriated for other purposes. But presidential emergency powers are much broader. The Brennan Center for Justice attempted to collect a comprehensive list of presidential emergency powers, and found 123 distinct statutory powers that may be exercised on the basis of a unilateral presidential declaration of emergency.[70] And while some of those powers are modest, others are extensive or even terrifying. The most nightmare-inducing example the Brennan Center delicately describes as the power to 'suspend the operation of provisions regulating the storage, transportation, disposal, procurement, handling, and testing of chemical and biological weapons, including the prohibition on testing such weapons on human subjects'. Would even the most fevered conspiracy theorists imagine that there is a law allowing the President to test secret superbugs on people?

---

[70] Brennan Center for Justice, 'A Guide to Emergency Powers and Their Use' (*Brennan Center for Justice*, 2019) www.brennancenter.org/sites/default/files/2019-10/2019_10_15_EmergencyPowersFULL.pdf.

Hafetz has plausibly suggested that national security law is functionally distinct from ordinary law in a way that undermines traditional rule of law values.[71] It lacks the traditional concern with facilitating public obedience – for national security law doesn't directly command the public – and thus does not provide courts with the incentive, present in more traditional cases, to progressively develop and clarify the law through ongoing adjudication. Instead, the courts are motivated to preserve executive flexibility in dealing with complex and evolving situations – that Schmittian emergency. This naturally leads to the softening of controls on executive power by the development and expansion of vague standards governing executive authority.

Yet emergency powers are a feature of all states, and the numerous gubernatorial emergency public health orders in response to the COVID-19 catastrophe have most recently revealed why they are necessary. Ultimately, the Schmittian dilemma of the executive – how to make it possible to respond to genuine emergencies without creating a dictator – will be present in every country, and it is manifestly present in the United States.

But we must also consider that Schmitt was not merely a theorist of executive power and emergencies, but also a theorist of sovereignty and of the infamous boundary between friends and enemies. For Schmitt, emergency executive power (the 'state of exception') was the core characteristic of sovereignty, and the exercise of this power in turn presupposes the capacity of a sovereign actor to claim authority on the basis of a bounded people defined against some other people.[72]

In the United States, these bounds have all too often been drawn on the basis of racialised ethno-national categories. Thus, we saw the ethno-racial legacy of the deprivation of Japanese immigrants of their property via alien land laws converted in World War II into the outright removal of Japanese-American US citizens from their homes as 'internment'. The notorious *Koremastu* case, which upheld the removal of Japanese-Americans from their homes, relied in turn on *Hirabayashi v United States*, upholding a curfew for Japanese-Americans, which explicitly appealed to a racialised allegation of existing ties between those citizens and Japan: 'There is support for the view that social, economic and political conditions which have prevailed since the close of the last century, when the Japanese began to come to this country in substantial numbers, have intensified their solidarity and have in large measure prevented their assimilation as an integral part of the white population.'[73]

---

[71] J Hafetz, 'A Problem of Standards? Another Perspective on Secret Law' (2016) 57 *William and Mary Law Review* 2141.

[72] If you believe Agamben, the modern administrative state, that other great executive *bête noire* of rule of law advocates, was also a product of wartime states of emergency, at least in the European tradition of which US law also partakes. G Agamben, *State of Exception* (University of Chicago Press, 2005), 12–13, 20–22.

[73] *Hirabayashi v United States* 320 US 81, 96 (1943); see also *Korematsu v United States*, 323 US 214 (1944).

Ironically, the Court in the same breath noted that America's own legal discrimination against Japanese-Americans may have contributed to this perceived disloyalty as failure to assimilate:

> As a result of all these conditions affecting the life of the Japanese, both aliens and citizens, in the Pacific Coast area, there has been relatively little social intercourse between them and the white population. The restrictions, both practical and legal, affecting the privileges and opportunities afforded to persons of Japanese extraction residing in the United States have been sources of irritation, and may well have tended to increase their isolation, and in many instances their attachments to Japan and its institutions.[74]

In a footnote, the Court lists discrimination in immigration laws, in naturalisation laws, in 'the privilege of owning land', and in laws regulating marriage. In other words: the *Hirabayashi-Korematsu* line of cases again illustrates the point I first noted in chapter two with respect to the Fugitive Slave Acts: legal caste tends to metastasize. Having relegated them to a subordinate legal status, the whites who dominated the United States government decided that it could not trust the loyalty of its Japanese-American citizens because they would resent their treatment. Thus, under pressure of external threat, the United States saw itself as having no real choice but to chase them out of their homes.

From *Korematsu*, we naturally turn to immigration and citizenship law. For it is in that conjoined area of law that the Schmittian identity of the people becomes most salient, for it is there that who counts as a member is defined today – and the delineation between who counts and who does not count becomes one between who is subject to arbitrary power as a presumptive enemy and who is entitled to legal process, to being addressed with reasons before being subject to government coercion as opposed to being simply subject to the raw force of the sovereign. Immigration is where the literal and the figurative borders of the American rule of law meet, and where *Korematsu* meets Chinese Exclusion in contemporary arbitrary executive power.[75]

---

[74] ibid 98.
[75] RS Chang, 'Whitewashing Precedent: From the Chinese Exclusion Case to Korematsu to the Muslim Travel Ban Cases' (2018) 68 *Case Western Reserve Law Review* 1183.

6

The Gavel and the Fist: The Problem of Sovereignty and Borders

I N 1943, A United States Department of State official named Josiah DuBois wrote an explosive report accusing the Department of culpability in the Holocaust. A key claim in this report is that the United States had imposed impossible red tape on Jewish refugees from Germany, requiring them to turn up 'among other things two affidavits of support and sponsorship to be furnished with each application for a visa. To each application for support and sponsorship there must be attached two letters of reference from two reputable American citizens'.[1] These requirements were imposed allegedly for 'security reasons', but DuBois observed that they operated as if they were 'specifically designed to prevent Jewish refugees from entering this country'. Herd and Moynihan detail still more requirements and explain why this looks like a deliberate imposition: the requirements were almost totally impossible for a refugee to satisfy.[2] For example, immigrants were obliged to collect all kinds of government documents from their home country, and the State Department enforced those requirements against Jews fleeing Germany – even though they obviously couldn't be expected to show up at their local Gestapo office to ask for a copy of their police record to take to the Americans.

Today, the use of bureaucracy as a weapon against refugees and other immigrants continues. Under the Trump administration, the United States Citizenship and Immigration Services quietly implemented a policy requiring immigrants to fill out every single field in their immigration paperwork, even if a field didn't apply, and rejecting applications if there are any black spaces at all. For example, a refugee who did not have a middle name would have their application rejected for leaving a blank middle name field rather than writing 'none' in it.[3] Journalists reported on one example of a rejection under this policy: an 8-year-old child

---

[1] R Medoff, *Blowing the Whistle on Genocide: Josiah E. Dubois, Jr., And the Struggle for a U.S. Response to the Holocaust* (Purdue University, 2009).

[2] P Herd and DP Moynihan, *Administrative Burden: Policymaking by Other Means* (Russell Sage Foundation, 2018) 5–9.

[3] C Rampell, 'This Latest Trick From the Trump Administration Is One of the Most Despicable Yet' (*Washington Post*, 13 February 2020) www.washingtonpost.com/opinions/the-trump-administrations-kafkaesque-new-way-to-thwart-visa-applications/2020/02/13/190a3862-4ea3-11ea-bf44-f5043 eb3918a_story.html.

who listed 'none' for employment history but left the dates of employment field blank.[4]

Not seriously publicising this new policy, of course, the Trump regime clearly adopted it not for the purposes of getting more complete or accurate information – the failure to write 'n/a' in the field for 'spouse' when one has already checked the box saying one is single deprives the government of no information whatsoever – but for the purposes of tricking people into filing applications that would be deemed invalid, and hence having an excuse to deny people immigration benefits to which the law entitled them. As of this writing, the Biden administration appears to have undone the rule, but its creation during the Trump years illustrates the persistence of the capacity to use bureaucratic power to deny basic human rights to immigrants from 1943 to the present.

This sort of blatant procedural malice also bears a troubling relationship to prominent elements of Jim Crow, such as the disenfranchisement techniques in which Black Americans were forced to answer byzantine trick quizzes in order to be allowed to vote.[5] But I submit that this resemblance is not coincidental: in immigration law, we can simultaneously see the heritage of slavery and Jim Crow, as well as of Indian Removal, filtered through utterly unconstrained executive power in its Kafkaesque bureaucratic face. This chapter aims to bring to light our most lawless area of contemporary American law in our immigration system.

The origins of our immigration law lie in the Chinese Exclusion Act era, which wrote open racism into federal law; its plenary power doctrine is shared with the covertly colonial relationship between the federal government and Native American Nations, and the openly colonial Insular Cases – both covering groups who have been represented as quasi-foreigners with subordinate legal rights. In many respects its formal characteristics are a reprise (albeit at a lower key) of many of the ways in which slavery and Jim Crow warped the American legal system. Immigration, like slavery, has been characterised by the rhetorical and legal creation of categories of legal non-subjects or outlaws who are excluded from the ordinary protections of due process and subject to the whims of both specially empowered public officials as well as private persons. And much as in the time of slavery, immigration law today creates perennial conflicts over federalism, as states struggle to be more or less protective of migrants than the federal government would permit. Slavery even raised the legal issue most characteristic of immigration law, deportation itself, as some contended that free Black Americans were noncitizens who could be forcibly removed from US territory or from specific states, or at least encouraged to leave.[6] In recent years

---

[4] ibid.

[5] eg, R Onion, 'Take the Impossible "Literacy" Test Louisiana Gave Black Voters in the 1960s' (*Slate Magazine*, 28 June 2013) slate.com/human-interest/2013/06/voting-rights-and-the-supreme-court-the-impossible-literacy-test-louisiana-used-to-give-black-voters.html.

[6] MS Jones, *Birthright Citizens: A History of Race and Rights in Antebellum America* (Cambridge University Press, 2018) ch 2.

the notion of 'self-deportation' has been popular on the political right in the form of the open desire to make conditions so unpleasant for immigrants that they leave of their own 'free will'. But this is a longstanding US policy that was also applied to Black Americans and to Native Americans.[7]

Much like the Fugitive Slave Act, in immigration too the existence of legal caste has compromised the procedural protections available to those whom the law targets as well as those adjacent; the immigration enforcement regime thereby poses a threat to the protections of law for citizens and others outside the immediate immigration context. The organisations tasked with immigration enforcement, like all bureaucracies, have a tendency to grow and to propagate the distinctive logic of their operation – in the case of the immigration agencies, a lack of internal legal culture and habit of ignoring individual rights. The willingness of political leaders, courts, and ordinary citizens to ignore the lawless behaviour of the immigration enforcement agencies has a corrupting effect on their collective capacity to check the lawless behaviour of other public officials. And the boundary between the categories of 'citizen' and 'non-citizen' is sufficiently porous, both conceptually and in practice, that citizens cannot safely assume that the misconduct of these officials will not be directed against them. Such is the argument of this chapter.

THE PLENARY POWER

Even the legal rules that supposedly regulate immigration themselves defy the ambition to legal order in American governance, although the defenders of its most harsh features claim that they are necessary to uphold the rule of law, represented as the effectiveness of the prohibition on unauthorised migration. Certain doctrines in US immigration law effectively represent the proposition that some migrants are outside the legal community entirely.

In particular, the plenary power doctrine, according to which Congressional legislation relating to immigration is largely immune from judicial review, seems to represent the view that migrants entirely lack legal rights.[8] The plenary power doctrine in immigration was born at the end of the nineteenth century in the famous *Chinese Exclusion Case*, in which the Court stepped aside to permit the political branches to implement the policy of excluding almost all immigrants from China, notwithstanding a case only three years before which held that race discrimination against Chinese people already in the country

---

[7] K-S Park, 'Self-Deportation Nation' (2019) 132 *Harvard Law Review* 1878; cf Jones (n 6) 44 for an 1831 example of Black Americans accusing the government of just that.

[8] The plenary power doctrine at its fullest expression only applies to would-be migrants seeking admission to the United States. Once an immigrant is in the United States, it is well established that they have some constitutional rights enforceable by a court. *Wong Yang Sung v McGrath* 339 US 33 (1950). However, those rights still seem to turn out to be substantially lower than those of citizens.

could be struck down under the Equal Protection Clause (a case and argument which the Court did not discuss, instead focusing on the Act's consistency with prior treaties).[9] Formally speaking, those cases were not inconsistent, for the Fourteenth Amendment's Equal Protection Clause only applies to the states, while Chinese exclusion was accomplished through federal legislation; it was not for many years until it became clear that Equal Protection doctrine would largely be applied against the federal government through 'reverse incorporation' under the Fifth Amendment's Due Process Clause.[10] Nonetheless, the moral, political, and policy inconsistency, if not the legal inconsistency, of the two cases is palpable, and plenary power is the justification that the Court adopted in order to rationalise that inconsistency by declaring migration largely outside the laws.

The Chinese Exclusion era was also a period of innovation in administrative law, particularly the development of the strategy of taking adjudications away from Article III courts and allocating them to administrative agencies to procure decisions which were both more informal (ie, absent procedural protections) and more biased in favour of the government.[11]

A key example of that strategy (which also further illustrates that Chinese exclusion was about race rather than allegiance) is the infamous 1905 case of *United States v Ju Toy*.[12] In that case, the executive branch was permitted to deport a 'person of Chinese descent' notwithstanding a District Court's ruling that he was a native-born US citizen. The Supreme Court sent *Ju Toy* into exile because Congress had stripped the federal courts of jurisdiction to review the determinations of executive branch immigration agents as to any deportations. The Court upheld that privative clause and undid the District Court's habeas corpus ruling on his citizenship, notwithstanding the almost entirely process-free character of the administrative determination, declaring that 'the almost necessary result of the power of Congress to pass exclusion laws' is that 'the decision may be entrusted to an executive officer and that his decision is due process of law'.

The dissent, by contrast, emphasised the character of the law as applying only to 'Chinese persons' (a characterisation which must, in view of the citizenship

---

[9] The *Chinese Exclusion Case* is more formally styled *Chae Chan Ping v United States* 130 US 581 (1889); the earlier case is *Yick Wo v Hopkins* 118 US 356 (1886). While the Court does not formally consider the race discrimination in play against an explicit constitutional challenge, it does endorse the racial motivations for the Act in dicta, noting that 'differences of race' exacerbated the conflict between native-born Americans and Chinese immigrants in the west, in part because of an alleged failure of the immigrants to assimilate. Congress's motivations for the Act are alleged to involve the fear 'that their immigration was in numbers approaching the character of an Oriental invasion, and was a menace to our civilization'. In short, federal plenary power was manifestly invoked to permit this open racism.

[10] *Bolling v Sharpe* 347 US 497 (1954).

[11] LE Salyer, *Laws Harsh as Tigers: Chinese Immigrants and the Shaping of Modern Immigration Law* (University of North Carolina Press, 1995).

[12] *United States v Ju Toy* 198 US 253 (1905).

of the petitioner, refer to race rather than to nationality) and explained the lawless character of the rules the executive was supposed to apply as follows:

> It will be seen that under these rules it is the duty of the immigration officer to prevent communication with the Chinese seeking to land by any one except his own officers. He is to conduct a private examination, with only the witnesses present whom he may designate. His counsel, if under the circumstances the Chinaman has been able to procure one, is permitted to look at the testimony but not to make a copy of it. He must give notice of appeal, if he wishes one, within two days, and within three days thereafter the record is to be sent to the Secretary at Washington; and every doubtful question is to be settled in favor of the Government. No provision is made for summoning witnesses from a distance or for taking depositions, and if, for instance, the person landing at San Francisco was born and brought up in Ohio, it may well be that he would be powerless to find any testimony in San Francisco to prove his citizenship. If he does not happen to have money he must go without the testimony, and when the papers are sent to Washington (three thousand miles away from the port, which in this case was the place of landing) he may not have the means of employing counsel to present his case to the Secretary. If this be not a star chamber proceeding of the most stringent sort, what more is necessary to make it one?

Ju Toy, thankfully, no longer reflects the present state of the law. Although it has not, as far as I can determine, been formally overruled, the Supreme Court made essentially the opposite holding as to the due process rights of American citizens stopped at the border 15 years later – continuing to permit the determination to be made by the executive, but at least requiring some rudiments of procedural justice to be observed in the process.[13] But the essential permission that the Court gave for even citizenship itself to be adjudicated within the executive branch remained, and, as Chin has shown, became a foundational holding for the doctrine of 'administrative finality' which permitted executive branch agencies to render final judgments without the involvement of any court.[14]

In post-Chinese-Exclusion cases, the plenary power doctrine and the closely related doctrine of 'consular nonreviewability' (providing that visa decisions by consular officers are immune from judicial review) have been used to justify a wide variety of egregious shortfalls from procedural justice that have frequently sank to the level of freeing the political branches from any real obligation to make immigration determinations according to the law. A particularly notable example *is Knauff v Shaughnessy*, which held that 'the alien wife of a citizen who had served honorably in the armed forces of the United States during World War II' could be refused admission on the basis of secret evidence, with no hearing, and 'solely upon a finding by the Attorney General that her admission would be prejudicial to the interests of the United States'.[15] In that case, the

---

[13] *Kwock Jan Fat v White* 253 US 454 (1920).

[14] GJ Chin, 'Regulating Race: Asian Exclusion and the Administrative State' (2002) 37 *Harvard Civil Rights-Civil Liberties Law Review* 1.

[15] *Knauff v Shaughnessy* 338 US 537 (1950).

Court declared that 'Whatever the procedure authorized by Congress is, it is due process as far as an alien denied entry is concerned.'

Commentators often talk as if the plenary power and consular nonreviewability doctrines are dead or dying, or securely locked up behind a wall of statutory interpretation.[16] Alas, the Supreme Court seems to think the opposite – it permitted consular officers to exclude the spouse of a US citizen on the bare allegation that he was involved in 'terrorism', not only without a hearing but without even an explanation of the basis for this allegation as recently as 2015.[17] And it upheld Donald Trump's infamous Muslim ban in 2018.

Shortly after his inauguration, Donald Trump fulfilled a campaign pledge to put a stop to Muslim immigration by issuing an executive order suspending entry from seven predominantly Muslim countries. Under pressure from lower-court injunctions, he issued two revised orders which created a Homeland Security review process and several iterations of the travel ban, ultimately including two countries without significant Muslim populations among a list of predominantly or largely Muslim countries. Under conventional constitutional religious discrimination doctrine under both the Establishment Clause and the Free Exercise Clause, such a course of events would have been quite likely to have been struck down. In both areas of doctrine, an extended course of behaviour indicating that some public act was motivated by religious goals or sectarian animus would be sufficient to render it unconstitutional.[18]

However, rather than rely on First Amendment doctrine, the Supreme Court first turned to *Kleindienst v Mandel*, an immigration case which had permitted the viewpoint-based exclusion of a Marxist professor who wanted to give a talk at Stanford on the basis of the 'facially legitimate and bona fide' alternative reason that the executive branch articulated, namely his violation of the conditions attached to a previous visa.[19] In a pregnant passage, the Court suggested that applying this review would be even *weaker* than the 'rational basis' standard that it applies to ordinary economic regulation legislation by Congress (under which it is generally supposed that the government almost always wins):

> The upshot of our cases in this context is clear: 'Any rule of constitutional law that would inhibit the flexibility' of the President 'to respond to changing world conditions should be adopted only with the greatest caution,' and our inquiry into matters of entry and national security is highly constrained. We need not define the precise contours of that inquiry in this case. A conventional application of Mandel, asking only whether the policy is facially legitimate and bona fide, would put an end

[16] M Kagan, 'Plenary Power is Dead! Long Live Plenary Power' (2015) 114 *Michigan Law Review First Impressions* 21; H Motomura, 'Immigration Law After a Century of Plenary Power: Phantom Constitutional Norms and Statutory Interpretation' (1990) 100 *Yale Law Journal* 545.
[17] *Kerry v Din* 576 US 86 (2015).
[18] *McCreary County v ACLU* 545 US 844 (2005); *Lukumi Babalu Aye v Hialeah* 508 US 520 (1993).
[19] *Kleindienst v Mandel* 408 US 753 (1972).

to our review. But the Government has suggested that it may be appropriate here for the inquiry to extend beyond the facial neutrality of the order. For our purposes today, we assume that we may look behind the face of the Proclamation to the extent of applying rational basis review. That standard of review considers whether the entry policy is plausibly related to the Government's stated objective to protect the country and improve vetting processes.[20]

Unsurprisingly, given that standard, the Supreme Court permitted the Muslim ban to stand, ruling that the Homeland Security review process on which it was nominally based was sufficient to show a plausible relationship to national security. In short, the plenary power and consular nonreviewability doctrines still exist – and even if the political branches must now utter some plausible reason other than sheer racial or religious animus, the power to exclude migrants may be exercised without the constitutional constraints that apply in every other domain of government action.

The conventional rationale for the plenary power and consular nonreviewability doctrines is articulated in the *Chinese Exclusion Case*; in essence, it is about sovereignty – that immigration is a foreign affairs power – that the political branches have the power to determine the United States's relations with foreign countries, relations which include decisions about whose nationals are to be admitted where, and also to make related decisions about the military security risks posed by decisions about who may cross the border.

The Courts of the Conqueror

The other main site of the contemporary plenary power doctrine is in Federal Indian Law, and the foreign affairs origin of the doctrine is visible there as well.[21] The plenary power in that domain fundamentally originates

---

[20] *Trump v Hawaii* 138 S Ct 2392, 2419–20 (2018) (internal citations omitted).

[21] See generally SH Cleveland, 'Powers Inherent in Sovereignty: Indians, Aliens, Territories, and the Nineteenth Century Origins of Plenary Power over Foreign Affairs' (2002) 81 *Texas Law Review* 1. A third context, which I briefly discuss at the end of this section, is over unincorporated territories. That context is less relevant to contemporary law, as the US no longer holds vast colonial possessions like the Philippines, but is still analytically important (and is still available to be used against territories such as Puerto Rico). Other important works on the conjunction of plenary power concepts include SB Coutin, J Richland and V Fortin, 'Routine Exceptionality: The Plenary Power Doctrine, Immigrants, and the Indigenous under U.S. Law' (2014) 4 *UC Irvine Law Review* 97; N Taylor Saito, *From Chinese Exclusion to Guantánamo Bay: Plenary Power and the Prerogative State* (University Press of Colorado, 2007); PP Frickey, 'Domesticating Federal Indian Law' (1996) 81 *Minnesota Law Review* 31. I use the term 'Indian Law' with some discomfort, as 'Indian' seems racist to me – a way of referring to the people who were in the US at the time of settlement by Europeans not by the names of their own nations but by an externally imposed colonial term, which, moreover, was just transposed from an entirely different country. However, legal scholars who are also members of Native American nations also use the term 'Federal Indian Law' referring to the body of federal law that came out of that colonial tradition, so I will defer to that usage. Outside of the legal context, where possible, we ought to refer to individuals by the name of the indigenous nation with which

from the 1823 case of *Johnson v M'Intosh*, in which the Supreme Court invalidated the sale of Native American land to a private party on the basis of a doctrine of 'discovery' according to which the United States, as successor in interest to the European nations who allegedly 'discovered' the continent, was the only party who could acquire land from Native Americans.[22] The court asserted that title in land could only originate from the United States, via the colonial charters that it absorbed in the revolution, and 'the Indian inhabitants are to be considered merely as occupants, to be protected, indeed, while in peace, in the possession of their lands, but to be deemed incapable of transferring the absolute title to others'. In other words, Native Americans, viewed as often-hostile nonmembers occupying the same space as citizens, would not be seen as capable of exercising property rights which American citizens need respect.[23]

Particularly striking in Chief Justice Marshall's opinion for the Court is the flat denial of law's universality in dealing with conquered lands: 'Conquest gives a title which the courts of the conqueror cannot deny, whatever the private and speculative opinions of individuals may be, respecting the original justice of the claim which has been successfully asserted.'[24] The construction 'the courts of the conqueror' lets the mask of the rule of law slip all the way off in a kind of foundational rejection of the idea of judicial impartiality familiar from domains like criminal law: because the sovereignty of the state is at stake, the courts cease to be neutral between the government and the person seeking a remedy and merely become agents of the conqueror. The sovereign conqueror, in other words, is very much judge in its own case, and, for Marshall, this is acceptable (or at least the way things are) because the sovereign does not stand in a *legal* relationship to conquered peoples, but only in a relationship of power. This construction sits in parallel to Madison's unification of 'the impartiality of judges' and 'the affection of friends' in Federalist 43's discussion of the federal government's power to put down slave revolts and serve as 'umpires' in civil conflict in which the enslaved have chosen a side: impartiality and friendship can only go together if we imagine that impartiality is a duty only owed to members, that is, that the United States speaks to the enslaved as a conqueror's court.

I contend that 'the courts of the conqueror' is the real theoretical root of the idea of plenary power. When the United States stands as a sovereign to an outsider, its courts and its legal system cease to offer the rule of law and become

---

they are affiliated. In general, I will use 'Native Americans' or 'members' to refer to individuals whose legally meaningful status is just that – their membership in some Native American nation. For similar reasons, I will refer to Native American 'nations' rather than 'tribes'.

[22] *Johnson v M'Intosh* 21 US 543 (1823).

[23] Ten years later, the Court moderated this view. Cleveland (n 21) 39–40, but the essential idea of the incapability of Native Americans to hold title to their lands, except at the sufferance of the federal government, remained, and reappeared as late as 1977. ibid 53.

[24] *Johnson v M'Intosh* 21 US 543, 588 (1823).

bureaucratic instrumentalities of raw force. Its ancient precedent is Thucydides's Melian dialogue: 'the strong do what they can, and the weak suffer what they must'. Its twenty-first century heir is Carl Schmitt's Political Theology – and immigration law.[25]

Expropriation in the Schmittian Judiciary

Unsurprisingly, given the centrality of property rights to the American rule of law, when the courts (and Congress) set aside their legal role and adopt their sovereign function of conquest, the protection of property has often been the first thing to go.

The instability of property rights on both a collective (ie, property of a given Native American nation) and an individual basis is a persistent theme of the use of plenary power in American Indian law – of which the whole course of Indian Removal stands as the most obvious example. Even after the removal period, and fluctuating depending on Congressional policy in any given decade, sometimes members might be obliged to hold individual land; sometimes they might be obliged to maintain land in the authority of their nation, but subject (of course) to the federal government. Harris and Carrillo each sketch versions of this insta-bility focused on the colonial notion that only the sorts of property associated with white Europeans could be protected by law – and that having individual property was itself associated with whiteness as membership.[26]

The Dawes Act of 1887 is a clear illustration both of the tie between prop-erty and legal status and of Congress's self-asserted power to dispose of Native American property however it pleased. In that legislation, Congress directly tied landholding to citizenship: Native Americans would be given 'allotments' of reservation land, which the US government would hold in trust for 25 years; after that period was over, those who had received allotments would acquire title to the land and citizenship.[27] Compounding the problem with arbitrary

---

[25] There are several existing Schmittian accounts of immigration law, including R Koulish, *Immigration and American Democracy: Subverting the Rule of Law* (Routledge, 2010) ch 2; M Coleman, 'Immigration Geopolitics Beyond the Mexico-US Border (2007) 39 *Antipode* 54; and PJ Pope and TM Garrett, 'America's Homo Sacer: Examining U.S. Deportation Hearings and the Criminalization of Illegal Immigration' (2013) 45 *Administration & Society* 167.

[26] CI Harris, 'Whiteness as Property' (1993) 106 *Harvard Law Review* 1707, 1921–24; J Carrillo, 'Identity as Idiom: Mashpee Reconsidered' (1995) 28 *Indiana Law Review* 511, 536–45.

[27] An Act To provide for the allotment of lands in severalty to Indians on the various reservations, and to extend the protection of the laws of the United States and the Territories over the Indians, and for other purposes, 24 Stat 388 (1887). See also An Act To amend section six of an Act approved February eighth, eighteen hundred and eighty-seven, entitled An Act to provide for the allotment of lands in severalty to Indians on the various reservations, and to extend the protection of the laws of the United States and the Territories over the Indians, and for other purposes ('Burke Act'), 34 Stat 182 (1906), which provided that citizenship would not pass at the issuing of the patent (as seems to be suggested by the quoted text), but extended only after the expiration of the trust period, while also conferring on the Secretary of the Interior the fully discretionary power to drop the trust period and convey full title to anyone 'competent and capable of managing his or her affairs'.

executive power, the President would have untrammelled discretion not only to decide which nations would be subject to the effective dissolution entailed by such allotment, but also to extend the 25-year 'trust' period and hence deprive any individual person of full land title for as long as he saw fit.

Taking up the 'allotment' would entitle a member to legal protection to go with their citizenship. This was written right into the text of the Dawes Act:

> That upon the completion of said allotments and the patenting of the lands to said allottees, each and every member of the respective bands or tribes of Indians to whom allotments have been made shall have the benefit of and be subject to the laws, both civil and criminal, of the State or Territory in which they may reside; and no Territory shall pass or enforce any law denying any such Indian within its jurisdiction the equal protection of the law. And every Indian born within the territorial limits of the United States to whom allotments shall have been made under the provisions of this act, or under any law or treaty, and every Indian born within the territorial limits of the United States who has voluntarily taken up, within said limits, his residence separate and apart from any tribe of Indians therein, and has adopted the habits of civilized life, is hereby declared to be a citizen of the United States, and is entitled to all the rights, privileges, and immunities of such citizens[.]

That passage could be the subject of a book all on its own. Note the clear linguistic references to the Fourteenth Amendment – effectively, the Act purported to extend the protections of that Amendment to members of Native American nations on the condition that they accept individualised rather than collective national property and abandon their culture. From the standpoint of the United States it seems to be extending property, and with it citizenship and legal standing, but only as an exercise of foreign affairs discretion to get rid of the pesky nations by chopping up their land and encouraging their people to abandon them. It's exactly the way a conqueror deals with property and persons of the conquered: absorb ('assimilate') those who are willing to join the conquering people and exclude the rest. (Recall the complaints of the court in the Chinese Exclusion Case that people from China wouldn't assimilate.) This sort of history explains why it can be confusing to try to figure out whether promoting the alienability of Native American land is good or terrible for their members (and as a non-Native-American I am not remotely competent to judge).[28] The Indian Reorganization Act of 1934 put a stop to allotments and tried to encourage constitution-making among the Native American nations – another shift in policy toward the notion of more independent sovereignty but also less emphasis on the individual members' rights

---

[28] Some of the debate about the extent to which restrictions on alienability were offensively paternalistic or necessary to protect individuals from exploitation and nations from dissolution – as well as the patently racist administration of the Secretary of the Interior's exercise of the discretion to confer fee title before the expiration of the statutory trust period, which was based on the belief that those with more 'white blood' were more intelligent – can be gleaned from JA McDonnell, *The Dispossession of the American Indian, 1887–1934* (Indiana University Press, 1991).

vis a vis the United States.[29] That Act explicitly restricted the alienability of land in Indian Country.[30]

The merger of immigration plenary power and Indian plenary power was achieved in *Lone Wolf v Hitchcock*.[31] In that case, the Kiowa sued seeking to strike down legislation providing for the allotment of their reservation as well as its sale to nonmembers, arguing that it was in violation of their treaty rights as well as their vested property interests as a nation under the Medicine Lodge Treaty of 1867. Citing the *Chinese Exclusion Case* as well as the nineteenth century caselaw about the mere occupancy rights of the Indians, the Court concluded that 'as Congress possessed full power in the matter, the judiciary cannot question or inquire into the motives which prompted the enactment of this legislation. If injury was occasioned, which we do not wish to be understood as implying, by the use made by Congress of its power, relief must be sought by an appeal to that body for redress, and not to the courts'.[32]

That statement bears a strong resemblance to similar statements in immigration law cases like the *Chinese Exclusion Case* and *Knauff v Shaughnessy*. Reading them together, we must see the instability of Native American property rights – and hence their marginal status as subjects of the law – to be a consequence of their semi-foreign status. As chapter 1 discussed, property rights in the United States were initially reserved to citizens. The notion that secure rights to landownership are inextricable from full-fledged republican citizenship, and hence unavailable to Native Americans, could be deployed to permit the legislative instability of land rights under Federal Indian law.

Immigration too is associated with a history of unstable property rights in addition to the alienage restrictions on land ownership at the time of the founding. As an outgrowth of Chinese exclusion, 'aliens ineligible to [naturalized] citizenship' – which meant nonwhite persons, and in practice was applied against Asians, particularly Japanese immigrants – were prohibited from owning land in many western states in the early twentieth century.[33] If a non-white immigrant acquired land, the state could bring an escheat action to seize it; moreover, under California's law, the state divested land by operation of law even after the 'alien

---

[29] An Act To conserve and develop Indian lands and resources; to extend to Indians the right to form business and other organizations; to establish a credit system for Indians; to grant certain rights of home rule to Indians; to provide for vocational education for Indians; and for other purposes, 48 Stat 984 (1934).

[30] 'Indian Country' is another term that I use only because it seems to be the preferred term when many Native American scholars and activists themselves refer to ancestral and/or reservation land. See eg National Congress of American Indians, 'NCAI Response to Usage of the Term 'Indian Country' (27 December 2019) www.ncai.org/news/articles/2019/12/27/ncai-response-to-usage-of-the-term-indian-country ('The term is used with positive sentiment within Native communities, by Native-focused organizations such as NCAI, and news organizations such as Indian Country Today.').

[31] *Lone Wolf v Hitchcock* 187 US 553 (1903).

[32] Fortunately, once again, this harsh ruling has been moderated somewhat. See Cleveland's (n 21) 78–81 discussion.

[33] K Aoki, 'No Right to Own?: The Early Twentieth-Century "Alien Land Laws" as a Prelude to Internment' (1998) 37 *Boston College Law Review* 37.

ineligible to citizenship' sold it, even to a citizen.[34] Such enactments would be unconstitutional under contemporary doctrine, in view of the fact that state law distinctions on the basis of alienage are generally subject to strict scrutiny (as, obviously, are the race based motivations) but there are still alien landownership restrictions on the books in most states.[35] Moreover, many of those in Mexican ethno-national groups now stereotyped as 'immigrants' lost their land at the hands of the courts of the conqueror after the Mexican-American war.[36]

Even today the de facto consequences of immigration enforcement can pose a serious threat to property ownership not only of migrants but also of their families: there is empirical evidence suggesting that immigration enforcement initiatives are an important factor leading to foreclosures in mixed-status households by depriving those households of income-earners,[37] and deported immigrants also regularly find that their personal property has disappeared in Immigration and Customs Enforcement (ICE) or Customs and Border Patrol (CBP) custody.[38]

Yet, paradoxically – and representing the grip of the property-focused conception of the rule of law even as the Court carries out lawlessness – the Supreme Court denied, in the *Chinese Exclusion Case*, that plenary power could undermine property rights. The Court had no compunctions about holding that the political branches had complete authority to abrogate a treaty and declare that a Chinese citizen who had left the country could be barred from returning at the naked will of the political branches and with no judicial scrutiny. But the Court balked at imagining that such a person could be deprived of property. In distinguishing the right to retain property from the right to return to the United States, the Court drew on a distinction later to be deployed by later rule of law critics of administrative law such as Gary Lawson who are interested in sorting out which sorts of economic monopolies (like patents) can count as property rights entitled to full procedural protections in adjudication, to wit, between a vested right and an expectancy:

> [In a prior case] the learned justice observes that, 'if real estate be purchased or secured under a treaty, it would be most mischievous to admit that the extinguishment of the treaty extinguished the right to such estate. In truth, it no more affects

[34] ibid 55, 59, 63.

[35] A Brownell Tirres, 'Property Outliers: Non-Citizens, Property Rights and State Power' (2012) 27 *Georgetown Immigration Law Journal* 77, 97–101. In 1948, the Supreme Court struck down some of the burdens those laws imposed on citizen children of immigrants in *Oyama v California* 332 US 633 (1948). This case was a landmark in establishing the legal right of even subordinated minorities (at least if they were citizens) to land ownership, and was cited as authority shortly thereafter in *Shelley v Kraemer*. R Cuison Villazor, 'Rediscovering Oyama v. California: At the Intersection of Property, Race, and Citizenship' (2010) 87 *Washington University Law Review* 979.

[36] GT Luna, 'Chicana/Chicano Land Tenure in the Agrarian Domain: On the Edge of a Naked Knife' (1989) 4 *Michigan Journal of Race & Law* 39.

[37] J Rugh and M Hall, 'Deporting the American Dream: Immigration Enforcement and Latino Foreclosures' (2016) 3 *Sociological Science* 1077.

[38] W Ewing and G Cantor, 'Deported With No Possessions: The Mishandling of Migrants' Personal Belongings by CBP and ICE' (*American Immigration Council*, 21 December 2006)

such rights than the repeal of a municipal law affects rights acquired under it.' Of this doctrine there can be no question in this court; but far different is this case, where a continued suspension of the exercise of a governmental power is insisted upon as a right, because, by the favor and consent of the government, it has not heretofore been exerted with respect to the appellant or to the class to which he belongs. Between property rights not affected by the termination or abrogation of a treaty, and expectations of benefits from the continuance of existing legislation, there is as wide a difference as between realization and hopes.[39]

There's one problem with this distinction: on the actual facts of the case before the Court, the plaintiff had been issued a certificate by a customs official, under the authority of pre-existing legislation, declaring that he was entitled to return to the US. The Court makes no effort to explain why the government might issue someone a piece of paper saying 'this is a patent to land, you have rights to it now' and not be able to extinguish it by the arbitrary will of a political official when the law changes, but can issue the almost identical piece of paper 'this is a patent to land *on our shores*, you have the right to do that now' and take it away afterward by pure fiat.[40] In a sense, the *Chinese Exclusion Case* encompasses the whole theoretical framework of this book in one go: even in cases that stand as monuments to arbitrary power, our courts still sing a paean to the legal protection of property rights – but what kinds of things get counted as property rights is entirely endogenous to pre-existing relations of political power and who is counted as a member of the legal community.[41]

In short, the US seems to have a consistent strategy in dealing with those who are present but considered external to the legal community. As Coutin et al aptly put it, citing both *Chae Chan Ping* and *Lone Wolf*:

Both immigrant and indigenous groups occupy a space of exception vis-a-vis U.S. law: as 'resident aliens' and 'dependent nations' they are inside and outside at the same time. Their presence demands law – the petition, the recognition claim – even as this demand simultaneously seeks an exception to law in that officials have the discretion to decide what presence means, acting according to what has been termed 'administrative grace' or the government's 'pleasure,' in a manner "not subject to be controlled by the judicial department.[42]

www.americanimmigrationcouncil.org/research/deported-no-possessions#:~:text=New%20 Survey%20Data%20Reveals%20That%20Migrants%20Are%20Routinely%20Removed%20 Without%20Their%20Personal%20Belongings&text=According%20to%20new%20data%20 from,their%20personal%20belongings%20were%20returned.

[39] *Chae Chan Ping v United States* 130 US 581, 610 (1889); *cf* G Lawson, 'Appointments and Illegal Adjudication: The America Invents Act through a Constitutional Lens' (2018) 26 *George Mason Law Review* 26.

[40] *cf* ibid 39–43.

[41] Maybe this helps reconcile the *Chinese Exclusion Case* with *Yick Wo v Hopkins*: in the earlier case, the discrimination against Chinese people was in their right to operate laundries in San Francisco – and hence threatened their capacity to use real estate. Indeed, much of the rhetoric in *Yick Wo* sounds eerily similar to that of *Lochner*.

[42] Coutin, Richland and Fortin (n 21) 99. C Saunt, *Unworthy Republic: The Dispossession of Native Americans and the Road to Indian Territory*, 1st edn (WW Norton & Company, 2020), has

Often, the categories of legal exclusion have overlapped. During the colonial and then antebellum periods, the statuses of 'alien,' of 'Indian,' and of slave could be intertwined. As early as 1670, Anthony Johnson, a Black person who had originally been carried over from Africa but had managed to become free and to acquire property, was subjected to alien land laws prohibiting his children from inheriting on the grounds that 'he was a Negroe and by consequence an alien'.[43] Black Americans also could sometimes claim Native American ancestry as a way to escape enslavement.[44] And many Native Americans themselves were enslaved – albeit mostly illegally – up to the Civil War.[45] Of course, the colonisation movement represented an outright effort to ascribe the status of alien on free Black Americans. Today, members of Native American nations whose ancestral lands occupied both sides of what are now US borders are still subject to legally liminal statuses as their citizenship status and movement rights sometimes renders them 'immigrants' to land their ancestors occupied long before the United States existed.[46] And this is precisely what we would expect in a society rooted in settler ideology, in which the conception of freedom at the root of American society required the creation of legally subordinated castes which lacked the right to property ownership, and hence to legal protection.[47]

The courts of the conqueror also intersect with slavery in that the theoretical tradition in which America's founders were embedded understood one of the main justifications of slavery to be property rights acquired by conquest. According to one common argument in the period, the victor in a war has the right to enslave those whom they would otherwise have a right to kill – a view that John Locke at least partially endorsed (albeit with some complexities), and which Montesquieu tried to refute.[48] Chief Justice Marshall's appeal to 'the courts of the conqueror' in *Johnson v M'Intosh* was followed two years later by his declaration that '[b]ut from the earliest times, war has existed, and war confers rights in which all have acquiesced. Among the most enlightened nations of antiquity, one of these was that the victor might enslave the vanquished'.[49] Hinshelwood completes the scholarly circle between slavery, conquest, and

---

recently done important work in connecting Native American removal to the concept of 'deportation' as applied to immigrants – and, not incidentally, in developing the relationship between this programme of deportation and the expansion of slavery, thus connecting the three great American failures of the rule of law.

[43] A de la Fuente and AJ Gross, *Becoming Free, Becoming Black: Race, Freedom, and Law in Cuba, Virginia, and Louisiana* (Cambridge University Press, 2020) 15.

[44] ibid 94–98.

[45] A Reséndez, *The Other Slavery: The Uncovered Story of Indian Enslavement in America*, 1st edn (Mariner Books, Houghton Mifflin Harcourt, 2017).

[46] EM Luna-Firebaugh, 'The Border Crossed Us: Border Crossing Issues of the Indigenous Peoples of the Americas' (2002) 17 *Wicazo Sa Review* 159.

[47] A Rana, *The Two Faces of American Freedom* (Harvard University Press, 2014).

[48] See W Uzgalis and N Zack, 'John Locke, Racism, Slavery, and Indian Lands' in *The Oxford Handbook of Philosophy and Race* (Oxford University Press, 2017); DJ Schaub, 'Montesquieu on Slavery' (2005) 34 *Perspectives on Political Science* 70.

[49] *The Antelope* 23 US 66, 120 (1825).

Native Americans by drawing out the relationship between Locke's theory of slavery and efforts to justify the enslavement of Native Americans in Carolina in the late seventeenth century.[50]

Another kind of merger of the way the US has interacted with Native Americans as the human impediments to an expanding empire and the way the US has interacted with immigrants as unwanted intruders can be perceived in its treatment of Filipinos in the early twentieth century, after it had acquired the Philippines in the Spanish-American war. These territorial acquisitions formed the basis for the third assertion of plenary power, the *Insular Cases*. Filipinos were characterised as 'tribal,' and hence unsuited for self-rule – much like Native American nations were – and the expressed goal was 'benevolent assimilation'.[51] Consistent with this goal, they were regarded by law as 'U.S. nationals' (not citizens), and permitted to travel to the mainland – but when they arrived, they were subjected to racially motivated violence on the basis of the familiar story, so prominent in today's anti-immigrant narrative, about competition for jobs. Filipinos also were the victims by transposition of many racist cultural tropes often applied to Black Americans, such as beliefs about sexual aggression.

The Supreme Court appealed directly to the authority of *Johnson v M'Intosh* in applying the plenary power doctrine to its newfound colonial empire, quoting a passage from Chief Justice Marshall's opinion in that case to justify maintaining a distinction between a conquered but separate people whose status is 'maintained by force' until such time as they are 'incorporated with the victorious nation'. It thus justified the different constitutional statuses of colonial territory and metropole on the same conquest and assimilation theory with which it justified the failure to respect Native American property rights.[52]

The Plenary Power Doctrine is Indefensible

Expressed as a proposition of foreign relations, the notion that there may be some sovereign 'plenary powers' has a substantial degree of historical support. Doubtless, many countries, including the United States, have coerced foreigners found abroad in numerous ways without offering them any kind of legal process – seizing their property, killing them in wartime, and otherwise treating

---

[50] B Hinshelwood, 'The Carolinian Context of John Locke's Theory of Slavery' (2013) 41 *Political Theory* 562.

[51] MM Ngai, *Impossible Subjects: Illegal Aliens and the Making of Modern America*, New Paperbook edn (Princeton University Press, 2014) 120–49.

[52] *Downes v Bidwell* 182 US 244, 281–82 (1901). One meaningful point of tension in this legacy connecting slavery and American colonialism of both Native American nations and the Philippines, however, is that the application of the plenary power doctrine to unincorporated federal territory is hardly consistent with the proposition in *Dred Scott* – critical to that case's outcome for the reasons described in chapter one – that Congress lacks the authority to legislate to determine the scope of permissible property interests in such territories.

them merely as objects of foreign policy rather than legal rightsholders. But the plenary power doctrine as a way of dealing with persons who are peacefully in the United States or at its borders ought to be rejected as wholly inconsistent with the rule of law.

First of all, it seems to me that the full application of such doctrines violates the United States's international commitments. The US has joined the Protocol Relating to the Status of Refugees and the Convention against Torture and Other Cruel, Inhuman or Degrading Treatment or Punishment. Those international agreements, and statutes that have been enacted to implement them, impose constraints on unbounded executive discretion even in admitting refugees at the border – although they ultimately do not constrain Congress, as it is well-established that an after-enacted Act of Congress can abrogate a treaty, their current legal status seems to me inconsistent with notions like plenary power and consular nonreviewability.

Moreover, the executive branch certainly acts as if it seeks to regulate immigration by law as opposed to as a sheer exercise of sovereign power: it offers many immigrants some kind of hearing; it calls those who bear responsibility for adjudicating immigration claims 'judges' and requires them to wear judicial robes and operate in buildings that it calls courtrooms.[53] Accordingly, the idea of the rule of law has some normative bite in the US framework of addressing immigrants by the country's own performative admission.

I would further argue that the US morally ought to treat prospective migrants as legal subjects. I have argued elsewhere that we ought to understand the obligations of the rule of law as attaching when a country wields monopolistic coercive force against another under a claim of right.[54] For the reasons noted above, when the US confronts migrants who seek admission to its territory, it does not simply present itself as entitled to do so for the reasons of the Athenians at Melos – it participates in a robust domestic and international legal regime governing cross-border travel.[55] Indeed, the US specifically purports to subject migrants' actions at the border not to its military power but to its ordinary

---

[53] See U.S. Department of Justice, Executive Office for Immigration Review, Memorandum from Chief Immigration Judge, Operating Policies and Procedures Memorandum Number 94-10: Wearing of the Robe During Immigration Judge Hearings (17 October 1994) www.justice.gov/eoir/efoia/ocij/oppm94/94-10.pdf; U.S. Department of Justice, Executive Office for Immigration Review, Memorandum from Chief Immigration Judge, Operating Policies and Procedures Memorandum Number 17-03: Guidelines for Immigration Court Cases Involving Juveniles, Including Unaccompanied Alien Children (20 December 2017).

[54] P Gowder, *The Rule of Law in the Real World* (Cambridge University Press, 2016) 9–10.

[55] This section in part responds to a more theoretical prior conversation in which Matt Lister and Chad Flanders have urged me to clarify my views on the conceptual applicability of the notion of the rule of law at the border. M Lister, 'Can the Rule of Law Apply at the Border? A Commentary on Paul Gowder's The Rule of Law in the Real World' (2018) 62 *Saint Louis University Law Journal* 323; C Flanders, 'Keeping the Rule of Law Simple: Comments on Gowder, The Rule of Law in the Real World' (2018) 62 *Saint Louis University Law Journal* 313, 319–21; P Gowder, 'Resisting the Rule of Men' (2018) 62 *Saint Louis University Law Journal* 333, 345; see also M Lister, 'Enforcing Immigration Law' (2020) 15 *Philosophy Compass* e12653.

criminal jurisdiction: it has established crimes with which many migrants can be charged simply on the basis of their entry – and hence has directly asserted that it stands in a legal relationship with those who pass its gates.[56]

Furthermore, notwithstanding the economic and military rise of China and the loss of American international prestige occasioned by the Trump regime, the reality is that the US does not stand in the same position as other nations in the international system. It is a global hegemon that has long had disproportionate weight in shaping the international legal and political system, and hence in setting the real-world structures that individuals must navigate in their efforts to cross borders. In effect, the US is a major regulator of persons globally.[57] Furthermore, American foreign policy has substantially contributed to the conditions that have prompted international migrant flows, most obviously (but far from exclusively) by starting destabilising wars in the Middle East and by promoting years of 'Washington consensus' international economic policies that have dictated the development paths of numerous foreign countries and created both the conditions for its own wealth and economic incentives to migration by facilitating the free movement of capital and the restricted movement of labour.

It is hardly unreasonable, in light of the immense entanglement that the lives of migrants have with US regulation and US power, to demand that the US at least meet some minimal legal standards with respect to those who cross its borders.

Frickey rightly suggests that Federal Indian Law represents 'the tension between colonization and American constitutionalism'.[58] Immigration law captures a similar tension, between constitutionalism and *empire*: as the

---

[56] See eg L Uhl, 'Prosecuting Illegal Reentry Cases Where Evidentiary Documents Are Missing or Incomplete: Everything You Never Wanted to Know about A-Files and Removal Documents and Were Not Afraid Not to Ask' (2017) 65 *United States Attorneys' Bulletin* 17.

[57] The US also engages in a substantial amount of extraterritorial regulation, particularly with respect to the financial system, although the Supreme Court has partly restrained the global reach of American law via an interpretive 'presumption against extraterritoriality'. P-H Verdier, 'The New Financial Extraterritoriality' (2019) 87 *George Washington Law Review* 239. Notwithstanding the Supreme Court's restraint, US citizens residing abroad, for example, notoriously find it difficult to open bank accounts because the US has leveraged its economic domination to force foreign banks to assume burdensome compliance obligations. SE Pippin, JA Wong and RM Mason, 'Perceived and Actual Consequences of the Foreign Account Tax Compliance Act: A Survey of Americans Living Abroad' in *Advances in Taxation*, vol 25 (Emerald Publishing Limited, 2018); G Williams, 'U.S. Expats Find Their Money Is No Longer Welcome at the Bank' (*Reuters*, 11 June 2014) www.reuters.com/article/us-banks-expats-idUSKBN0EM16V20140611. Its Foreign Corrupt Practices Act regulates businesses all over the world. H Lowell Brown, 'Extraterritorial Jurisdiction Under the 1998 Amendments to the Foreign Corrupt Practices Act: Does the Government's Reach Now Exceed its Grasp' (2001) 26 *North Carolina Journal of International Law and Commercial Regulation* 239. And it even extends its non-financial criminal jurisdiction to many acts done abroad that are perceived to affect American security interests. M Farbiarz, 'Accuracy and Adjudication: The Promise of Extraterritorial Due Process' (2016) 116 *Columbia Law Review* 625; SA Koh, 'Foreign Affairs Prosecutions' (2019) 94 *New York University Law Review* 340.

[58] PP Frickey, 'Marshalling Past and Present: Colonialism, Constitutionalism, and Interpretation in Federal Indian Law' (1993) 107 *Harvard Law Review* 381, 383.

United States has expanded its global hegemony and the scale of the noncitizen individuals whom its policies affect, it becomes more and more difficult to understand its relationships with those persons as merely those of a sovereign interacting at a kind of Westphalian arms-length with foreigners. The state comes to people who are, via its power, partially integrated into its community; but, because that integration is only partial, it still has a taste of Melos to it in the form of a kind of Schmittian reserve capacity to treat them as invaders or conquered people (or sometimes, as with Mexicans crossing over into land in Texas which the United States grabbed from Mexico in the first place, both) and replace the gavel with a fist. This cannot be permitted in a country that purports to be a nation of laws.

IMMIGRATION 'COURT': BARELY ADJUDICATION AT ALL

The canonical way that any dispute between an immigrant and the government about the lawful character of their admission or presence is adjudicated is via a hearing before an 'immigration judge' within the Department of Justice, with an appeal thereafter to the Board of Immigration Appeals (BIA), and thereafter to a federal court of appeals. As will be seen, there are many categories of case that do not follow that route, but we may take it as the normative system. Of course, there is always a substantial drop-off at each level of an appeal, so the primary adjudicator with whom most immigrants subjected to exclusion or deportation will be concerned is an immigration judge.[59]

Richard Posner once bluntly declared from the bench that the immigration courts have 'fallen below the minimum standards of legal justice'.[60] Posner's primary theory for this failure, as he articulated in another case, was 'its severe underfunding by Congress, which has resulted in a shortage of immigration judges that has subjected them to crushing workloads'.[61]

But these workloads themselves represent policy choices; immigration adjudication is an example of the Kafkaesque teeth of the administrative state in the form of its control over things like budgets and personnel rules, which itself operates as a site for the exercise of potentially arbitrary power.

---

[59] According to the Department of Justice, in fiscal year 2017, the 'immigration courts' within the department received 405,947 I-862 (deportation, exclusion) cases, while the BIA received 33,503 cases. Department of Justice Executive Office for Immigration Review Statistics Yearbook for Fiscal Year 2017, www.justice.gov/eoir/page/file/1107056/download (Accessed 19 April 2021). I cannot find statistics for how many cases from the BIA were appealed to federal court, but, assuming a similar proportion drop off at this second level of appellate review, that would entail that 99% of immigrants deported and excluded never see any kind of adjudication outside the executive branch. On the President's control over immigration adjudication more generally, see CY Kim, 'The President's Immigration Courts' (2018) 68 *Emory Law Journal* 1.

[60] *Benslimane v Gonzales* 430 F3d 828 (7th Cir 2005).

[61] *Chavarria-Reyes v Lynch* 845 F3d 275 (7th Cir 2016) (dissenting opinion).

As an example of this power, in late 2002, the BIA was some 56,000 cases behind, so then-Attorney General Ashcroft ordered them to catch up and gave them a deadline of March 2003. Obeying the order, the Board drastically accelerated its review process, leading single BIA judges to dispose of a case as fast as one every ten minutes and increasing the Board's affirmation rate of immigration judges from 59 per cent to 86 per cent.[62] Thus, by issuing a bureaucratic time management order, the Attorney General was able to deprive thousands of immigrants of any genuine opportunity for administrative review of their cases.

More recently, the Department of Justice imposed performance standards on its immigration judges requiring them to clear 700 cases a year or be punished, even while increasing their adjudicative burden by prohibiting them from administratively closing cases. Assuming 262 workdays a year, this amounts to a requirement that immigration judges clear 2.6 cases a day, rain or shine, and regardless of their complexity or any other duties they may need to carry out.[63] A telling indication of exactly how the immigration adjudication system is oriented toward racing through cases can be gleaned from one immigration judge's suggestion in an interview with Amit Jain that the process of judicial review of their decisions imposed pressure to 'do these lengthy decisions citing cases …. And so decisions that used to be quick now were taking 35, 40, 50, 60 minutes or more'.[64] Citing legal authority is evidently perceived as an unbearable burden, and thirty-five minutes per case is evidently considered slow.

In light of this crushing workload, immigration judges are frequently criticised for providing barely-serious hearings to the people before them. For example, in the case that so exercised Judge Posner, the 7th Circuit upheld (Posner was writing in dissent) the results of an adjudication in which the immigration judge 'never invited [*Chavarria-Reyes*] to present evidence on his own behalf'.

Immigrants who have legal representation tend to fare much better than those who do not: 'represented detained noncitizens were 10.5 times more likely to succeed in removal proceedings than their pro se counterparts'.[65] There's probably some selection bias in that ratio – counsel are probably more likely to offer their services to clients with strong cases. But there's some evidence suggesting a causal element too: a pilot programme providing universal representation to

[62] L Getter and J Peterson, 'Speedier Rate of Deportation Rulings Assailed' (*Los Angeles Times*, 5 January 2003) www.latimes.com/archives/la-xpm-2003-jan-05-na-immig5-story.html.

[63] I take the 262 workdays a year figure from the U.S. Office of Personnel Management, 'Fact Sheet: Computing Hourly Rates of Pay Using the 2,087-Hour Divisor' www.opm.gov/policy-data-oversight/pay-leave/pay-administration/fact-sheets/computing-hourly-rates-of-pay-using-the-2087-hour-divisor/.

[64] A Jain, 'Bureaucrats in Robes: Immigration Judges and the Trappings of Courts' (2019) 33 *Georgetown Immigration Law Journal* 261, 286.

[65] American Bar Association, '2019 Update Report: Reforming the Immigration System: Proposals to Promote Independence, Fairness, Efficiency, and Professionalism in the Adjudication of Removal Cases' (American Bar Association Commission on Immigration, March 2019) 5–3 www.americanbar.org/content/dam/aba/publications/commission_on_immigration/2019_reforming_the_immigration_system_volume_2.pdf.

migrants in New York yielded a substantial increase in successful adjudicatory outcomes for migrants.[66] Another study found that, after controlling for factors like a detainee's criminal record and employment history (which may be part of the indica of merit that immigration lawyers use to select cases), detainees represented by counsel were more than three times more likely to be released on bond.[67] Yet immigrants typically don't receive court-appointed representation in the process, and while some 61 per cent are represented, substantially fewer of those who are detained manage to find representation.[68]

Compounding the problem is the famous complexity of American immigration law – so complex that non-specialist lawyers screw it up in drastic ways; for example, criminal defence lawyers can easily fail to correctly advise their clients about the immigration consequences of criminal convictions.[69] Unrepresented – possibly non-English-speaking and desperately poor – immigrants who may be in detention and hence unable without extreme difficulty to do things like conduct legal research and gather evidence are almost certainly unaware of such rights as they may enjoy. Ryo reports that large proportions of surveyed detainees did not know why they were in removal proceedings and did not understand the contents of bond notices.[70]

While an immigrant may ultimately appeal an immigration judge's determination to the BIA and thereafter to a real court, the factual determinations made in the immigration judge's hasty hearing are reviewed under a deferential standard, and a court is prohibited from remanding for additional fact-finding.[71] Moreover, the BIA review level may be minimal. Under existing regulations, a single BIA member is authorised to affirm an immigration court decision in summary fashion, with no written opinion.[72] And Congress has specifically stripped the real courts of jurisdiction over a number of determinations.[73] Access to an appeal from the executive to the judiciary is further impaired by the fact that a final administrative decision renders a migrant immediately deportable in the absence of a stay – the government can whisk even an

---

[66] ibid 5–10.

[67] E Ryo, 'Detained: A Study of Immigration Bond Hearings' (2016) 50 *Law & Society Review* 117, 139.

[68] American Bar Association (n 65) 5–8 to 5–9.

[69] JA Cade, 'The Plea-Bargain Crisis for Noncitizens in Misdemeanor Court Part VI: Immigration Litigation Issues' (2013) 34 *Immigration and Nationality Law Review* 597. The Supreme Court, in *Padilla v Kentucky* 559 US 356 (2010), held that it constitutes ineffective assistance of counsel to fail to advise clients of 'succinct and straightforward' immigration consequences – but explicitly recognised that the complexity of immigration law is such that even a skilled criminal defence lawyer could miss 'situations in which the deportation consequences of a particular plea are unclear or uncertain' without the conviction being unconstitutional under the Sixth Amendment, as long as they advise the client that there *might* be immigration consequences.

[70] E Ryo, 'Fostering Legal Cynicism through Immigration Detention' (2017) *Southern California Law* Review 999, 1034–36.

[71] 8 USC § 1252(b)(4)(B); 8 USC § 1252(a)(1).

[72] 8 CFR § 1003.1(e).

[73] 8 USC § 1252(a)(2).

unrepresented immigrant thousands of miles away from any court the minute the administrative process is done unless they're savvy enough to ask for a stay quickly and lucky enough to get it.[74]

Immigration adjudication is also notoriously lacking in independence.[75] Unlike many other executive branch adjudicators, immigration judges lack the protections provided by the Administrative Procedure Act.[76] Catherine Kim and Amy Semet have provided empirical evidence suggesting that the president in office at the time of a particular adjudication exercises more influence over immigration judges' rulings than the president who appointed an immigration judge – ie, when a more or less immigrant-friendly president is in power, the decisions of the judges shift.[77] It's no surprise then that a qualitative study of immigration court judges found that they largely experience their role as bureaucratic cogs rather than as independent adjudicators.[78]

The compromises to judicial independence in immigration adjudication have run even deeper. In conjunction with the 2002 speedup, Ashcroft reduced the size of the BIA and reassigned some of its members to other duties. Those who were reassigned were heavily weighted toward those known to make 'liberal' decisions.[79] In one case from the period, a senior immigration judge stepped in to take over an immigration case and reverse the rulings of a judge who had determined in favour of the immigrant – after *ex parte* contact from the government's lawyers.[80] More recently, during the Trump administration, the Department of Justice replaced an immigration judge midway through the adjudicative process because it was annoyed that the judge was making a serious effort to have notice of a hearing served on a child.[81] There have been allegations – which, due to a 'lack of transparency', cannot be investigated – that the Department of Justice uses political criteria as a basis for the selection of adjudicators.[82]

---

[74] American Bar Association (n 65) 3–15, 4–3.

[75] SH Legomsky, 'Deportation and the War on Independence' (2006) 26 *Journal of the National Association of Administrative Law Judiciary* 387.

[76] Those protections, and other procedural requirements, are given by 5 USC § 554. It has been established that they do not apply in immigration cases since *Marcello v Bonds* 349 US 302 (1955). For discussions of the difference between 'Administrative Law Judges' and 'Administrative Judges', and the lack of procedural protections in the latter, see K Barnett, 'Against Administrative Judges' (2016) 49 *UC Davis Law Review* 1643; M Asimow, 'Five Models of Administrative Adjudication' (2015) 63 *American Journal of Comparative Law* 3.

[77] CY Kim and A Semet, 'Presidential Ideology and Immigrant Detention' (2020) 69 *Duke Law Journal* 1855.

[78] Jain (n 64).

[79] Legomsky (n 75) 376–77.

[80] E Schmitt, '2 Judges Do Battle in an Immigration Case' (*New York Times*, 21 June 2001) www.nytimes.com/2001/06/21/us/2-judges-do-battle-in-an-immigration-case.html.

[81] T Kopan, 'Immigrant Ordered Deported After Justice Department Replaces Judge' (CNN, 7 August 2018) www.cnn.com/2018/08/07/politics/immigration-judge-replaced-deportation-case-justice-department/index.html. The Attorney General used poor Mr Castro-Tum's case as an excuse to make new rules regarding the practice of administrative closure. *Matter of Castro-Tum* 27 I&N Dec 271 (AG 2018).

[82] American Bar Association (n 65) 2–19.

From those facts, it is impossible to avoid the conclusion that there are no fair hearings in immigration court. Rather, a presidential administration – like the Trump administration – bent on excluding and deporting as many immigrants as possible has the power to largely ignore underlying law by acting as judge in its own case.

Even if the designated adjudicators themselves were independent, the immigration system contains one further feature that makes it incompatible with any serious notion of judicial independence: the Attorney General is entitled to exercise what is known as the 'self-referral power' to order any case transferred from the BIA to himself, after which he may unilaterally adjudicate it in any fashion he pleases. This is frequently used as a direct instrument of executive branch policy, including for the purpose of setting determinative legal rules through precedential adjudication.[83]

The Attorney General's referral authority can be exercised in an arbitrary fashion, with no procedural protections whatsoever. The Third Circuit described the process in one such case: 'Despite requests by Silva-Trevino's counsel, the Attorney General refused to identify the issues to be considered, to define the scope of his review, to provide a briefing schedule, or to apprise counsel of the applicable briefing procedure.'[84]

Accordingly, a political appointee of the president has the authority to dictate the outcome of any adjudication determining an individual's legal right to be present in the United States based on nothing more than short-term political considerations. Moreover, the Attorney General might apply those political considerations retroactively – the Attorney General may announce a new rule, disadvantageous to the immigrant, and motivated solely by what we might call 'reasons of state', and immediately (ie, retroactively) apply that rule in a case they have referred to themselves, depriving the immigrant of a neutral adjudicator and using that immigrant's fate as nothing more than a means for the pursuit of broader policy goals.

This power was used repeatedly by the Trump administration, surely the most anti-immigrant US presidency in modern history. For example, consider *Matter of A-B-*, in which the Attorney General declared that domestic violence is not group-based persecution for purposes of asylum.[85] Or *Matter of Castro-Tum*, in which Jeff Sessions overruled two precedential decisions to determine that immigration judges lack the power to suspend or close cases on their own.[86]

---

[83] AR Gonzales and P Glen, 'Advancing Executive Branch Immigration Policy through the Attorney General's Review Authority' (2016) 101 *Iowa Law Review* 841, 841–94, review the history and uses of the referral authority. Stella Elias and I have a more extensive discussion of the lawless character of the self-referral authority in a working paper currently entitled 'Lawless Lawmaking: The Attorney General Self-Referral Power and the Rule of Law'.

[84] *Jean-Louis v Attorney General* 582 F3d 462, 470 n 11 (3d Cir 2009).

[85] *Matter of A-B-* 27 I&N Dec 316 (AG 2018).

[86] *Matter of Castro-Tum* 27 I&N Dec 271 (AG 2018). In addition to undermining the capacity of judges to manage their dockets, the facts of *Castro-Tum* are troubling. The judge in *Castro-Tum*

Regardless of the substantive correctness or incorrectness of such rulings, in their political context it's impossible to understand them as anything other than politically motivated retroactive changes to immigration law, carried out as a matter of executive prerogative.

Expedited Removal: For When Executive Adjudication is Still Too Fair

Yet immigration courts represent a relatively generous extension of procedural protections for immigrants compared to the main alternative under existing law, namely, the 'expedited removal' process. If subjected to 'expedited removal', an immigrant may be deported without any appearance before a judicial officer, or even a quasi-judicial immigration 'judge', whatsoever. Expedited removal has grown to account for some 35-40 per cent of removals.[87] The process applies to anyone stopped at the border allegedly without proper documentation – and, under Trump administration regulations expanding the scope of expedited review to the limits of its statutory authority, to anyone allegedly without proper documentation found in the US within two years of entry – with narrow exceptions relating to asylum claims, claims of citizenship or lawful permanent residence, and the like.[88]

Lest the reader think that expedited removal is merely a process that applies to persons who sneak across the physical border in the dead of night or who procure admission through forged documents, it should be noted that it also applies to migrants who (are alleged to have) crossed the border in a wide variety of other unlawful ways – for example, immigrants who enter claiming to be tourists while actually intending to stay, or even people whose passports do not have six months of validity remaining.[89] The Seventh Circuit has recognised that the inquiry as to a person's intent at the border is a giant hole in the process: some immigration official can arbitrarily dump someone in the expedited review category without any judicial scrutiny at all by deciding that, even though the individual insists that they're entering the country for some non-immigrant purpose and intend to leave, they're really an 'intending immigrant'.[90] Moreover, the burden of proof even when a person is apprehended

had ordered the proceedings be closed because they were not convinced that the respondent had been successfully notified of the hearing, and were not satisfied with the reliability of the Department of Homeland Security's address database. The Attorney General ruled that there was a presumption that notice had been carried out because it had been mailed to an address that the immigrant – a 17-year-old unaccompanied child – had given the government.

[87] American Immigration Council, 'A Primer on Expedited Removal' (*American Immigration Council*, 3 February 2017) www.americanimmigrationcouncil.org/research/primer-expedited-removal.

[88] HR Smith, 'Expedited Removal of Aliens: Legal Framework' (Congressional Research Service, 2019) R45314 10–11.

[89] ibid 12; *Smith v US Customs & Border Prot* 741 F3d 1016 (9th Cir 2014).

[90] *Khan v Holder* 608 F3d 325, 329–30 (7th Cir 2010).

in the interior is on the immigrant to show that they are not subject to expedited removal for being in the US less than two years, or have been admitted to the US as opposed to having entered without permission.[91] 'Burden of proof' in this context really just means a near-total lack of legal protection, since the person to whom an immigrant must prove their status is a potentially biased or legally untrained immigration official. Thus, in reality, expedited removal processes may apply far beyond their intended bounds.

Yet, despite offering migrants no procedural protections, expedited removal carries significant collateral legal consequences. An immigrant who is subjected to expedited removal is subject to a five-year or longer bar to re-entry and becomes guilty of a felony if they re-enter the US later, just the same as an immigrant who is removed under normal procedures that provide them with a real opportunity to contest the grounds for removal.[92]

THE TENDENCY OF ARBITRARY POWER
TO METASTASIZE THROUGHOUT THE LEGAL SYSTEM

In arguing that 'the principle that unadmitted aliens have no constitutionally protected rights defies rationality', Justice Thurgood Marshall, dissenting in *Jean v Nelson*, pointed out that 'the Fourteenth Amendment was specifically intended to overrule a legal fiction similar to that undergirding [plenary power doctrine cases] *Knauff*, *Chew*, and *Mezei* – that freed slaves were not "people of the United States"'.[93] Justice Marshall identified a condition of outlawry connecting the enslaved and those who seek admission to the United States.[94]

The connections between immigration and slavery cannot be explored fully in this volume. One important aspect of those connections is grimly paradoxical: it would be fair to say that the Chinese Exclusion regime which spawned

---

[91] 8 USC § 1225(b)(1)(a)(iii)(II); 8 CFR 235.3(b)(6).

[92] Smith (n 88) 13; J Lee Koh, 'When Shadow Removals Collide: Searching for Solutions to the Legal Black Holes Created by Expedited Removal and Reinstatement' (2018) 96 *Washington University Law Review* 337; 8 USC § 1225(b)(1); 8 USC § 1326. However, there is some possibility for collateral attack of the underlying order of removal in such a criminal proceeding. *United States v Villarreal Silva* 931 F3d 330 (4th Cir 2019); *United States v Mendoza-Lopez* 481 US 828 (1987); Smith (n 88) 35–36.

[93] *Jean v Nelson* 472 US 846, 874–75 (1985) (Marshall J, dissenting) (quoting *Dred Scott v Sandford* at the end).

[94] A number of scholars have compared the immigration regime to the Fugitive Slave Act. See KM McKanders, 'Immigration Enforcement and the Fugitive Slave Acts: Exploring Their Similarities' (2012) 61 *Catholic University Law Review* 921; J Stevens, 'The Alien Who Is a Citizen' in BN Lawrance and J Stevens (eds), *Citizenship in Question: Evidentiary Birthright and Statelessness* (Duke University Press, 2017) 225; N Lasch, 'Rendition Resistance' (2013) 92 *North Carolina Law Review* 149. Actually, the very first comparison between immigration adjudication and the Fugitive Slave Acts was made in 1921: in that year, the *Yale Law Journal* printed an article defending the constitutionality of the Fugitive Slave Acts (!) via an analogy to the result in cases like *Ju Toy* where biased administrators could adjudicate the right to enter the country of citizens of Chinese descent. A Johnson, 'The Constitutionality of the Fugitive Slave Acts' (1921) 31 *Yale Law Journal* 161, 182.

contemporary immigration law itself was in part an outgrowth of *abolition*. Historians have identified that Chinese Exclusion was rooted in part in post-Civil-War Republican fears about the importation of unfree labourers – although straightforward racism was also implicated.[95]

Yet in many other ways the immigration regime stands as a betrayal of the legacy of abolition, as it resurrects many of the legal and social conditions of slavery, albeit in less egregious form. Let's start with the superficial, albeit particularly shocking: even though the Thirteenth Amendment only carves out an exception to its prohibition on involuntary servitude for 'punishment for crime whereof the party shall have been duly convicted', and even though immigration detention and removal is nominally a civil rather than a criminal process, immigrant detainees labour on behalf of the private companies who manage ICE detention facilities for little or no pay.[96]

Nor are detained immigrants the only ones who are subject to forced or quasi-forced labour. Many industries, such as agriculture, meatpacking, construction, and nail salons, frequently employ undocumented workers under coercive conditions.[97] The National Employment Law Project conducted a 2009 study of low-wage workers in America's three largest cities, and found that almost 39 per cent were undocumented.[98] It turns out that when someone is an outlaw

[95] On the association between Chinese immigrants and unfree labour, see M-H Jung, 'Outlawing 'Coolies': Race, Nation, and Empire in the Age of Emancipation' (2005) 57 *American Quarterly* 677. For a general survey of the influences on Chinese exclusion cogently discussing both the fear of unfree labourers and the racism, see L VanderVelde and GJ Chin, 'Sowing the Seeds of Chinese Exclusion as the Reconstruction Congress Debates Civil Rights Inclusion' (2020) 12 *Tsinghua China Law Review* 185.

[96] J Stevens, 'One Dollar Per Day: The Slaving Wages of Immigration Jail, From 1943 to Present' (2015) 29 *Georgetown Immigration Law Journal* 391; J Booth, 'Ending Forced Labor In ICE Detention Centers: A New Approach' (2020) 34 *Georgetown Immigration Law Journal* 573; A Sinha, 'Slavery by Another Name: 'Voluntary' Immigrant Detainee Labor and the Thirteenth Amendment' (2015) 11 *Stanford Journal of Civil Rights and Civil Liberties* 1; J Stevens, 'One Dollar Per Day: A Note on Recent Forced Labor and Dollar-Per-Day Wages in Private Prisons Holding People Under Immigration Law' (2018) 52 *Valparaiso University Law Review* 343. Detention bears many other similarities to criminal imprisonment. Detainees are subject to the physical and symbolic conditions of imprisonment such as shackles, jumpsuits, strict rules on visitation and touching, strip searches, arbitrary discipline, and even enforced social hierarchies between themselves and guards such as rules about who is allowed to speak to and look directly at whom. Ryo (n 70) 1027–34; E Ryo, 'Understanding Immigration Detention: Causes, Conditions, and Consequences' (2019) 15 *Annual Review of Law and Social Science* 97, 104; L Ricciardelli et al, 'A Snapshot of Immigration Court at Stewart Detention Center:' (2019) 20 *Critical Social Work* 57. The length of detention too can more resemble prison than temporary adjudicative detention, with the average being over a month but with substantial numbers of immigrants being detained for years. E Ryo and I Peacock, 'A National Study of Immigration Detention in the United States' (2018) 92 *Southern California Law Review* 1, 32.

[97] See E Fussell, 'The Deportation Threat Dynamic and Victimization of Latino Migrants: Wage Theft and Robbery' (2011) 52 *The Sociological Quarterly* 593; E Schlosser, 'In the Strawberry Fields' (*The Atlantic*, November 1995) www.theatlantic.com/magazine/archive/1995/11/in-the-strawberry-fields/305754; S Maslin Nir, 'The Price of Nice Nails' (*New York Times*, 7 May 2015) www.nytimes.com/2015/05/10/nyregion/at-nail-salons-in-nyc-manicurists-are-underpaid-and-unprotected.html.

[98] A Bernhardt, R Milkman and N Theodore, 'Broken Laws, Unprotected Workers: Violations of Employment and Labor Laws in America's Cities' (*National Employment Law Project*, 2019) 15

who can be deported if they come into contact with the government, they don't really have anyone to turn to in order to protect them from their employers – and so employers are frequently caught subjecting undocumented immigrants to wage theft, passport withholding, and debt peonage.[99]

The forced labour of noncitizen workers has been going on at least since emancipation – the Radical Republicans enacted an anti-peonage statute in 1867 to try to stop the forced labour of Mexicans and Native Americans in New Mexico.[100] Authorised workers can be little better off than the undocumented – the 'Bracero' guest-worker programme of the mid-twentieth century has been widely criticised for creating exploitative and at least quasi-coercive labour conditions.[101] Today, we have the H-visa system, but Ontiveros argues that such guest worker programmes serve a similar economic function as coerced labour, and lead to similar treatment of workers.[102] And largely immigrant workers in agriculture and in domestic labour are excluded from important protections of federal labour law, an exclusion that traces directly back to Jim Crow and was, Perea has convincingly argued, intended to secure the votes of Southern Democrats for the passage of the National Labor Relations Act by excluding Black workers.[103]

Immigration Outlawry Harms Citizens Too

Introducing procedural injustice into a system on a caste basis inevitably spills over to those who are nominally protected by the law, for a person who is falsely accused of being in the group that lacks legal protections can easily find themselves subjected to outlaw procedures and hence without any ability to defend themselves. We saw this first in the kidnapping of Black Northerners under the

---

www.nelp.org/publication/broken-laws-unprotected-workers-violations-of-employment-and-labor-laws-in-americas-cities/.

[99] K Kim, 'The Coercion of Trafficked Workers' (2011) 96 *Iowa Law Review* 409; B Azmy, 'Unshackling the Thirteenth Amendment: Modern Slavery and a Reconstructed Civil Rights Agenda' (2002) 71 *Fordham Law Review* 981. For an extreme example of the abuse to which immigrants can be subjected, see *United States v Alzanki* 54 F3d 994 (1st Cir 1995), concerning a Sri Lankan domestic worker held in what I must characterise as outright slavery. Of course, that sort of treatment, which included copious physical violence, is a crime, and the enslaver in Alzanki was rightly convicted – but the point is that their status as quasi-outlaws makes immigrants, and especially undocumented immigrants, vulnerable to this kind of criminal enslavement because they – rationally – fear the state.

[100] A Soifer, 'Old Lines in New Battles: An Overlooked Yet Useful Statute to Confront Exploitation of Undocumented Workers by Employers and by ICE' (2018) 19 *Nevada Law Journal* 397.

[101] eg, RL Mize Jr, 'Reparations for Mexican Braceros – Lessons Learned from Japanese and African American Attempts at Redress' (2005) 52 *Cleveland State Law Review* 273, 283–91.

[102] ML Ontiveros, 'Noncitizen Immigrant Labor and the Thirteenth Amendment: Challenging Guest Worker Programs' (2007) 38 *University of Toledo Law Review* 923.

[103] JF Perea, 'The Echoes of Slavery: Recognizing the Racist Origins of the Agricultural and Domestic Worker Exclusion from the National Labor Relations Act' (2011) 72 *Ohio State Law Journal* 95.

Fugitive Slave Act regime: in view of the lack of procedural protections before federal commissioners, a kidnapped free Northerner could easily be unable to put up a defence and end up enslaved.[104] We also saw that in the Chinese Exclusion era in cases like *Ju Toy*, where a US citizen could be deported because the process for proving his citizenship began with the presumption that he was not a citizen, and hence deprived him of the capacity to prove his entitlement to process itself.

Today, lawful permanent residents and even US citizens who are subject to the scrutiny of the immigration authorities for whatever reason may find themselves caught up in the expedited removal process. Consider the case of Sharon McKnight, a native-born New Yorker who made the mistake of visiting family in Jamaica – and who was arrested at JFK airport upon her return, detained, and deported back to Jamaica the next day, despite presenting her perfectly valid US passport to border patrol officers – and despite the heroic efforts of her family, who showed up at the airport with her birth certificate, which the federal agents also disbelieved. Despite her manifest and perfectly documented citizenship, she was subjected to expedited removal, and only made it back to the US via the intercession of a member of Congress.[105] If it can happen to her, it can happen to any of us – or at least any of us with the markers of 'foreignness' as they might be perceived by the sort of person who works for the Border Patrol (about whom see below) – markers which the Supreme Court declared in *United States v Brignoni-Ponce* can even include race.[106]

This happens outside the expedited removal process as well. Consider the case of Mark Daniel Lyttle: a US citizen with psychiatric disabilities, he was taken from a mental health ward in a North Carolina jail by ICE agents who ignored his insistence that he was a US citizen, brought before an immigration court judge before whom he 'did not have an opportunity to present evidence or challenge the evidence of Mexican citizenship brought against him', and then deported to Mexico, where he 'wandered around Central America for 125 days, sleeping in the streets, staying in shelters, and being imprisoned and abused in Mexico, Honduras, and Nicaragua because he had no identity or proof of citizenship'.[107]

Mr Lyttle's case shares commonalities with other deportations of US citizens, particularly mentally disabled citizens who have pieces of paper shoved in front of them by ICE and CBP agents with no effort to determine whether

---

[104] J Oliver Horton and LE Horton, 'A Federal Assault: African Americans and the Impact of the Fugitive Slave Law of 1850' (1993) 68 *Chicago-Kent Law Review* 1179, 1189–90.

[105] I James, 'Wrongly Deported, American Citizen Sues INS for $8 Million' (*Los Angeles Times*, 3 September 2000) www.latimes.com/archives/la-xpm-2000-sep-03-mn-14714-story.html.

[106] *United States v Brignoni-Ponce* 422 US 873, 887 (1975) euphemistically declared that 'Mexican appearance' is 'a relevant factor' in detaining an individual.

[107] The quotations are from the district court opinion in Mr Lyttle's ultimate suit for damages as a result of this conduct. *Lyttle v United States* 867 FSupp2d 1256 (2012).

they understand or agree with what they are signing. Another example is Los Angeles-born Peter Guzman, who had a 'voluntary departure' form shoved under his nose which was then used to deport him to Mexico, despite the fact that he only could read at a second-grade level. In Mexico, '[h]e frequently ate out of garbage cans and for the most part slept outside without adequate shelter or warmth, bathing in rivers'.[108]

Supposed voluntary departure and other documentary concessions of alienage brought about by coercion or manipulation seems to be a common fact pattern in deportations of US citizens.[109] In this respect, immigration law's resemblance to the Fugitive Slave Act regime can be supplemented by its resemblance to coercive plea bargaining: the overwhelming power of government officials who hold a person in detention can be used to extract false confessions – in plea bargaining, of criminal guilt; in immigration, of alienage; accordingly, the majority of the US citizens Stevens found who had falsely signed statements declaring themselves noncitizens did so as a way to get out of custody or as a result of intimidation by federal agents.[110] And once a citizen has been removed via the unfair immigration process, they lose effective access to the processes that may have protected their claim to citizenship (if only they had known how to invoke them) while they were in the US.[111]

One prominent study estimates that upwards of 20,000 US citizens were detained by ICE or deported between 2003 and 2010.[112] And even detention without deportation can cause serious harms. Consider the case of Davino Watson, a US citizen who was held in immigration detention for three years while ICE and the Department of Justice tried to sort out who his parents were and what the government thought about his citizenship status.[113] This power may have even been deployed for the purpose of retaliation against citizens who report human rights abuses: as I write this, it has come out that Alma Bowman, an ICE detainee who blew the whistle on forced hysterectomies of detainees at the facility in which she is housed, actually is a US citizen. She's been detained for two years, and was put on the deportation schedule after her whistleblowing.[114]

---

[108] Testimony of JJ Brosnahan and MD Rosenbaum, Submitted to the Subcommittee on Immigration, Citizenship, Refugees, Border Security, and International Law of the House Judiciary Committee, 13 February 2008, www.aclu.org/other/testimony-mark-rosenbaum-and-james-brosnahan-about-deportation-us-citizen-peter-guzman.

[109] J Stevens, 'U.S. Government Unlawfully Detaining and Deporting U.S. Citizens as Aliens' (2011) 18 *Virginia Journal of Social Policy & the Law* 606, 621, 627, 630–32.

[110] ibid 627.

[111] C Burke Robertson and ID Manta, 'Litigating Citizenship' (2020) 73 *Vanderbilt Law Review* 757, 778.

[112] Stevens (n 109) 608.

[113] *Watson v United States* 865 F3d 123 (2d Cir 2017).

[114] J Washington and J Olivares, 'ICE Medical Misconduct Witness Slated for Deportation Is a U.S. Citizen, Says Lawyer' (*The Intercept*, 2 November 2020) theintercept.com/2020/11/02/ice-medical-misconduct-us-citizen-deportation/.

Immigration Outlawry Corrupts the System as a Whole

When enforcement agencies are created to operate in spaces of legal liminality or even outlawry, their interactions with those who possess legal rights are bound to be infected by that culture. ICE and CBP agents typically interact with those who have weakened or no due process rights under the plenary power doctrine. Those agents, accordingly, have developed a culture of disregard for individual rights and an expectation of impunity.[115] This is perhaps most saliently highlighted by the recent Supreme Court case of *Hernandez v Mesa*, in which a border patrol officer was granted impunity from civil liability for firing across the border and killing a 15-year-old child.[116] But it is psychologically and sociologically unrealistic to expect officials who operate in such an environment to seamlessly switch modes from the bureaucratic priority to get rid of an intruder as efficiently as possible when interacting with a noncitizen to providing due process and the respect owed to a fellow legal subject when interacting with a person who says they're a citizen, when they may be encountered in a similar location and may have similar ascriptive characteristics (ie, ethnicity) and behave similarly to noncitizens. This goes not just for front-line enforcement officials but also for adjudicators: how could we realistically expect them to internalise two such radically different modes of interacting with the persons who appear before them? Instead, they carry on their assembly-line processing of noncitizens even when a citizen appears before them, with the results described.

This too is a commonality between slavery and the contemporary immigration regime. Even the Southern courts recognised that compromises to legal procedures to permit the harsh treatment of slaves could leak out into the treatment of whites if not closely guarded.[117] One particularly important manifestation of what we might call the leakage of lawlessness thesis that can be found in abolitionist literature is that slavery corrupted the moral character of masters and overseers.[118]

Thomas Jefferson recognised this psychological fact:

> The parent storms, the child looks on, catches the lineaments of wrath, puts on the same airs in the circle of smaller slaves, gives a loose to his worst of passions, and thus nursed, educated, and daily exercised in tyranny, cannot but be stamped by it with odious peculiarities. The man must be a prodigy who can retain his manners and morals undepraved by such circumstances. And with what execration should the statesman be loaded, who permitting one half the citizens thus to trample on the

---

[115] EF Cohen, *Illegal: How America's Lawless Immigration Regime Threatens Us All*, 1st edn (Basic Books, 2020) ch 1.

[116] *Hernandez v Mesa* 140 S Ct 735 (2020).

[117] M Tushnet, *The American Law of Slavery, 1810–1860: Considerations of Humanity and Interest* (Princeton University Press, 1981) 122.

[118] DG Matthews, 'The Abolitionists on Slavery: The Critique Behind the Social Movement' (1967) 33 *The Journal of Southern History* 163, 179–80; LF Leach, 'Roots and the Trope of the Good Slaveholder' (2019) 40 *Slavery & Abolition* 361, 362, 371.

rights of the other, transforms those into despots, and these into enemies, destroys the morals of the one part, and the amor patriae of the other.[119]

Jefferson probably learned this argument from Montesquieu, who observes that a master 'grows accustomed to failing in all the moral virtues, because he grows proud, curt, harsh, angry, voluptuous, and cruel'.[120] Jefferson and Montesquieu were obviously right. Exercising unconstrained power over other human beings and telling oneself that those others lack basic rights as a justification for that unconstrained power is inherently corrupting because it trains one to disregard the humanity of others.[121] This folk-psychological insight is consistent with current research in psychology on cognitive dissonance reduction and moral disengagement, through which people who find themselves engaging in reprehensible behaviour develop stories to justify that behaviour to themselves and decline to subject their actions to moral scrutiny.[122]

Now consider that the immigration enforcement agencies commit cruelties like destroying caches of water left for the survival of people in the desert and arresting members of humanitarian groups who try to keep border-crossers alive.[123] Those agencies participated in a deliberate practice of separating parents from their children for the purposes of deterrence and holding those children in overcrowded cages.[124] What kinds of habits of moral judgement and perceptions of the world must someone who engages in such behaviour adopt, and how might they carry those habits into their interactions with others?[125]

Actually, we've already seen one example of the moral corruption of immigration enforcers, and with it, seen that deportation is not the only way that

---

[119] T Jefferson, *Notes on the State of Virginia* (John Stockdale, 1787) 271.

[120] C de Secondat Montesquieu in AM Cohler, BC Miller and H Samuel Stone (eds), *The Spirit of the Laws* (Cambridge University Press, 1989) 246.

[121] Immanuel Kant recognised this point with respect to animals as well, arguing that cruelty to animals was impermissible because of the way it twisted the characters of the people who engaged in it. AW Wood, 'Kant on Duties Regarding Nonrational Nature' (1998) 72 *Aristotelian Society Supplementary Volume* 189, 194.

[122] A Bandura, 'Moral Disengagement in the Perpetration of Inhumanities' (1999) 3 *Personality and Social Psychology Review* 193; S Shalvi et al, 'Self-Serving Justifications: Doing Wrong and Feeling Moral' (2015) 24 *Current Directions in Psychological Science* 125.

[123] AB Wang, 'Border Patrol Agents Were Filmed Dumping Water Left for Migrants. Then Came a "Suspicious" Arrest' (*Washington Post*, 24 January 2018) www.washingtonpost.com/news/post-nation/wp/2018/01/23/border-patrol-accused-of-targeting-aid-group-that-filmed-agents-dumping-water-left-for-migrants/.

[124] MD Shear, K Benner and MS Schmidt, '"We Need to Take Away Children", No Matter How Young, Justice Dept. Officials Said' (*The New York Times*, 6 October 2020) www.nytimes.com/2020/10/06/us/politics/family-separation-border-immigration-jeff-sessions-rod-rosenstein.html; C Domonoske and R Gonzalez, 'What We Know: Family Separation And "Zero Tolerance" At The Border' (*National Public Radio*, 19 June 2018) www.npr.org/2018/06/19/621065383/what-we-know-family-separation-and-zero-tolerance-at-the-border.

[125] Another important location for examining the corrupting effect of power is policing. Police exist in a hyper-masculine culture in which they are trained to display constant dominance over others. They also have a marked propensity to commit acts of domestic violence off the job. L Goodmark, 'Hands up at Home: Militarized Masculinity and Police Officers Who Commit Intimate Partner Abuse' (2015) 2015 *Brigham Young University Law Review* 1183.

the corruption of the immigration regime spills out to deprive even US citizens of their legal rights. The violent and lawless culture of the Border Patrol has been brought into the interior: during the summer 2020 protests in Portland, Oregon, the Trump administration deployed 'BORTAC' special forces troopers into streets of the city, where they – perhaps with other federal agents (it is not clear) – went on a Pinochet-style rampage: arresting people without probable cause, sticking hoods on them, and stuffing them into vans; brutally beating a 53-year-old Navy veteran who merely came to the protests to peacefully ask the federal officers how their behaviour comported with their oath to uphold the Constitution.[126] But what else would we expect when we take troops whose ordinary job is to deal out brutality to stigmatised and racialised foreigners with zero legal rights and deploy them on the streets of a city?[127]

In less immediately violent terms, the compromise of legality occasioned by the immigration regime also operates geographically. Racial profiling is specifically permitted in immigration enforcement, just so long as it isn't the *only* excuse a Border Patrol officer can give for their stop and search of a private person.[128] Now further consider that the Border Patrol claims the authority to operate anywhere within 100 air miles of the US border – and that 'border' in this context includes not just the Canadian and Mexican borders, but also the coastline, the Great Lakes, and the like; and hence most major US population centres are in that region.[129] Accordingly, the majority of US citizens are potentially subject to arbitrary stops and searches by the Border Patrol on the basis of suspicion, not of any kind of crime, but merely of being an immigrant without papers, and where the basis for that suspicion can include the person's race.

Plano, Illinois is a tiny midwestern town so stereotypically American that it was used in a Superman movie as the site for 'Smallville', the fictional rural American town where the Man of Steel was raised to love truth, justice, and the

---

[126] E Pilkington, '"These Are His People": Inside the Elite Border Patrol Unit Trump Sent to Portland' (*The Guardian*, 27 July 2020) www.theguardian.com/us-news/2020/jul/27/trump-border-patrol-troops-portland-bortac; S Olmos, M Baker and Z Kanno-Youngs, 'Federal Agents Unleash Militarized Crackdown on Portland' (*The New York Times*, 17 July 2020) www.nytimes.com/2020/07/17/us/portland-protests.html; J Ismay, 'A Navy Veteran Had a Question for the Feds in Portland. They Beat Him in Response' (*The New York Times*, 20 July 2020) www.nytimes.com/2020/07/20/us/portland-protests-navy-christopher-david.html; T Jawetz, PE Wolgin and C Flores, '5 Immediate Steps To Rein in DHS in the Wake of Portland' (*Center for American Progress*, 2 September 2020) www.americanprogress.org/issues/immigration/reports/2020/09/02/489934/5-immediate-steps-rein-dhs-wake-portland/.

[127] See also J Levy, 'Law and Border' (*Niskanen Center Blog*, 25 July 2018) www.niskanencenter.org/law-and-border/; Cohen (n 115) 20–21; DW Carbado and CI Harris, 'Undocumented Criminal Procedure' (2011) 58 *UCLA Law Review* 1543.

[128] *United States v Brignoni-Ponce* 422 US 873 (1975).

[129] D Anthony, 'The U.S. Border Patrol's Constitutional Erosion in the 100-Mile Zone' (2020) 124 *Penn State Law Review* 391. The ACLU, 'ACLU Factsheet on Customs and Border Protection's 100-Mile Zone' (*American Civil Liberties Union*) www.aclu.org/other/aclu-factsheet-customs-and-border-protections-100-mile-zone, estimates that this border region contains 2/3 of the US population.

American Way. But Plano is only about 60 miles from Lake Michigan. If you believe the Department of Homeland Security, it's actually part of the border and hence perfectly fair game for all kinds of searches, seizures, and miscellaneous harassment and racial profiling.[130]

Immigration law also serves as a site for experimentation with techniques of lawlessness to be later deployed elsewhere. For example, the indefinite incarceration of people believed to be associated with terrorism in the legal black hole of the Guantanamo Bay military base in Cuba during the War on Terror has rightly subjected the United States to intense criticism.[131] But that was the second use of Gitmo to arbitrarily detain people: a decade beforehand, during the Haitian refugee crisis, the Coast Guard and the INS interdicted refugees on the high seas and held them there, denying them access to counsel or correct information about the right to seek asylum; the Eleventh Circuit held that because the refugees had never reached US soil, they were not entitled to any procedural rights.[132] The Bush Administration tried to use the very same idea of a space which the writ of US law would not reach, applied to the very same military base, to defend its far more famous use of Gitmo as a black hole for accused terrorists in *Rasul v Bush*.[133] Small mercy: the government lost the second time around.

Lawless Racism: The Challenge to Birthright Citizenship

Even the constitutional foundations of citizenship are under attack by those who seek to subordinate immigrants. A number of extreme rightist commentators, some in the academy (or recently departed the academy, as did John Eastman, formerly of Campbell University, who resigned in early 2021 in disgrace after speaking at the rally that lead to the 6 January 2021 coup attempt), have advanced frivolous arguments according to which the birthright (*jus soli*) citizenship clause of the Fourteenth Amendment does not apply to US born children of undocumented immigrants on the putative grounds that they were not born under the 'jurisdiction' of the United States – thus directly attacking one of the core achievements of the Black freedom movement.[134] This argument is

---

[130] See also Cohen (n 115) 47–54.

[131] eg, R Alford, *Permanent State of Emergency: Unchecked Executive Power and the Demise of the Rule of Law* (McGill University Press, 2017) 110–27.

[132] *Haitian Refugee Center v Baker* 953 F3d 1498, 1505-09 (11th Cir 1992); GL Neuman, 'Anomalous Zones' (1996) 48 *Stanford Law Review* 1197.

[133] *Rasul v Bush* 542 US 466 (2004).

[134] eg JC Eastman, 'From Feudalism to Consent: Rethinking Birthright Citizenship' (*Heritage Foundation*, 2006) www.heritage.org/the-constitution/report/feudalism-consent-rethinking-birthright-citizenship. This argument appeared some decades before Eastman in PH Schuck and RM Smith, *Citizenship Without Consent: Illegal Aliens in the American Polity* (Yale University Press, 1985). As to the Schuck/Smith book, N Gotanda, 'Race, Citizenship, and the Search for Political Community

so blatantly nonsensical that it can be dispatched in a blog post – and I have – and even far-right legal scholars have rejected it.[135] Nonetheless, Donald Trump went so far as to claim that he could strip away citizenship from the US-born children of immigrants by executive order.[136]

The legal debates about this argument (such as it is), however, are not pertinent to this book. Rather, my point in introducing it is to illustrate the reprise of legal and political ideas first used against freedpeople to the case of immigrants and their children. The theoretical basis of the contemporary attack on birthright citizenship is the idea that citizenship cannot be achieved except by the 'consent' of those who are already present; because the American people allegedly have not consented to the presence of undocumented immigrants in the territory, they cannot have consented to including their children as citizens.[137] But the 'consent' argument has been tried before – indeed, we can plausibly interpret the Fourteenth and Fifteenth Amendments as in part a response to it. In 1866, Andrew Johnson opposed Black demands for the vote by assuming 'the people' of the South meant white people only and then insisting that he could not force Black members on that community without the consent of that 'people'.[138] The affinity of the argument against Black suffrage and the argument against birthright citizenship today can also be seen in the form of at least one contemporary scholar who has gone so far as to reprise the citizenship by consent argument as a defence of Johnson's and ex-Confederate resistance to Black citizenship after the Civil War: according

Among "We the People" – A Review Essay on Citizenship Without Consent' (1997) 76 *Oregon Law Review* 233 and GL Neuman, 'Back to Dred Scott' (1987) 24 *San Diego Law Review* 485, conclusively dispatch the arguments therein. Fortunately, Smith seems to have moderated his position somewhat, and he has sensibly argued in RM Smith, 'Living in a Promiseland?: Mexican Immigration and American Obligations' (2011) 9 *Perspectives on Politics* 545, that the coercive character of the United States's relationship with Mexican immigrants in particular entitles them to substantial solicitude in immigration and citizenship law.

[135] P Gowder, 'Reading the Plain Text of the Birthright Clause in the Fourteenth Amendment' (*Niskanen Center*, 1 November 2018) www.niskanencenter.org/reading-the-plain-text-of-the-birthright-clause-in-the-fourteenth-amendment/; JC Ho, 'Defining "American": Birthright Citizenship and the Original Understanding of the 14th Amendment' (2006) 9 *Green Bag* 359; J Yoo, 'Settled Law: Birthright Citizenship and the 14th Amendment' (*American Enterprise Institute*, reprinted from The *American Mind*, 25 October 2018) www.aei.org/articles/settled-law-birthright-citizenship-and-the-14th-amendment/.

[136] J Wagner, J Dawsey and F Sonmez, 'Trump Vows Executive Order to End Birthright Citizenship, a Move Most Legal Experts Say Would Run Afoul of the Constitution' (*Washington Post*, 30 October 2018) www.washingtonpost.com/politics/trump-eyeing-executive-order-to-end-citizenship-for-children-of-noncitizens-born-on-us-soil/2018/10/30/66892050-dc29-11e8-b3f0-62607289efee_story.html.

[137] Eastman (n 134) 6–7.

[138] J Gray Pope, 'Snubbed Landmark: Why United States v. Cruikshank (1876) Belongs at the Heart of the American Constitutional Canon' (2014) 49 *Harvard Civil Rights-Civil Liberties Law Review* 385, 396–97. A contemporaneous newspaper account of Johnson trotting out these arguments in a meeting with George Downing and Frederick Douglass is in the 8 February 1866 *National Intelligencer*, available at www2.vcdh.virginia.edu/saxon/servlet/SaxonServlet?source=/xml_docs/valley_news/newspaper_catalog.xml&style=/xml_docs/valley_news/news_cat.xsl&level=edition&paper=rv&year=1866&month=02&day=16&edition=rv1866/va.au.rv.1866.02.16.xml.

to one Thomas G West of Hillsdale College, giving the vote to Black people was just like forcing a group of immigrants on a community without their consent.[139]

The consent argument also showed up with respect to Indian removal: at least once in the South the notion that the federal government could confer citizenship on Native Americans was taken to entail that the states would no longer be able to exercise control over whom they admitted to their own political communities and ultimately seemed to risk the threat that the enslaved, too, would come to citizenship.[140] In the words of an editorialist in the Southern Recorder, admitting that the federal government had the power to include Native Americans 'would, in the end, deprive the States of all power in deciding what should be the condition, and character, and rights of any description of their inhabitants'.[141] We all know which 'inhabitants' the editorialist had in mind.

In the United States, protestations of a right to withhold consent on behalf of the white-identified, European/coloniser descended, group that sees itself as the community whose consent is to be sought have always been particularly dishonest, since, of course, the land that group occupies was first taken by military force from the Native American nations, who are also addressed with the 'plenary power' doctrine of immigration law and whose members then became just another outsider group to be granted citizenship only by statute rather than by constitutional provision.[142] And, of course, those freed by the Thirteenth Amendment were around only because their ancestors were brought here and incorporated into the territory and the economy by the very people who wanted to later claim the right to 'consent' to their sharing of political power. Similarly with respect to the Mexican people who are the victims of the chief stereotypes about 'illegal immigration', immigration courts often are also the courts of the conqueror: the US outright seized most of the Southwest from Mexico in the first place via fomenting revolution in, then annexing, Texas and then going to war and seizing more land still in the Treaty of Guadalupe Hidalgo. That's why Mexican activists often say 'we didn't cross the border, the border crossed us'.

The US has purposefully availed itself of its immigrants, documented or undocumented, in numerous ways; for example, by operating industries that depend on undocumented immigrant labour with a nudge and a wink. And Black abolitionists raised precisely this point as an argument for their own citizenship, with or without the 'consent' of whites: in 1852, Martin Delany argued

---

[139] TG West, *Vindicating the Founders: Race, Sex, Class, and Justice in the Origins of America* (Rowman & Littlefield Publishers, 2001) 28–30.

[140] Saunt (n 42) 39–40.

[141] Quoted by Saunt from an unsigned editorial of 9 April 1827, which is available in an online archive at gahistoricnewspapers.galileo.usg.edu/lccn/sn82016415/1827-04-09/ed-1/seq-1/.

[142] Cleveland (n 21) 48, 56–58.

that Black Americans had 'a birthright citizenship – natural claims upon the country – claims common to all others of our fellow citizens'.[143] The basis for his argument was in substantial part the contributions that Black labour had made to the country – contributions made because Europeans had brought their ancestors from Africa in order to procure them.[144] While immigrants are here more-or-less voluntarily – certainly relative to the enslaved – Delany's argument about the rightful claim to citizenship of those who are here to do necessary labour that nobody else is able or willing to do applies just as well to the locally-born children of the former as it did to the latter.[145]

The birthright citizenship argument illustrates the roots of our contemporary discourse of immigration and alienage in white nationalism and the incompatibility of that white nationalism with the rule of law. The people constructed by law have consented through their laws to the application of the birthright principle in the very text of the Fourteenth Amendment. The only way I can interpret the shocking difficulty that the 'scholarly' critics of the birthright principle associated with far-right/West Coast Straussian institutions like the Claremont Institute and Hillsdale College seem to have in understanding that the consent they demand was given a century and a half ago – though I do not claim to know their individual racial attitudes or the contents of their innermost thoughts – is to suppose that they implicitly operate from an assumption similar to that of Andrew Johnson, ie, that the people constituted by law are not the *real* people. And – again with the caveat that I speak here of my interpretation of their arguments and claim no knowledge of their personal dispositions – it's hard not to suspect that their notions of the true American people are ethno-nationally defined. And because general legal rules neutrally applied do not permit the moment-by-moment rule of the sovereign group (white people), they seem to interpret the neutral application of the Fourteenth Amendment as anti-democratic and anti-national. In short, white people must consent on a moment-by-moment basis to the inclusion of political others; they cannot bind themselves by law in a way that would alienate their control of and identification with the state as nation, nor even make binding commitments to expand the identity of the nation to encompass people other than their own ethnic group.

---

[143] M Robison Delany, *The Condition, Elevation, Emigration, and Destiny of the Colored People of the United States Politically Considered* (Published by the Author, 1852) 48–49.

[144] ibid 49–51, 63–66.

[145] In light of the system of global economic hegemony that the US operates, one could fairly deny that immigrants are truly here of their own free will. Notably, Emily Ryo found in interviews with immigrants both that they often experienced their migration to be a matter of necessity and that they understood the violation of immigration laws to be distinct from the violation of criminal laws because immigrants are coming not to harm the community but to benefit it, with honorable and fair work. E Ryo, 'Less Enforcement, More Compliance: Rethinking Unauthorized Migration' (2015) 62 *UCLA Law Review* 622, 650–56.

All this talk about 'consent' and 'allegiance' should be exposed for what it is: another version of the phenomenon that Charles Tilly named 'opportunity hoarding'.[146] Ultimately the two themes of this book come together in the way that the dominant groups within the United States have since the founding treated membership in the legal community itself as a kind of property, to which they have some kind of pre-existing claim of natural right – and hence have twisted the universalistic ambitions of law for the purpose of the benefit of their own narrow group. But here I need do no more than to cite Cheryl Harris, who has made this point with great force.[147]

---

[146] C Tilly, *Durable Inequality* (University of California Press, 1999).
[147] Harris (n 26).

Conclusion: Is there Any Hope for an American Rule of Law?

A DECADE AGO, Stephen Holmes predicted that no high Bush Administration officials would ever be prosecuted for committing the crime of torture, despite presiding over the following conduct:

> Detainees in U.S. custody were stripped naked, exposed to hypothermia, hung by their arms till their shoulders became dislocated, threatened with ferocious dogs, and placed in the cramped confinement of boxes for hours. Their heads were smashed against walls, and they were threatened with guns to the neck and with the revving of an electrical drill. Some were told that their children would be killed and their mothers raped.[1]

Holmes confidently – and accurately, at least thus far – predicted that those at the highest levels of our government would enjoy impunity for such events (although some low-level soldiers did get convicted) for the simple reason that legal rules tend to be enforced against the powerless rather than the powerful. Holmes also gave an account of the government's special ability to deploy impunity. For example, it could manipulate good faith immunity doctrines by writing memos (as lawyers say, 'papering the file') filled with frivolous legal arguments for the permissibility of torture – memos on which executive branch officials could thereafter 'reasonably' rely. This contingency of the enforceability as well as interpretation of law on relations of hierarchy and power is, of course, well known, but when it goes to an extreme we end up with a state in which legal order itself is nothing more than a cynical pretence. Is the United States at that extremity?

To conclude this volume, I raise that critical question and explore its implications externally and then internally.

THE WASHINGTON CONSENSUS: HERE COMES PROPERTY AGAIN

The deep connection between the American rule of law and the notion of property rights that existed at the founding reappears in its international development efforts. For many years, an ideology commonly known as

---

[1] S Holmes, 'The Spider's Web: How Government Lawbreakers Routinely Elude the Law' in A Sarat and N Hussain (eds), *When Governments Break the Law: The Rule of Law and the Prosecution of the Bush Administration* (New York University Press, 2010) 127.

'the Washington consensus' – associated, as the name obviously suggests, primarily with the United States – dominated international development efforts. That ideology focused on capitalist market reforms, and once again joined the rule of law with extensive private property rights.[2] The idea, broadly speaking, is that the rule of law is particularly useful for the enforcement of property rights as well as contracts, which in turn are useful for economic development insofar as they create a safer environment for capital investment. In accordance with that idea, the United States has taken an active leadership role in promoting the development of the rule of law abroad through both government organisations such as USAID, and through NGOs supporting those efforts.

US rule of law (and democracy) promotion has been criticised for representing a form of neo-colonialism in which the export of US institutions and ideas serves as a cover for political and economic domination.[3] Strikingly, however, America's first foray into rule of law development was an instance of *actual* colonialism, and was carried out internally: I refer to the Indian Reorganization Act of 1934, based at least in part on a 'vacuum' theory according to which at least some of the Native American nations lacked effective self-government (although the details are contested) and hence were pressured to adopt constitutions under the tutelage of the Bureau of Indian Affairs.[4] At least one contemporary participant interviewed for an edited volume on Native American constitutional reform believed that Native nations are engaging in constitutional reform for the same reason that countries submit to Washington Consensus-style development efforts: to provide reassurances to external investors.[5] So American rule of law

---

[2] For general discussion, see I Glinavos, 'Neoliberal Law: Unintended Consequences of Market-Friendly Law Reforms' (2008) 29 *Third World Quarterly* 1087. According to a World Bank report, the Washington Consensus, while originating at a meeting in Washington in 1990, was actually led by Latin-American and Caribbean policymakers. S Javed Burki and G Perry, *Beyond the Washington Consensus: Institutions Matter* (World Bank, 1998) 1, however, when the term was coined in J Williamson, 'What Washington Means by Policy Reform' in J Williamson (ed), *Latin American Adjustment: How Much Has Happened?* (Institute for International Economics, 1990), it was specifically associated with Washington qua the United States as well. It's also worth noting that the boundaries of the 'Washington consensus' are a bit fuzzy, and certainly not bounded by Williamson's original article – I shall use it to also incorporate the institution-based reforms described by Burki and Perry (above), even though they themselves distinguish those reforms from the Washington consensus proper. The term 'neoliberal' is also frequently used in this context, but I shall avoid it here, for it has lately seemed to serve as a kind of general derogatory description of capitalism among left-wing scholars and commentators; it's not clear what the specific content of 'neoliberalism' as such might be. For a helpful discussion of all of this terminological muddle, see B Fine and A Saad-Filho, 'Politics of Neoliberal Development: Washington Consensus and the Post-Washington Consensus' in H Weber (ed), *The Politics of Development: A Survey*, 1st edn (Routledge, 2014).

[3] eg U Mattei and L Nader, *Plunder: When the Rule of Law Is Illegal* (Blackwell Publishing, 2008).

[4] E Rusco, 'The Indian Reorganization Act and Indian Self-Government' in ED Lemont (ed), *American Indian Constitutional Reform and the Rebuilding of Native Nations*, 1st edn (University of Texas Press, 2006) 50.

[5] J Peters Jr, 'Firsthand Account' in ED Lemont (ed), *American Indian Constitutional Reform and the Rebuilding of Native Nations*, 1st edn (University of Texas Press, 2006).

export, and the challenge to that effort as a form of colonialism, is some decades older than most of us think.

The 'vacuum' theory resembles Teemu Ruskola's concept of 'legal orientalism', according to which western observers engaging in motivated reasoning falsely come to the belief that China lacks law.[6] The US also conducted a weird form of quasi-export of the rule of law in China. Because the United States didn't believe that China had real law, it negotiated the 1844 Treaty of Wanghia, under which US citizens in China were only subject to trial by US officials.[7] From 1906, there was even a US District Court located in China for the sole purpose of adjudicating cases involving Americans. The same sort of colonial distrust characterises current US legal attitudes with respect to Native American governments, who are not allowed to exercise criminal jurisdiction over non-Native Americans on the reservation.[8]

Not all of America's rule of law development efforts are shamelessly colonial. Some might genuinely facilitate the self-governance of those who might otherwise be subjected to violence or oppression. I have previously cited, as admirable examples, programmes in Liberia and Afghanistan that appear to genuinely treat local leaders and the so-called 'informal' norms under which they operate with respect and aim to empower those leaders to protect the legal interests of community members.[9]

But even well-intentioned and otherwise-effective efforts may be undermined by lawlessness at home. If America fails to present itself to outsiders as a genuine rule of law state, the credibility of its external rule of law promotion efforts may be undermined. This is a familiar worry about American credibility with some historical importance: the international imperatives of the Cold War were an important element in the US's efforts to remedy the vestiges of Jim Crow, in part because its efforts to promote its ideology abroad were undermined by the visibly hypocritical implementation of that ideology at home.[10] The US could not seriously be seen as a credible promoter of freedom and democracy when it denied freedom and democracy to Black Americans; its racial injustice provided propaganda victories for the Soviets, and Black Americans appealed to the international community in order to pressure the US to deliver some simulacrum of justice.

The credibility challenge the US faces today is exacerbated by the fact that the most outward-facing aspect of its legal system is also its most lawless – I refer, of course, to the immigration system described in the previous chapter,

---

[6] T Ruskola, *Legal Orientalism: China, the United States, and Modern Law* (Harvard University Press, 2013).

[7] T Ruskola, 'Colonialism Without Colonies: On the Extraterritorial Jurisprudence of the U.S. Court for China' (2008) 71 *Law and Contemporary Problems* 217, 220.

[8] *Oliphant v Suquamish Indian Tribe* 435 US 191 (1978).

[9] P Gowder, *The Rule of Law in the Real World* (Cambridge University Press, 2016) 174–75.

[10] ML Dudziak, *Cold War Civil Rights: Race and the Image of American Democracy* (Princeton University Press, 2011).

which makes a mockery of America's claims to embody the rule of law. Can the United States truly be a credible promoter of the rule of law in war-torn and impoverished countries when refugees from those countries, presenting themselves at our shores, are subject to lengthy detention in harsh conditions culminating in a kangaroo-court process and then promptly flown back to those countries with that negative experience fresh in their minds? Ryo argues that 'immigrant detainees [and immigrants in general], as individuals embedded in domestic and transnational networks, have the potentially to widely disseminate deference and trust, or alternatively cynicism and delegitimating beliefs, about the US legal system and authorities – not only within the United States but around the world'.[11] And, as Ryo describes, the current message that America's immigration system is communicating to the world is decidedly negative.

America has long held out in its legal system as a model for the world. In the early stages of the writing of this manuscript, I returned to Ronald Cass's almost-two-decades ago treatment of the American rule of law.[12] Toward the beginning of that book, the reader is treated to a story of Ronald Reagan's meeting with Mikhail Gorbachev and proudly boasting of America's tradition of free criticism of our leaders. In Cass's retelling of the story, 'Reagan observed that anyone in the United States could stand directly in front of the White House, the very seat of government power, and criticise the American president and his policies, in the harshest terms imaginable, without fear of punishment'.[13] For Cass, it was clear both that Reagan's pride in American political freedom was justified, and that it arose from the rule of law and its function of establishing a well-defined and predictable set of individual liberties:

> In fact, protestors outside the White House can know well before they get to Lafayette Park the general contours of (very substantial) constitutional constraints on the president's power to punish critics. Freedom to criticize the president is not a function of judges' and law enforcers' hostility to the president or their sympathy for the critics but of accepted free speech doctrine. All of the following were safe bets: police officers who idolized Ronald Reagan would not arrest critics condemning him in the vilest terms; if arrests were made, prosecutors whose sympathies were strongly with Reagan would not take such cases to court; and if the cases got to court, judges, including those who owed their appointment to Reagan, would not allow his critics to be punished.[14]

Stories about Russians gazing at our legal system with childlike admiration seem to have been a staple of the period. A few years later, Chief Justice John Roberts began his 2007 year-end report on the judiciary with a story about a Russian Supreme Court Justice who went to Arlington National Cemetery to lay

---

[11] E Ryo, 'Fostering Legal Cynicism through Immigration Detention' (2017] *Southern California Law Review* 999, 1002.
[12] R A Cass, *The Rule of Law in America* (Johns Hopkins University Press, 2003).
[13] ibid 27.
[14] ibid 28.

a wreath on Chief Justice Rehnquist's grave.[15] Roberts recounts how Rehnquist had inspired that Russian jurist to drive reforms in his home country, and went on to trumpet the idea that the American judiciary is a model for the world:

> Few could have imagined these episodes a mere 25 years ago. Justice Sidorenko's words are poignant, but his actions in seeking to reform the Russian judiciary reflect a more fundamental truth that should resonate with all Americans: When foreign nations discard despotism and undertake to reform their judicial systems, they look to the United States Judiciary as the model for securing the rule of law.

> In recent years, even mature democracies with established traditions have modified their judicial systems to incorporate American principles and practices. For example, Great Britain, which exported its common law system to the American colonies some 400 years ago, has recently imported the distinctly American concept of separation of powers. It has transferred the House of Lords' judicial review functions to an independent Supreme Court. Japan has adopted trial procedures inspired by American jury practice, while South Korea is increasingly employing American-style oral advocacy in its judicial review proceedings. But perhaps most important, our federal courts provide the benchmark for emerging democracies that seek to structure their judicial systems to protect basic rights that Americans have long enjoyed as the norm.

I re-read Cass's words on 13 June 2020. Two weeks previously, President Donald Trump had shut Lafayette Park down in order to spare himself the sight of people condemning his response to the protestors who had for weeks been convulsing America's cities in response to the police murder of George Floyd.[16]

On 1 June, Trump decided he wanted to take a photo opportunity at a church which had been damaged in the unrest. But there were protestors in Lafayette Square who would have inconvenienced his photo op. So Attorney General William Barr ordered them attacked.[17]

In the words of the *New York Times*:

> What ensued was a burst of violence unlike any seen in the shadow of the White House in generations. As he prepared for his surprise march to the church, Mr. Trump first went before cameras in the Rose Garden to declare himself 'your president of law and order' but also 'an ally of all peaceful protesters,' even as peaceful protesters just a block away and clergy members on the church patio were routed by smoke and flash

[15] The year end report is available at www.supremecourt.gov/publicinfo/year-end/2007year-endreport.pdf.

[16] M Lefrak, 'The White House And Lafayette Park Went From "Public Square" To "Veritable Fortress"' (*NPR*, 5 June 2020) www.npr.org/local/305/2020/06/05/870877297/the-white-house-and-lafayette-park-went-from-public-square-to-veritable-fortress.

[17] D Gregorian, C Kube and CE Lee, 'Trump Says He Will Deploy Military If State Officials Can't Contain Protest Violence' (*NBC News*, 1 June 2020) www.nbcnews.com/politics/white-house/trump-considering-move-invoke-insurrection-act-n1221326; T Gjelten, 'Peaceful Protesters Tear-Gassed To Clear Way For Trump Church Photo-Op' (*NPR*, 1 June 2020) www.npr.org/2020/06/01/867532070/trumps-unannounced-church-visit-angers-church-officials; L King, 'Secret Service Admits It Used Pepper Spray to Clear Protesters Prior to Trump Photo Op at St. John's Church' (*USA Today*, 13 June 2020) www.usatoday.com/story/news/politics/2020/06/13/floyd-protests-secret-service-used-pepper-spray-trump-photo-op/3184223001.

grenades and some form of chemical spray deployed by shield-bearing riot officers and mounted police.[18]

Alas for Cass's happy confidence in the refusal of officials to illegally suppress the individual rights protected by the Constitution, there's no evidence that anyone in the legions of police agencies who gassed protesters refused to obey orders. Let's hope the Russians aren't still taking notes.

THE CRISIS OF THE AMERICAN RULE OF LAW:
REFLECTIONS ON DONALD TRUMP

The problems with America's existing rule of law run deep. Institutionally, we seem to lack the tools necessarily to effectively control the abuse of power; culturally, a combination of polarisation and mutual distrust rooted in inequality may make it impossible for the American people to use the tools they have.

On the institutional side, one easy claim to make is that executive officials just have too much power. Prosecutors can essentially dictate convictions via plea bargain without the benefit of jury due to the threat of life-ruining sentences if a defendant dares roll the dice on a trial; the Attorney General can command the outcomes of immigration cases; the President can declare a bogus state of emergency and build a wall without congressional appropriation. These are concrete institutional powers written into law; we can write them back out again.

Yet at the same time, American government is also too weak. The President can do malicious harm to individuals or hated groups within the polity but cannot convince Congress and the states to make policy. As Howell and Moe cogently argue, people turn to populist demagogues when their governments are ineffective at responding to their (real or perceived) problems.[19] But American government is notoriously ineffective. The federal government is unable – in contrast to the rest of the world's liberal democracies – to finance health care without bankrupting citizens when they get sick. The states and localities are perennially broke – and that governmental penury provokes more rule of law catastrophes, as they abuse their tax and criminal justice systems to expropriate their citizens.[20] Moreover, this penury is radically unevenly distributed, leading to human rights catastrophes like the poisoning of the water supply in Flint, Michigan. Our transit infrastructure is crumbling. Anyone with the money to get their children out of our public schools does so at the earliest opportunity. No surprise that the people have started looking for someone to make the trains run on time.

---

[18] P Baker, M Haberman, K Rogers, Z Kanno-Youngs and K Benner, 'How Trump's Idea for a Photo Op Led to Havoc in a Park' (*New York Times*, 2 June 2 2020) (updated 17 September 2020) www.nytimes.com/2020/06/02/us/politics/trump-walk-lafayette-square.html.
[19] WG Howell and TM Moe, *Presidents, Populism, and the Crisis of Democracy* (University of Chicago Press, 2020).
[20] B Atuahene, 'Predatory Cities' (2020) 108 *California Law Review* 107.

Culturally, one of the consequences of this weakness has been shocking inequality, both economic and legal. I say that this inequality is a consequence as well as a cause of the underlying governmental weakness because the United States, unlike most other developed countries, has been incapable of creating a sufficient social safety net to prevent its worst-off from experiencing extreme suffering – as the unique phenomenon of widespread medical bankruptcies again dramatically illustrates.[21] Another important example is the inability even of progressive politicians such as numerous centre-left mayors of major cities to break the power of police unions and control racially disparate police violence. As I have argued elsewhere, this inequality is likely, especially in conjunction with the elite polarisation that we see in America's current political environment, to make it impossible for ordinary citizens to act collectively to backstop their institutions and hold their officials to compliance with the law.[22] At the same time, inequality also undermines institutional reform and exacerbates the problem of misgovernance. Racial inequality and white resentment about enacting policies from which non-whites might benefit is doubtless part of the reason the US has not been able to build a functioning social safety net.

Such inequality is also at the heart of the rule of law crisis in America, for its cruellest manifestations – racially disparate criminal justice and immigration law – rest on a system of racial and economic caste. Only in a caste system are poor Black and Brown Americans geographically segregated from richer Americans of more privileged races and vulnerable to the development of distinctive strategies of policing bound to stigmatised neighbourhoods. And only as the continuing global side of such a system (originating, as it did, in colonialism and empire) are entire countries of Black and Brown human beings subject to a kind of economic segregation in which capital, pursuant to the Washington Consensus, is entitled to freely cross borders to seek out the cheapest labour at will, while labour is locked in place, and when the actual human beings try to cross borders to go to the rich country, they are subjected to an immigration regime that is barely a parody of a legal process.

Even property itself, qua core of the American rule of law, turns against the poor as public and private power combine in arbitrary regulation-by-landlord. Consider what are known as 'nuisance property' or 'chronic nuisance' ordinances. Under those ordinances, landlords are obliged on pain of penalty to 'abate' the nuisances caused by properties that generate, for example, too many police calls. Advocates for victims of domestic violence have been particularly vocal about the harms these laws can inflict by punishing crime victims for the misconduct of their victimisers, and have highlighted scandals, such as the infamous case of Lakisha Briggs, who was evicted by her landlord under pressure

---

[21] DU Himmelstein et al, 'Illness and Injury as Contributors to Bankruptcy' (2005) 24 *Health Affairs* W5.

[22] P Gowder, 'The Dangers to the American Rule of Law Will Outlast the Next Election' (2020) 2020 *Cardozo Law Review de novo* 126.

from the police when a neighbour called 911 to report that she had been stabbed by her abusive boyfriend.[23] Public housing tenants have also been evicted for the crimes of their relatives.[24] These cases represent an analytically striking inversion of the traditional role of property in the American rule of law – rather than being a basis for the protection of a person's legal rights, property law becomes the back door through which criminal sanctions are inflicted on individuals whom the state could not lawfully punish via ordinary law. Not only is the jury evaded – so is the judge and even the prosecutor, as police authorities go through landlords to achieve ends unfathomable to ordinary criminal law.

The Danger of Legal Alienation

On every side, the promises of the American rule of law seem to be illusory. In segregated communities, the police act like an occupying military force. For the most vulnerable in the United States, interactions with government bureaucracies are filled with Kafkaesque menace. Public and private power merge as the state uses landlords as a law enforcement tool, while companies may freely rewrite the law and deprive individuals of their ordinary legal entitlements through legal doctrines that permit, for example, the use of putative contracts entered without any real assent to strip away individuals' rights to a judicial remedy for civil wrongs, or the use of captured federal agencies to preempt individuals' ordinary common-law remedies in tort and contract.[25]

Yet, at the same time, it is unquestionably true that the United States, driven in large part though not exclusively by Black liberation movements, has made substantial strides over its history toward a genuine achievement of its rule of law ideals. Lynching is not an ordinary part of Southern racialised criminal justice any more. The Supreme Court has, since 1963, forced the states to fund lawyers for criminal defendants who cannot pay for their own, although the effective delivery of that promise of access to law has been undermined both by the plea-bargaining power of prosecutors and the egregious underfunding of many public defence systems.[26] And while the insecurity of property rights through mechanisms like civil asset forfeiture is a serious problem, it's nothing

---

[23] K Moran-McCabe, A Gutman and S Burris, 'Public Health Implications of Housing Laws: Nuisance Evictions' (2018) 133 *Public Health Reports* 606; G Arnold and M Slusser, 'Silencing Women's Voices: Nuisance Property Laws and Battered Women' (2015) 40 *Law & Social Inquiry* 908; M Desmond and N Valdez, 'Unpolicing the Urban Poor: Consequences of Third-Party Policing for Inner-City Women' (2013) 78 *American Sociological Review* 117.

[24] R Austin, 'Step on a Crack, Break Your Mother's Back: Poor Moms, Myths of Authority, and Drug-Related Evictions from Public Housing' (2002) 14 *Yale Journal of Law and Feminism* 273.

[25] See generally, MJ Radin, *Boilerplate* (Princeton University Press, 2012)); *AT&T Mobility v Concepcion* 563 US 333 (2011); *Northwest Inc v Ginsberg* 572 US 273 (2014).

[26] *Gideon v Wainwright* 372 US 335 (1963); B Mock, 'New Orleans to Poor Criminal Defendants: We Can't Defend You' (*The Atlantic*, January 2016) www.theatlantic.com/politics/archive/2016/01/new-orleans-to-poor-criminal-defendants-we-cant-defend-you/458856/.

like Jim Crow. Criminal defence lawyers do manage to win their trials and have their clients set free (and public defenders tend to be among the most skilled, notwithstanding their egregious overwork). The infliction of quasi-peonage on undocumented migrant labourers is a crime, and when employers are caught doing it, they are at least sometimes punished. Men are no longer entitled to inflict private 'discipline' on their wives, and although efforts to use the criminal justice system to remedy gender-based private domination have backfired, at least the state is trying.[27] As I have detailed at length in this book, the United States has a long way to go. But it has also come a long way.

A key problem, it seems to me, is that this progress doesn't manifest itself in the ways that ordinary people interact with the law on a day-to-day basis. A lot of people, especially those people who happen to be not white, still have strong reason to fear the police when they encounter them on the street, reason that has nothing to do with whether they've committed any kind of crime. I experience this fear myself: when I pass a police officer walking down the streets of Chicago, I always find myself feeling a kind of mental compulsion to attempt to make eye contact with them and nod in a friendly fashion, to communicate (falsely) that I'm not afraid to see them, that I have nothing to hide – and hence that I am not a 'suspicious' person who should be stopped, harassed, and perhaps arrested. And this is so even though I'm a law professor at an elite university who lives in one of the richest neighbourhoods in the city – after all, my being a lawyer didn't stop the New Orleans police officer who falsely arrested me in 2003 on a made-up marijuana charge after pulling me over for a broken taillight. I'm also more than a little bit afraid that the Border Patrol will retaliate against me for the contents of the previous chapter the next time I return to the US from abroad. But others – poorer, lacking law degrees or even citizenship – have much more reason to fear.

For the relatively well-off, the law's intrusions in our lives also seem to come predominantly in a series of endless petty public and private oppressions. Everything we do on a day-to-day basis is structured by a contract imposed on us by some corporation without any real alternatives – you or I undoubtedly enter into hundreds of contracts per day, so pervasively that some scholars have worried that it might be training us out of the habit of autonomous decision-making.[28] When we have to deal with the government, it presents itself to us in the form of some hostile and arbitrary-seeming bureaucratic hassle: we have

---

[27] On the backfire, see A Gruber, 'A Neo-Feminist Assessment of Rape and Domestic Violence Law Reform' (2012) 15 *Journal of Gender, Race & Justice* 583; L Goodmark, 'Reimagining VAWA: Why Criminalization Is a Failed Policy and What a Non-Carceral VAWA Could Look Like' (2020) 27 *Violence Against Women* 84. On reasons to think that protecting the victims of gender-based private violence is an important rule of law goal, see R West, 'Paul Gowder's Rule of Law' (2018) 62 *Saint Louis University Law Journal* 303, 309–11; P Gowder, 'Resisting the Rule of Men' (2018) 62 *Saint Louis University Law Journal* 333, 352–56).

[28] BM Frischmann and E Selinger, *Re-Engineering Humanity* (Cambridge University Press, 2018) ch 5.

to hire accountants to do our taxes, because Turbo Tax has hired lobbyists to make sure that the government doesn't dare simplify the process; we have to take a day off work to be glared at in a motor vehicle office to renew our drivers' licences. And when someone has wronged us – when, for example, the student loan servicer has screwed up our payments – we're forced to appear before yet another agonising and inaccessible bureaucracy as supplicants to have the wrong corrected, because our civil legal system is so expensive that there's no realistic path to calling upon the law to enforce even the rights of the wealthy in the absence of a truly dire injury.

For the poor, those same bureaucratic hassles are deadly traps: taking a day off work to go to the DMV could mean losing the job; the failure to pay a ridiculous 'occupancy permit' tax in Ferguson, Missouri, could mean going to jail, and then losing the driver's licence altogether because of the inability to pay the court fees on top of the occupancy permit, and then going to jail again for driving without a licence to get to work, and so on and so on, in an endless course of bureaucratically mediated criminal justice financial vampirism.[29] Because of the outrageous misallocation of law enforcement resources, while people with law professor incomes are the ones who can hire accountants to do their taxes, people with McDonald's incomes are vastly more likely to be the target of a tax audit that they lack the resources to defend.[30] The poor may also find themselves in things that call themselves courts, but which really operate assembly-line systems with little legal process used to punish or extract resources from them, like municipal criminal courts or eviction courts.[31]

For those reasons, it seems to me that a key source of the threat of degeneration rather than progress in American legality takes the form of what I will call 'legal alienation.' When the daily face of the law presents itself to ordinary, not-rich, people as nothing more than unilateral exercises of power – governments and companies shoving pieces of paper in their faces with magic incantations that take away whatever legal rights they happen to have – how do we expect ordinary people to maintain a minimum degree of respect for the legal system?[32] The rule of law depends on mass collective action to hold officials to the law.[33] But when the only experience ordinary people have with the legal system is that they have no rights, they cannot expect fair treatment from any government

---

[29] On occupancy permits, see my previous discussion in Gowder (n 9) 246–47.

[30] 'In 2017, [Earned Income Tax Credit – a credit for the working poor] recipients were audited at twice the rate of taxpayers with income between $200,000 and $500,000.' P Kiel and J Eisinger, 'Who's More Likely to Be Audited: A Person Making $20,000 – or $400,000?' (*ProPublica*, 12 December 2018) www.propublica.org/article/earned-income-tax-credit-irs-audit-working-poor?token=Tu5C70R2p CBv8Yj33AkMh2E-mHz3d6iu.

[31] M Desmond, *Evicted: Poverty and Profit in the American City*, 1st edn (Crown Publishers, 2016) 304; A Natapoff, 'Criminal Municipal Courts' (2021) 134 *Harvard Law Review* 964.

[32] Compare the worlds portrayed in TR Tyler, *Why People Obey the Law* (Yale University Press, 1990); and D Graeber, *The Utopia of Rules: On Technology, Stupidity, and the Secret Joys of Bureaucracy* (Melville House, 2016).

[33] Gowder (n 9) chs 6, 8.

agency or private company, they will be held to the letter of every single form shoved in front of their faces but the government and companies are under no obligations whatsoever, why would we ever expect them to come to the defence of the legal system when, for example, that legal system declares that a politician whom they support is breaking the law?

I think we have seen the consequences of legal alienation in the political domain. In the 2016 presidential debates, when Hillary Clinton criticised Donald Trump for avoiding income taxes, his response was 'that makes me smart'.[34] And millions of voters apparently thought that was a perfectly fine thing to say.[35] But are ordinary Americans wrong to see the legal system as Donald Trump evidently treats it – as a bunch of meaningless argle-bargle that certain kinds of coastal elites can utter in order to seize advantage from others, but which may be safely ignored by those with power? Why shouldn't Donald Trump cheat on his taxes? Our tax system is filled with endless loopholes for the benefit of the rich, and even the miserable *process* of filling out tax forms is a canonical example of corrupted law in which the lobbyists for the tax preparation industry have successfully blocked legislation to simplify it.[36] Is this really the sort of thing that ordinary citizens ought to perceive as legitimate, such that they should really be expected to punish a politician who casually flouts it?

Burke explained the danger long ago – ironically in a letter on the American Revolution itself: 'People crushed by law have no hopes but from power. If laws are their enemies, they will be enemies to laws; and those who have much to hope and nothing to lose will always be dangerous, more or less.'[37]

Returning to America's founding dichotomy between republican and liberal citizenship, we can see this kind of attitude as the failure state of extreme liberalism. At the limit, a legally alienated citizen sees the law not as an element of a co-created civic identity but as a hostile external force that must be monitored because of the threat it poses. Statements of legal rules are just utterances about stuff that powerful people will do to you if you make them mad, and are meaningful only to the extent they enable one to make predictions about those top-down exercises of power: an individual has their personal plans, and those

---

[34] C Vinograd, '2016 Presidential Debate: Donald Trump's Remark About Paying Taxes Raises Eyebrows' (*NBC News*, 27 September 2016) www.nbcnews.com/storyline/2016-presidential-debates/presidential-debate-donald-trump-s-remark-about-paying-taxes-raises-n655261.

[35] They also evidently thought his boasting about being able to 'stand in the middle of Fifth Avenue and shoot someone', J Johnson, 'Donald Trump: They Say I Could "Shoot Somebody" and Still Have Support' (*Washington Post*, 23 January 2016) www.washingtonpost.com/news/post-politics/wp/2016/01/23/donald-trump-i-could-shoot-somebody-and-still-have-support/, and 'grab [women] by the pussy', D Paquette, 'Why the Most Outrageous Part of Donald Trump's "Hot Mic" Comments Isn't the Vulgar Language' (*Washington Post*, 7 October 2016) www.washingtonpost.com/news/wonk/wp/2016/10/07/the-real-issue-with-donald-trump-saying-a-man-can-do-anything-to-a-woman/ – ie sexually assault them – was just fine.

[36] P Herd and DP Moynihan, *Administrative Burden: Policymaking by Other Means* (Russell Sage Foundation, 2018) 9–11.

[37] E Burke, letter to Charles James Fox, 8 October 1777, in *The Works of The Right Honorable Edmund Burke*, vol. XI (Little, Brown and Company, 1899), 147.

plans will have to be adjusted if an external thing called 'the legal system' signals to one that people with guns may garnish one's bank account or put one in a cage for engaging in certain activities.

When those legal rules are also substantively unjust; when they do real world harm on a regular basis to the vulnerable; when they provide the framework for a profoundly unequal social order; it's hard to really blame some 60 million people for voting for a guy for the highest office in the land whose entire campaign was a gleeful celebration of crime. If the critical legal studies scholars are right about what American law is, then perhaps the people ought to abandon it.

Long before CLS, Walter Benjamin, confronting much grimmer circumstances, articulated what we might take as a concise summary of the negative side of this volume in his eighth thesis on the philosophy of history:

> The tradition of the oppressed teaches us that the 'state of emergency' in which we live is not the exception but the rule. We must attain to a conception of history that is in keeping with this insight. Then we shall clearly realize that it is our task to bring about a real state of emergency, and this will improve our position in the struggle against Fascism. One reason why Fascism has a chance is that in the name of progress its opponents treat it as a historical norm. The current amazement that the things we are experiencing are 'still' possible in the twentieth century is not philosophical. This amazement is not the beginning of knowledge – unless it is the knowledge that the view of history which gives rise to it is untenable.[38]

Those words are not fully suitable for our current situation. For the United States rule of law has come a long way from slavery, from Indian Removal, from Chinese Exclusion – largely thanks to the tireless work of Black activists and other activists of colour for self-liberation. But there is still a long way to go before the US satisfies the rule of law ideals against which its institutions have been framed. And it is incumbent on those of us who value what the American legal system could be to seek its reform – to demand an end to the big abuses, like police violence against Black Americans and kangaroo-court immigration adjudications, and to the little but pervasive abuses, like the corporate use of contracts to evade traditional common-law individual legal rights – and to demand real progress toward the social and economic equality without which the rule of law cannot be sustained – in order that the American rule of law may ultimately grow into the virtues that its advocates have always said it has.

---

[38] W Benjamin in Hannah Arendt (ed) and Harry Zorn (trans), *Illuminations* (Schocken Books, 1968) 259.

References

'Breonna Taylor: What Happened on the Night of Her Death?' (*BBC News*, 8 October 2020) www.bbc.com/news/world-us-canada-54210448.

Ackerman S, 'Bad Lieutenant: American Police Brutality, Exported from Chicago to Guantánamo' (*The Guardian*, 18 February 2015) www.theguardian.com/us-news/2015/feb/18/american-police-brutality-chicago-guantanamo.

——, 'Guantánamo Torturer Led Brutal Chicago Police Regime of Shackling and Confession' (*The Guardian*, 18 February 2015) www.theguardian.com/us-news/2015/feb/18/guantanamo-torture-chicago-police-brutality.

——, 'How Chicago Police Condemned the Innocent: A Trail of Coerced Confessions' (*The Guardian*, 19 February 2015) www.theguardian.com/us-news/2015/feb/19/chicago-police-richard-zuley-abuse-innocent-man.

——, 'Chicago's Homan Square "Black Site": Surveillance, Military-Style Vehicles and a Metal Cage' (*The Guardian*, 24 February 2015) www.theguardian.com/us-news/2015/feb/24/chicago-homan-square-black-site.

——, 'Homan Square Detainee: I Was Sexually Abused by Police at Chicago "Black Site"' (*The Guardian*, 14 May 2015) www.theguardian.com/us-news/2015/may/14/homan-square-detainee-police-abuse.

Adams J, *The Works of John Adams, Second President of the United States*, vol 3 (Charles Francis Adams ed, Little, Brown and Company, 1865).

Agamben G, *State of Exception* (University of Chicago Press, 2005).

Alexander GS, 'Time and Property in the American Republican Legal Culture' (1991) 66 *New York University Law Review* 273.

Alexander M, *The New Jim Crow: Mass Incarceration in the Age of Colorblindness* (The New Press, 2012).

Alford R, *Permanent State of Emergency: Unchecked Executive Power and the Demise of the Rule of Law* (McGill University Press, 2017).

Alschuler AW and Deiss AG, 'A Brief History of the Criminal Jury in the United States' (1994) 61 *University of Chicago Law Review* 867.

Amar AR, 'Of Sovereignty and Federalism' (1987) 96 *Yale Law Journal* 1425.

American Bar Association, '2019 Update Report: Reforming the Immigration System: Proposals to Promote Independence, Fairness, Efficiency, and Professionalism in the Adjudication of Removal Cases' (*American Bar Association Commission on Immigration*, 2019) www.americanbar.org/content/dam/aba/publications/commission_on_immigration/2019_reforming_the_immigration_system_volume_2.pdf.

American Civil Liberties Union, 'ACLU Factsheet on Customs and Border Protection's 100-Mile Zone' (*American Civil Liberties Union*) www.aclu.org/other/aclu-factsheet-customs-and-border-protections-100-mile-zone.

American Immigration Council, 'A Primer on Expedited Removal' (*American Immigration Council*, 3 February 2017) www.americanimmigrationcouncil.org/research/primer-expedited-removal.

Anderson E, *The Imperative of Integration* (Princeton University Press, 2010).

——, 'Moral Bias and Corrective Practices: A Pragmatist Perspective' (2015) 89 *Proceedings and Addresses of the American Philosophical Association* 21.

Andrews KT, 'The Impacts of Social Movements on the Political Process: The Civil Rights Movement and Black Electoral Politics in Mississippi' (1997) 62 *American Sociological Review* 800.

——, 'Social Movements and Policy Implementation: The Mississippi Civil Rights Movement and the War on Poverty, 1965 to 1971' (2001) 66 *American Sociological Review* 71.

Anthony D, 'The U.S. Border Patrol's Constitutional Erosion in the 100-Mile Zone' (2020) 124 *Penn State Law Review* 391.

Aoki K, 'No Right to Own?: The Early Twentieth-Century "Alien Land Laws" as a Prelude to Internment' (1998) 37 *Boston College Law Review* 37.

Appleman LI, 'The Plea Jury' (2010) 85 *Indiana Law Journal* 731.

Arnold G and Slusser M, 'Silencing Women's Voices: Nuisance Property Laws and Battered Women' (2015) 40 *Law & Social Inquiry* 908.

Asimow M, 'Five Models of Administrative Adjudication' (2015) 63 *American Journal of Comparative Law* 3.

Atuahene B, 'Predatory Cities' (2020) 108 *California Law Review* 107.

Austin R, 'Step on a Crack, Break Your Mother's Back: Poor Moms, Myths of Authority, and Drug-Related Evictions from Public Housing' (2002) 14 *Yale Journal of Law and Feminism* 273.

Azmy B, 'Unshackling the Thirteenth Amendment: Modern Slavery and a Reconstructed Civil Rights Agenda' (2002) 71 *Fordham Law Review* 981.

Baker HR, 'The Fugitive Slave Clause and the Antebellum Constitution' (2012) 30 *Law and History Review* 1133.

Baldwin Clark L, 'Beyond Bias: Cultural Capital in Anti-Discrimination Law' (2018) 53 *Harvard Civil Rights-Civil Liberties Law Review* 381.

Balko R, *Rise of the Warrior Cop: The Militarization of America's Police Forces*, pbk edn (PublicAffairs, 2014).

Bandura A, 'Moral Disengagement in the Perpetration of Inhumanities' (1999) 3 *Personality and Social Psychology Review* 193.

Barnes ML and Chemerinsky E, 'The Once and Future Equal Protection Doctrine' (2011) 43 *Connecticut Law Review* 1059.

Barnett K, 'Against Administrative Judges' (2016) 49 *UC Davis Law Review* 1643.

Barnett RE, 'Was Slavery Unconstitutional Before the Thirteenth Amendment?: Lysander Spooner's Theory of Interpretation' (1997) 28 *Pacific Law Journal* 977.

Bass S, 'Policing Space, Policing Race: Social Control Imperatives and Police Discretionary Decisions' (2001) 28 *Social Justice* 156.

Baude W, 'Is Qualified Immunity Unlawful' (2018) 106 *California Law Review* 45.

Bell DA, 'Brown v. Board of Education and the Interest-Convergence Dilemma' (1980) 93 *Harvard Law Review* 518.

——, *And We Are Not Saved: The Elusive Quest for Racial Justice* (Basic Books, 1989).

Bell MC, 'Police Reform and the Dismantling of Legal Estrangement' (2017) 126 *Yale Law Journal* 2054.

——, 'Anti-Segregation Policing' (2020) 95 *New York University Law Review* 650.

Bell RL and Savage JD, 'Our Land is Your Land: Ineffective State Restriction of Alien Land Ownership and the Need for Federal Legislation' (1980) 13 *John Marshall Law Review* 679.

Benjamin SB, 'The Significance of the Massachusetts Constitution of 1780' (1997) 70 *Temple Law Review* 883.

Benjamin W, *Illuminations* (H Arendt, ed, H Zorn, trans, Schocken Books, 1968) 259.

Benton L, 'Just Despots: The Cultural Construction of Imperial Constitutionalism' (2013) 9 *Law, Culture and the Humanities* 213.

Berger R, 'Congressional Contraction of Federal Jurisdiction' (1980) 1980 *Wisconsin Law Review* 801.

Bernhardt A, Milkman R and Theodore N, 'Broken Laws, Unprotected Workers: Violations of Employment and Labor Laws in America's Cities' (*National Employment Law Project*, 21 September 2019) www.nelp.org/publication/broken-laws-unprotected-workers-violations-of-employment-and-labor-laws-in-americas-cities/.

Bernstein DE, *Lawless: The Obama Administration's Unprecedented Assault on the Constitution and the Rule of Law*, 1st American edn (Encounter Books, 2015).

Biggs M and Andrews KT, 'Protest Campaigns and Movement Success: Desegregating the U.S. South in the Early 1960s' (2015) 80 *American Sociological Review* 416.

Binder G, 'The Slavery of Emancipation Bondage, Freedom and the Constitution: The New Slavery Scholarship and Its Impact on Law and Legal Historiography' (1995) 17 *Cardozo Law Review* 2063.

Blenz P, 'Hamad v. Gates and the Continuing Interpretation of Boumediene: A Note on 732 F.3d 990 (9th Cir. 2013)' (2015) 35 *Journal of the National Association of Administrative Law Judiciary* 443.

Bloom J and Martin, Jr WE, *Black Against Empire: The History and Politics of the Black Panther Party*, 2nd edn (University of California Press 2016).

Booth J, 'Ending Forced Labor In ICE Detention Centers: A New Approach' (2020) 34 *Georgetown Immigration Law Journal* 573.

Boutrous TJ Jr and Evanson BH, 'The Enduring and Universal Principal of Fair Notice' (2013) 86 *Southern California Law Review* 193.

Bradley CA and Goldsmith JL, 'Obama's AUMF Legacy' (2016) 110 *American Journal of International Law* 628.

Brady PS, 'Slavery, Race, and the Criminal Law in Antebellum North Carolina: A Reconsideration of the Thomas Ruffin Court' (1979) 10 *North Carolina Central Law Journal* 248.

Bratton WJ, 'The New York City Police Department's Civil Enforcement of Quality-of-Life Crimes' (1995) 3 *Journal of Law and Policy* 447.

Brennan Center for Justice, 'A Guide to Emergency Powers and Their Use' (*Brennan Center for Justice*, 2019) www.brennancenter.org/sites/default/files/2019-10/2019_10_15_EmergencyPowersFULL.pdf.

Brennan-Marquez K, 'Extremely Broad Laws' (2019) 61 *Arizona Law Review* 641.

Bromell NK, *The Powers of Dignity: The Black Political Philosophy of Frederick Douglass* (Duke University Press, 2021).

Brown HL, 'Extraterritorial Jurisdiction under the 1998 Amendments to the Foreign Corrupt Practices Act: Does the Government's Reach Now Exceed its Grasp' (2001) 26 *North Carolina Journal of International Law and Commercial Regulation* 239.

Brown P, 'Parents' House Seized After Son's Drug Bust', *CNN Digital* (3 September 2014) www.cnn.com/2014/09/03/us/philadelphia-drug-bust-house-seizure/index.html.

Burke E, *The Works of The Right Honorable Edmund Burke*, vol. XI (Little, Brown and Company, 1899).

Burki SJ and Perry G, *Beyond the Washington Consensus: Institutions Matter* (World Bank, 1998).

Burns H, 'The Rule of Law in the South' (1965) 40 *Commentary* 80.

Burns N, *The Formation of American Local Governments: Private Values in Public Institutions* (Oxford University Press, 1994).

Butler P, 'Racially Based Jury Nullification: Black Power in the Criminal Justice System' (1995) 105 *Yale Law Journal* 677.

Button JW, *Blacks and Social Change.* (Princeton University Press, 1989).

Cade JA, 'The Plea-Bargain Crisis for Noncitizens in Misdemeanor Court Part VI: Immigration Litigation Issues' (2013) 34 *Immigration and Nationality Law Review* 597.

Campbell SW, *The Slave Catchers: Enforcement of the Fugitive Slave Law, 1850–1860* (University of North Carolina Press, 1970).

Capers B, 'Policing, Place, and Race' (2009) 44 *Harvard Civil Rights – Civil Liberties Law Review* 43.

——, 'Rethinking the Fourth Amendment: Race, Citizenship, and the Equality Principle' (2011) 46 *Harvard Civil Rights-Civil Liberties Law Review* 1.

Carbado DW, 'Blue-on-Black Violence: A Provisional Model of Some of the Causes' (2016) 104 *Georgetown Law Journal* 1479.

——, 'From Stopping Black People to Killing Black People: The Fourth Amendment Pathways to Police Violence' (2017) 105 *California Law Review* 125.

——, 'Predatory Policing' (2017) 85 *UMKC Law Review* 545.

Carbado DW and Harris CI, 'Undocumented Criminal Procedure' (2011) 58 *UCLA Law Review* 1543.

Carrillo J, 'Identity as Idiom: Mashpee Reconsidered' (1995) 28 *Indiana Law Review* 511.

Carroll JE, 'Nullification as Law' (2014) 102 *Georgetown Law Journal* 579.

Cass RA, *The Rule of Law in America* (Johns Hopkins University Press, 2003).

Chang RS, 'Whitewashing Precedent: From the Chinese Exclusion Case to Korematsu to the Muslim Travel Ban Cases' (2018) 68 *Case Western Reserve Law Review* 1183.

Chapman NS and Mcconnell MW, 'Due Process as Separation of Powers' (2012) 121 *Yale Law Journal* 1672.

Chernega J, 'Black Lives Matter: Racialised Policing in the United States' (2016) 14 *Comparative American Studies An International Journal* 234.

Chesney RM, 'State Secrets and the Limits of National Security Litigation' (2007) 75 *George Washington Law Review* 1249.

Chin GJ, 'Regulating Race: Asian Exclusion and the Administrative State' (2002) 37 *Harvard Civil Rights-Civil Liberties Law Review* 1.

Clegg J and Foley D, 'A Classical-Marxian Model of Antebellum Slavery' (2019) 43 *Cambridge Journal of Economics* 107.

Cleveland SH, 'Powers Inherent in Sovereignty: Indians, Aliens, Territories, and the Nineteenth Century Origins of Plenary Power over Foreign Affairs' (2002) 81 *Texas Law Review* 1.

Cohen EF, *Illegal: How America's Lawless Immigration Regime Threatens Us All*, 1st edn (Basic Books, 2020).

Cohen J, 'The Arc of the Moral Universe' (1997) 26 *Philosophy & Public Affairs* 91.

Cohen W, 'Thomas Jefferson and the Problem of Slavery' (1969) 56 *The Journal of American History* 503.

Cole D, *No Equal Justice: Race and Class in the American Criminal Justice System* (New Press, 1999).

Coleman M, 'Immigration Geopolitics Beyond the Mexico-US Border (2007) 39 *Antipode* 54.

Constable M, *The Law of the Other: The Mixed Jury and Changing Conceptions of Citizenship, Law, and Knowledge* (University of Chicago Press, 1994).

Cornelius J, '"We Slipped and Learned to Read": Slave Accounts of the Literacy Process, 1830–1865' (1983) 44 *Phylon (1960–)* 171.

Courtright JA, 'Rhetoric of the Gun: An Analysis of the Rhetorical Modifications of the Black Panther Party' (1974) 4 *Journal of Black Studies* 249.

Coutin SB, Richland J and Fortin V, 'Routine Exceptionality: The Plenary Power Doctrine, Immigrants, and the Indigenous under U.S. Law' (2014) 4 *UC Irvine Law Review* 97.

Cover RM, *Justice Accused: Antislavery and the Judicial Process* (Yale University Press, 1975).

Cox L, 'The Promise of Land for the Freedmen' (1958) 45 *The Mississippi Valley Historical Review* 413.

Coyne CJ and Hall AR, *Tyranny Comes Home: The Domestic Fate of U.S. Militarism* (Stanford University Press, 2018).

Crespo AM, 'The Hidden Law of Plea Bargaining' (2018) 118 *Columbia Law Review* 1303.

Davies C and Edwards C, '"A Jury of Peers": A Comparative Analysis' (2004) 68 *The Journal of Criminal Law* 150.

Davis AJ, 'Racial Fairness in the Criminal Justice System: The Role of the Prosecutor' (2007) 39 *Columbia Human Rights Law Review* 202.

Delany MR, *The Condition, Elevation, Emigration, and Destiny of the Colored People of the United States Politically Considered* (Published by the Author, 1852).

——, *Martin R. Delany, A Documentary Reader* (RS Levine ed, University of North Carolina Press 2003).

Desmond M, *Evicted: Poverty and Profit in the American City*, 1st edn (Crown Publishers, 2016).

Desmond M and Valdez N, 'Unpolicing the Urban Poor: Consequences of Third-Party Policing for Inner-City Women' (2013) 78 *American Sociological Review* 117.

Dicey AV, *Introduction to the Study of the Law of the Constitution* (Liberty Fund, 1982).

Domar ED, 'The Causes of Slavery or Serfdom: A Hypothesis' (1970) 30 *Journal of Economic History* 18.

Domonoske C and Gonzalez R, 'What We Know: Family Separation And "Zero Tolerance" At The Border' (*National Public Radio*, 19 June 2018) www.npr.org/2018/06/19/621065383/what-we-know-family-separation-and-zero-tolerance-at-the-border.

Donald BB and Davis PJ, 'To This Tribunal the Freedman Has Turned: The Freedmen's Bureau's Judicial Powers and the Origins of the Fourteenth Amendment' (2018) 79 *Louisiana Law Review* 1.

Douglass F, *My Bondage and My Freedom* (Miller, Orton & Co, 1857).

——, *The Frederick Douglass Papers. Ser. 1 Vol. 3: Speeches, Debates and Interviews 1855–63* (John W Blassingame ed, Yale University Press 1985).

——, *Frederick Douglass: Selected Speeches and Writings*, 1st edn (Philip Sheldon Foner and Yuval Taylor eds, Lawrence Hill Books, 1999).

——, 'The Constitution of the United States: Is It Pro-Slavery or Anti-Slavery?1' in Philip Sheldon Foner and Yuval Taylor (eds), *Frederick Douglass: Selected Speeches and Writings*, 1st edn (Lawrence Hill Books, 1999).

Dowell S, *A History and Explanation of the Stamp Duties: Containing Remarks on the Origin of Stamp Duties, a History of the Duties in This Country ... An Explanation of the System and Administration of the Tax, Observations on the Stamp Duties in Foreign Countries and the Stamp Laws at Present in Force in the United Kingdom, with Notes, Appendices, and a Copious Index* (Butterworths, 1873).

Dripps DA, 'Akhil Amar on Criminal Procedure and Constitutional Law: Here I Go Down That Wrong Road Again' (1996) 74 *North Carolina Law Review* 1559.

——, 'Guilt, Innocence, and Due Process of Plea Bargaining' (2016) 57 *William & Mary Law Review* 1343.

Du Bois WEB, *The Souls of Black Folk: Essays and Sketches*, 4th edn (AC McClurg & Co, 1904).

——, *Black Reconstruction: An Essay Toward a History of the Part Which Black Folk Played in the Attempt to Reconstruct Democracy in America, 1860–1880* (Harcourt, Brace & Co, 1935).

Dudziak ML, *Cold War Civil Rights: Race and the Image of American Democracy* (Princeton University Press 2011).

Duquette E, 'Tyranny in America, or, the Appeal to the Coloured Citizens of the World' (2021) 33 *American Literary History* 1.

Dworkin R, 'The Law of the Slave-Catchers' (1975) 3847 *Times Literary Supplement* 1437.

Dyzenhaus D, *The Constitution of Law: Legality in a Time of Emergency* (Cambridge University Press, 2012).

Eastman JC, 'From Feudalism to Consent: Rethinking Birthright Citizenship' (*Heritage Foundation*, 2006) www.heritage.org/the-constitution/report/feudalism-consent-rethinking-birthright-citizenship.

Epstein RA, *Design for Liberty: Private Property, Public Administration, and the Rule of Law* (Harvard University Press, 2011).

——, 'The Perilous Position of the Rule of Law and the Administrative State' (2013) 36 *Harvard Journal of Law & Public Policy* 5.

——, 'Structural Protections for Individual Rights: The Indispensable Role of Article III – Or Even Article I – Courts in the Administrative State' (2019) 26 *George Mason Law Review* 777.

Ewing W and Cantor G, 'Deported With No Possessions: The Mishandling of Migrants' Personal Belongings by CBP and ICE' (*American Immigration Council*, 2006) www.americanimmigrationcouncil.org/research/deported-no-possessions#:~:text=New%20Survey%20Data%20Reveals%20That%20Migrants%20Are%20Routinely%20Removed%20Without%20Their%20Personal%20Belongings&text=According%20to%20new%20data%20from,their%20personal%20belongings%20were%20returned.

Fagan J and Ash E, 'New Policing, New Segregation: From Ferguson to New York' (2017) 106 *Georgetown Law Journal Online* 33.

Farber DA, 'A Fatal Loss of Balance: Dred Scott Revisited' (2011) 39 *Pepperdine Law Review* 13.

Farbiarz M, 'Accuracy and Adjudication: The Promise of Extraterritorial Due Process' (2016) 116 *Columbia Law Review* 625.

Fassin D, *Enforcing Order: An Ethnography of Urban Policing.* (Wiley, 2013).

Fede A, 'Legitimized Violent Slave Abuse in the American South, 1619–1865: A Case Study of Law and Social Change in Six Southern States' (1985) 29 *American Journal of Legal History* 93.

Felber G, *Those Who Know Don't Say The Nation of Islam, the Black Freedom Movement, and the Carceral State* (2020).

Feldman LC, 'Police Violence and the Legal Temporalities of Immunity' (2017) 20 *Theory & Event* 329.

Figueira T, 'Helotage and the Spartan Economy', *A Companion to Sparta* (John Wiley & Sons, Ltd, 2017).

Fine B and Saad-Filho A, 'Politics of Neoliberal Development: Washington Consensus and the Post-Washington Consensus' in Heloise Weber (ed), *The Politics of Development: A Survey*, 1st edn (Routledge, 2014).

Finkelman P, *An Imperfect Union: Slavery, Federalism, and Comity* (University of North Carolina Press, 1981).

——, 'Slavery and the Northwest Ordinance: A Study in Ambiguity' (1986) 6 *Journal of the Early Republic* 343.

——, 'Sorting Out Prigg v. Pennsylvania' (1993) 24 *Rutgers Law Journal* 605.

—— (ed), *Milestone Documents in African American History: Exploring the Essential Primary Sources* (Schlager Group, 2010).

Finley MI, 'Slavery' in DL Sills (ed), *International Encyclopedia of the Social Sciences*, vol 14 (Macmillan Co and Free Press, 1968).

Fisk C and Richardson S, 'Police Unions' (2017) 85 *George Washington Law Review* 712.

Flanders C, 'Keeping the Rule of Law Simple: Comments on Gowder, The Rule of Law in the Real World' (2018) 62 *Saint Louis University Law Journal* 313.

Foner E, 'Rights and the Constitution in Black Life During the Civil War and Reconstruction' (1987) 74 *The Journal of American History* 863.

——, *Reconstruction: America's Unfinished Revolution, 1863–1877*, Updated edn (HarperPerennial, 2014).

——, *The Second Founding: How the Civil War and Reconstruction Remade the Constitution*, 1st edn (WW Norton & Company 2019).

Forman J, *Locking Up Our Own: Crime and Punishment in Black America*, 1st edn (Farrar, Straus and Giroux, 2017).

Forret J, 'Slaves, Poor Whites, and the Underground Economy of the Rural Carolinas' (2004) 70 *The Journal of Southern History* 783.

Francis MM, *Civil Rights and the Making of the Modern American State* (Cambridge University Press 2014).

French D, 'Anti-Cop Rioters Don't Care about "Justice"' (*National Review*, September 2016) www.nationalreview.com/2016/09/black-lives-matter-rioters-rule-law-under-attack/.

Frickey PP, 'Marshalling Past and Present: Colonialism, Constitutionalism, and Interpretation in Federal Indian Law' (1993) 107 *Harvard Law Review* 381.

——, 'Domesticating Federal Indian Law' (1996) 81 *Minnesota Law Review* 31.

Frischmann BM and Selinger E, *Re-Engineering Humanity* (Cambridge University Press, 2018).

Fuente A de la and Gross AJ, *Becoming Free, Becoming Black: Race, Freedom, and Law in Cuba, Virginia, and Louisiana* (Cambridge University Press, 2020).

Fuller LL, *The Morality of Law*, Revised edn (Yale University Press, 1969).

Fussell E, 'The Deportation Threat Dynamic and Victimization of Latino Migrants: Wage Theft and Robbery' (2011) 52 *The Sociological Quarterly* 593.

Gambone JG, 'Ex Parte Milligan: The Restoration of Judicial Prestige?' (1970) 16 *Civil War History* 246.

Garrow DJ, 'Picking up the Books: The New Historiography of the Black Panther Party' (2007) 35 *Reviews in American History* 650.

Gaston S and Brunson RK, 'Reasonable Suspicion in the Eye of the Beholder: Routine Policing in Racially Different Disadvantaged Neighborhoods' (2020) 56 *Urban Affairs Review* 188.

Gienapp J, 'Beyond Republicanism, Back to Constitutionalism: The Creation of the American Republic at Fifty' (2020) 93 *The New England Quarterly* 275.

Gilchrist GM, 'Plea Bargains, Convictions and Legitimacy' (2011) 48 *American Criminal Law Review* 143.

Gillion DQ, 'Protest and Congressional Behavior: Assessing Racial and Ethnic Minority Protests in the District' (2012) 74 *The Journal of Politics* 950.

Glinavos I, 'Neoliberal Law: Unintended Consequences of Market-Friendly Law Reforms' (2008) 29 *Third World Quarterly* 1087.

Graeber D, The Utopia of Rules: On Technology, Stupidity, and the Secret Joys of Bureaucracy (Melville House, 2016).

Godsil RD, 'Race Nuisance: The Politics of Law in the Jim Crow Era' (2006) 105 *Michigan Law Review* 505.

Goldsmith J and Sunstein CR, 'Military Tribunals and Legal Culture: What a Difference Sixty Years Makes' (2002) 19 Constitutional Commentary 261.

Goldstein J and Haughney C, 'Relax, If You Want, but Don't Put Your Feet Up' (*The New York Times*, 6 January 2012) www.nytimes.com/2012/01/07/nyregion/minor-offense-on-ny-subway-can-bring-ticket-or-handcuffs.html.

Goluboff RL, 'The Thirteenth Amendment and the Lost Origins of Civil Rights' (2001) 50 *Duke Law Journal* 1609.

——, *Vagrant Nation: Police Power, Constitutional Change, and the Making of the 1960s* (Oxford University Press, 2016).

Gonzales AR and Glen P, 'Advancing Executive Branch Immigration Policy through the Attorney General's Review Authority' (2016) 101 *Iowa Law Review* 841.

Goodell W, *The American Slave Code in Theory and Practice: Its Distinctive Features Shown by Its Statutes, Judicial Decisions, and Illustrative Facts* (American and Foreign Anti-Slavery Society, 1853).

Goodman P, 'Hero and Inmate: Work, Prisons, and Punishment in California's Fire Camps' (2012) 15 *Working USA* 353.

Goodmark L, 'Hands up at Home: Militarized Masculinity and Police Officers Who Commit Intimate Partner Abuse' (2015) 2015 *Brigham Young University Law Review* 1183.

——, 'Reimagining VAWA: Why Criminalization Is a Failed Policy and What a Non-Carceral VAWA Could Look Like' (2020) 27 *Violence Against Women* 84.

Gotanda N, 'Race, Citizenship, and the Search for Political Community Among "We the People" – A Review Essay on Citizenship Without Consent' (1997) 76 *Oregon Law Review* 233.

Gowder P, 'The Rule of Law and Equality' (2013) 32 *Law and Philosophy* 565.

——, 'Equal Law in an Unequal World' (2014) 99 *Iowa Law Review* 1021.

——, 'Institutional Values, or How to Say What Democracy Is' (2014) 30 *Southwest Philosophy Review* 235.

——, 'Racial Classification and Ascriptive Injury' (2015) 92 *Washington University Law Review* 325.

——, 'What the Laws Demand of Socrates – and of Us' (2015) 98 *The Monist* 360.

——, *The Rule of Law in the Real World* (Cambridge University Press, 2016).

——, 'Resisting the Rule of Men' (2018) 62 *Saint Louis University Law Journal* 333.

——, 'Reading the Plain Text of the Birthright Clause in the Fourteenth Amendment' (*Niskanen Center*, 1 November 2018) www.niskanencenter.org/reading-the-plain-text-of-the-birthright-clause-in-the-fourteenth-amendment/.

——, 'Reconstituting We the People: Frederick Douglass and Jürgen Habermas in Conversation' (2019) 114 *Northwestern University Law Review* 335.

——, 'The Dangers to the American Rule of Law Will Outlast the Next Election' (2020) 2020 *Cardozo Law Review de novo* 126.

——, 'Untitled Review of Cass Sunstein and Adrian Vermeule, Law and Leviathan: Redeeming the Administrative State' (2021) 31 *Law and Politics Book Review* 12.

Graber MA, 'Desperately Ducking Slavery: Dred Scott and Contemporary Constitutional Theory' (1997) 14 *Constitutional Commentary* 271.

Green CR, 'The Original Sense of the (Equal) Protection Clause: Pre-Enacting History' (2008) 19 *George Mason University Civil Rights Law Journal* 1.

Gross AJ, *Double Character: Slavery and Mastery in the Antebellum Southern Courtroom* (Princeton University Press, 2000).

Gruber A, 'A Neo-Feminist Assessment of Rape and Domestic Violence Law Reform' (2012) 15 *Journal of Gender, Race & Justice* 583.

Guinier L and Torres G, 'Changing the Wind: Notes toward a Demosprudence of Law and Social Movements' (2014) 123 *Yale Law Journal* 2740.

Hafetz J, 'Calling the Government to Account: Habeas Corpus in the Aftermath of Boumediene' (2011) 57 *Wayne Law Review* 99.

——, 'A Problem of Standards? Another Perspective on Secret Law' (2016) 57 *William and Mary Law Review* 2141.

Hahn S, *A Nation Under Our Feet: Black Political Struggles in the Rural South, From Slavery to the Great Migration* (Belknap Press of Harvard University Press, 2003).

Hamburger P, *Is Administrative Law Unlawful?* (University of Chicago Press, 2014).

Hamilton DC and Hamilton CV, 'The Dual Agenda of African American Organizations Since the New Deal: Social Welfare Policies and Civil Rights' (1992) 107 *Political Science Quarterly* 435.

Hamilton DW, *The Limits of Sovereignty: Property Confiscation in the Union and the Confederacy during the Civil War* (University of Chicago Press, 2014).

Hardy DT, 'Dred Scott, John San(d)ford, and the Case for Collusion' (2014) 41 *Northern Kentucky Law Review* 37.

Harmon R, 'Why Arrest?' (2016) 115 *Michigan Law Review* 307.

Harrington MP, 'The Legacy of the Colonial Vice-Admiralty Courts (Part I)' (1995) 26 *Journal of Maritime Law and Commerce* 581.

Harris CI, 'Whiteness as Property' (1993) 106 *Harvard Law Review* 1707.

Hayek FA, *The Constitution of Liberty* (University of Chicago Press, 1960).

Herd P and Moynihan DP, *Administrative Burden: Policymaking by Other Means* (Russell Sage Foundation, 2018).

Heyman SJ, 'The First Duty of Government: Protection, Liberty and the Fourteenth Amendment' (1991) 41 *Duke Law Journal* 507.

Higginbotham AL and Kopytoff BK, 'Property First, Humanity Second: The Recognition of the Slave's Human Nature in Virginia Civil Law' (1989) 50 *Ohio State Law Journal* 511.

Himmelstein DU et al, 'Illness and Injury as Contributors to Bankruptcy' (2005) 24 *Health Affairs* W5.

Hinshelwood B, 'The Carolinian Context of John Locke's Theory of Slavery' (2013) 41 *Political Theory* 562.

Ho JC, 'Defining "American": Birthright Citizenship and the Original Understanding of the 14th Amendment' (2006) 9 *Green Bag* 359.

Holden-Smith B, 'Lynching, Federalism, and the Intersection of Race and Gender in the Progressive Era' (1996) 8 *Yale Journal of Law and Feminism* 31.

Holmes MD and Smith BW, 'Intergroup Dynamics of Extra-Legal Police Aggression: An Integrated Theory of Race and Place' (2012) 17 *Aggression and Violent Behavior* 344.

Holmes S, 'The Spider's Web: How Government Lawbreakers Routinely Elude the Law' in Austin Sarat and Nasser Hussain (eds), *When Governments Break the Law: The Rule of Law and the Prosecution of the Bush Administration* (New York University Press, 2010).

Hooker J, '"A Black Sister to Massachusetts": Latin America and the Fugitive Democratic Ethos of Frederick Douglass' (2015) 109 *American Political Science Review* 690.

——, 'Black Lives Matter and the Paradoxes of U.S. Black Politics: From Democratic Sacrifice to Democratic Repair' (2016) 44 *Political Theory* 448.

Horton JO and Horton LE, 'A Federal Assault: African Americans and the Impact of the Fugitive Slave Law of 1850' (1993) 68 *Chicago-Kent Law Review* 1179.

Horwitz MJ, 'The Rule of Law: An Unqualified Human Good?' (1977) 86 *Yale Law Journal* 561.

——, *The Transformation of American Law, 1780–1860* (Harvard University Press, 1977).

Howell WG and Moe TM, *Presidents, Populism, and the Crisis of Democracy* (University of Chicago Press, 2020).

Huhn WR, 'The Legacy of Slaughterhouse, Bradwell, and Cruikshank in Constitutional Interpretation' (2009) 42 *Akron Law Review* 1051.

Human Rights Watch, 'An Offer You Can't Refuse: How US Federal Prosecutors Force Drug Defendants to Plead Guilty' (5 December 2013) www.hrw.org/report/2013/12/05/offer-you-cant-refuse/how-us-federal-prosecutors-force-drug-defendants-plead.

Husak DN, *Overcriminalization: The Limits of the Criminal Law* (Oxford University Press, 2008).

Ismay J, 'A Navy Veteran Had a Question for the Feds in Portland. They Beat Him in Response' (*The New York Times*, 20 July 2020) www.nytimes.com/2020/07/20/us/portland-protests-navy-christopher-david.html.

Jacobs H, *Incidents in the Life of a Slave Girl (Written Under the Pen Name Linda Brent)* (L Maria Child ed, Published for the Author, 1861).

Jagmohan D, 'Peculiar Property: Harriet Jacobs on the Nature of Slavery' [Forthcoming] *Journal of Politics* 25.

Jain A, 'Bureaucrats in Robes: Immigration Judges and the Trappings of Courts' (2019) 33 *Georgetown Immigration Law Journal* 261.

James I, 'Wrongly Deported, American Citizen Sues INS for $8 Million' (*Los Angeles Times*, 3 September 2000) www.latimes.com/archives/la-xpm-2000-sep-03-mn-14714-story.html.

Jawetz T, Wolgin PE and Flores C, '5 Immediate Steps To Rein in DHS in the Wake of Portland' (Center for American Progress, 2 September 2020) www.americanprogress.org/issues/immigration/reports/2020/09/02/489934/5-immediate-steps-rein-dhs-wake-portland/.

Jefferson T, *Notes on the State of Virginia* (John Stockdale, 1787).

Johnson A, 'The Constitutionality of the Fugitive Slave Acts' (1921) 31 *Yale Law Journal* 161.

Johnson J, 'Donald Trump: They Say I Could "Shoot Somebody" and Still Have Support' (*Washington Post*, 23 January 2016) www.washingtonpost.com/news/post-politics/wp/2016/01/23/donald-trump-i-could-shoot-somebody-and-still-have-support/.

Johnson KR, 'How Racial Profiling in America Became the Law of the Land: United States v. Brignoni-Ponce and Whren v. United States and the Need for Truly Rebellious Lawyering' (2010) 98 *Georgetown Law Journal* 1005.

Johnson W (ed), *The Chattel Principle: Internal Slave Trades in the Americas* (Yale University Press, 2004).

Jones MS, *Birthright Citizens: A History of Race and Rights in Antebellum America* (Cambridge University Press, 2018).

Jones N, '"The Regular Routine": Proactive Policing and Adolescent Development Among Young, Poor Black Men' (2014) 2014 *New Directions for Child and Adolescent Development* 33.

Jones RL, 'Terry v. Ohio: Its Failure, Immoral Progeny, and Racial Profiling' (2018) 54 *Idaho Law Review* 511.

Julian GW, *Later Speeches on Political Questions With Select Controversial Papers* (Grace Julian Clarke ed, Carlon & Hollenbeck, 1889).

Jung M-H, 'Outlawing "Coolies": Race, Nation, and Empire in the Age of Emancipation' (2005) 57 *American Quarterly* 677.

Kadish SH, 'The Crisis of Overcriminalization' (1967) 374 *The ANNALS of the American Academy of Political and Social Science* 157.

Kagan M, 'Plenary Power is Dead! Long Live Plenary Power' (2015) 114 *Michigan Law Review First Impressions* 21.

Kato D, 'Strengthening the Weak State: Politicizing the American State's "Weakness" on Racial Violence' (2012) 9 *Du Bois Review: Social Science Research on Race* 457.

——, *Liberalizing Lynching: Building a New Racialized State* (Oxford University Press, 2016).

Katz SN, 'Thomas Jefferson and the Right to Property in Revolutionary America' (1976) 19 *The Journal of Law & Economics* 467.

Kelling GL and Wilson JQ, 'Broken Windows: The Police and Neighborhood Safety' (*The Atlantic*, March 1982) www.theatlantic.com/magazine/archive/1982/03/broken-windows/304465/.

Kennedy D, 'The Critique of Rights in Critical Legal Studies' in Wendy Brown and Janet E Halley (eds), *Left Legalism/Left Critique* (Duke University Press, 2002).

Kennedy R, *Race, Crime, and the Law*, 1st Vintage Books edn (Vintage Books, 1998).

Kennington KM, *In the Shadow of Dred Scott: St. Louis Freedom Suits and the Legal Culture of Slavery in Antebellum America* (The University of Georgia Press, 2017).

Kenyon CM, 'Men of Little Faith: The Anti-Federalists on the Nature of Representative Government' (1955) 12 *The William and Mary Quarterly* 3.

Kerr-Ritchie J, 'Forty Acres, or, An Act of Bad Faith' (2003) 5 *Souls* 8.

Kidane W, 'The Alienage Spectrum Disorder: The Bill of Rights from Chinese Exclusion to Guantanamo' (2010) 20 *Berkeley La Raza Law Journal* 89.

Kiel P and Eisinger J, 'Who's More Likely to Be Audited: A Person Making $20,000 – or $400,000?' (*ProPublica*, 12 December 2018) www.propublica.org/article/earned-income-tax-credit-irs-audit-working-poor?token=Tu5C70R2pCBv8Yj33AkMh2E-mHz3d6iu.

Kim CY, 'The President's Immigration Courts' (2018) 68 *Emory Law Journal* 1.

Kim CY and Semet A, 'Presidential Ideology and Immigrant Detention' (2020) 69 *Duke Law Journal* 1855.

Kim K, 'The Coercion of Trafficked Workers' (2011) 96 *Iowa Law Review* 409.

King ML, *Why We Can't Wait*, Signet Classics edn (New American Library, 2000).

Klarman MJ, 'The Racial Origins of Modern Criminal Procedure' (2000) 99 *Michigan Law Review* 48.

Kleintop AL, 'Life, Liberty, and Property in Slaves: White Mississippians Seek "Just Compensation" for Their Freed Slaves in 1865' (2018) 39 *Slavery & Abolition* 383.

Knox D, Lowe W and Mummolo J, 'Administrative Records Mask Racially Biased Policing' (2020) 114 *American Political Science Review* 619.

Knox D and Mummolo J, 'Toward a General Causal Framework for the Study of Racial Bias in Policing' (2020) 1 *Journal of Political Institutions and Political Economy* 341.

Koh JL, 'When Shadow Removals Collide: Searching for Solutions to the Legal Black Holes Created by Expedited Removal and Reinstatement' (2018) 96 *Washington University Law Review* 337.

Koh SA, 'Foreign Affairs Prosecutions' (2019) 94 *New York University Law Review* 340.

Koulish RE, *Immigration and American Democracy: Subverting the Rule of Law* (Routledge, 2010).

Kreimer SF, 'Federalism and Freedom' (2001) 574 *The ANNALS of the American Academy of Political and Social Science* 66.

Krivo LJ, Peterson RD and Kuhl DC, 'Segregation, Racial Structure, and Neighborhood Violent Crime' (2009) 114 *American Journal of Sociology* 1765.

Lacey N and Soskice D, 'Crime, Punishment and Segregation in the United States: The Paradox of Local Democracy' (2015) 17 *Punishment & Society* 454.

Langer M, 'Rethinking Plea Bargaining: The Practice and Reform of Prosecutorial Adjudication in American Criminal Procedure' (2006) 33 *American Journal of Criminal Law* 223.

Lasch N, 'Rendition Resistance' (2013) 92 *North Carolina Law Review* 149.

Lawson G, 'Appointments and Illegal Adjudication: The America Invents Act through a Constitutional Lens' (2018) 26 *George Mason Law Review* 26.

Lawson G and Calabresi S, 'The Depravity of the 1930s and the Modern Administrative State' (2018) 94 *Notre Dame Law Review* 821.

Leach LF, 'Roots and the Trope of the Good Slaveholder' (2019) 40 *Slavery & Abolition* 361.

Lederman MS, 'The Law (?) Of the Lincoln Assassination' (2018) 118 *Columbia Law Review* 323.

Lee T, *Mobilizing Public Opinion: Black Insurgency and Racial Attitudes in the Civil Rights Era* (University of Chicago Press, 2002).

Legomsky SH, 'Deportation and the War on Independence' (2006) 26 *Journal of the National Association of Administrative Law Judiciary* 387.

Lemann N, *Redemption: The Last Battle of the Civil War*, 1st edn (Farrar, Straus and Giroux, 2006).

Leonard G, 'Iredell Reclaimed: Farewell to Snowiss's History of Judicial Review' (2006) 81 *Chicago-Kent Law Review* 867.

Leonardatos CD, 'California's Attempts to Disarm the Black Panthers' (1999) 36 *San Diego Law Review* 947.

Lerner RL, 'The Troublesome Inheritance of Americans in Magna Carta and Trial by Jury' in R Hazell and J Melton (eds), *Magna Carta and its Modern Legacy* (Cambridge University Press, 2015).

Levin RM, 'The Administrative Law Legacy of Kenneth Culp Davis' (2005) 42 *San Diego Law Review* 315.

Levy J, 'Law and Border' (*Niskanen Center Blog*, 25 July 2018) www.niskanencenter.org/law-and-border/.

Levy LW, 'Property as a Human Right' (1988) 5 *Constitutional Commentary* 169.

Lister M, 'Can the Rule of Law Apply at the Border – A Commentary on Paul Gowder's The Rule of Law in the Real World' (2018) 62 *Saint Louis University Law Journal* 323.

——, 'Enforcing Immigration Law' (2020) 15 *Philosophy Compass* e12653.

Litman LM, 'The Myth of the Great Writ' (forthcoming 2022) 100 *Texas Law Review*_____.

Lopez CE, 'Disorderly (Mis)Conduct: The Problem with Contempt of Cop Arrests' (2010) 4 *Advance* 71.

López IFH, 'Post-Racial Racism: Racial Stratification and Mass Incarceration in the Age of Obama' (2010) 98 *California Law Review* 1023.

Luban D, 'Difference Made Legal: The Court and Dr. King' (1989) 87 *Michigan Law Review* 2152.

Lubet S, *Fugitive Justice: Runaways, Rescuers, and Slavery on Trial* (Belknap Press of Harvard University Press, 2010).

——, *The 'Colored Hero' of Harpers Ferry: John Anthony Copeland and the War Against Slavery* (Cambridge University Press, 2015).

Luna E, 'The Overcriminalization Phenomenon' (2005) 54 *American University Law Review* 703.

Luna GT, 'Chicana/Chicano Land Tenure in the Agrarian Domain: On the Edge of a Naked Knife' (1989) 4 *Michigan Journal of Race & Law* 39.

Luna-Firebaugh EM, 'The Border Crossed Us: Border Crossing Issues of the Indigenous Peoples of the Americas' (2002) 17 *Wicazo Sa Review* 159.

Magnusson P, 'FBI Knew Policeman Was Leak to Klan on Freedom Riders' (*Washington Post*, 20 August 1978) www.washingtonpost.com/archive/politics/1978/08/20/fbi-knew-policeman-was-leak-to-klan-on-freedom-riders/b7c9511b-8805-4ff6-a4dd-3da31a05f1af/.

Malamud DC, 'The Strange Persistence of Affirmative Action Under Title VII' (2015) 118 *West Virginia Law Review* 1.

Maltz EM, 'Fourteenth Amendment Concepts in the Antebellum Era' (1988) 32 *The American Journal of Legal History* 305.

Mancini MJ, 'Race, Economics, and The Abandonment of Convict Leasing' (1978) 63 *The Journal of Negro History* 339.

Markle MM, 'Jury Pay and Assembly Pay at Athens' (1985) 6 *History of Political Thought* 265.

Matsuda MJ, 'When the First Quail Calls: Multiple Consciousness as Jurisprudential Method' (1989) 11 *Women's Rights Law Reporter* 7.

Mattei U and Nader L, *Plunder: When the Rule of Law Is Illegal* (Blackwell Publishing, 2008).

Matthews DG, 'The Abolitionists on Slavery: The Critique Behind the Social Movement' (1967) 33 *The Journal of Southern History* 163.

Mazumder S, 'The Persistent Effect of U.S. Civil Rights Protests on Political Attitudes' (2018) 62 *American Journal of Political Science* 922.

McDonnell JA, *The Dispossession of the American Indian, 1887–1934* (Indiana University Press, 1991).

McKanders KM, 'Immigration Enforcement and the Fugitive Slave Acts: Exploring Their Similarities' (2012) 61 *Catholic University Law Review* 921.

Meares TL, 'Rewards for Good Behavior: Influencing Prosecutorial Discretion and Conduct with Financial Incentives' (1995) 64 *Fordham Law Review* 851.

Medoff R, *Blowing the Whistle on Genocide: Josiah E. Dubois, Jr., And the Struggle for a U.S. Response to the Holocaust* (Purdue University, 2009).

Meehan AJ and Ponder MC, 'Race and Place: The Ecology of Racial Profiling African American Motorists' (2002) 19 *Justice Quarterly* 399.

Mettraux G, 'US Courts-Martial and the Armed Conflict in the Philippines (1899–1902): Their Contribution to National Case Law on War Crimes' (2003) 1 *Journal of International Criminal Justice* 135.

Minter PH, '"The State of Slavery": Somerset, The Slave, Grace, and the Rise of Pro-Slavery and Anti-Slavery Constitutionalism in the Nineteenth-Century Atlantic World' (2015) 36 *Slavery & Abolition* 603.

Mitchell AB, 'Self-Emancipation and Slavery: An Examination of the African American's Quest for Literacy and Freedom.' (2008) 2 *Journal of Pan African Studies* 78.

Mize RL Jr, 'Reparations for Mexican Braceros – Lessons Learned from Japanese and African American Attempts at Redress' (2005) 52 *Cleveland State Law Review* 273.

Mock B, 'New Orleans to Poor Criminal Defendants: We Can't Defend You' (*The Atlantic*, January 2016) www.theatlantic.com/politics/archive/2016/01/new-orleans-to-poor-criminal-defendants-we-cant-defend-you/458856/.

Montesquieu C de S, *The Spirit of the Laws* (AM Cohler, BC Miller and HS Stone eds, Cambridge University Press, 1989).

Moran-McCabe K, Gutman A and Burris S, 'Public Health Implications of Housing Laws: Nuisance Evictions' (2018) 133 *Public Health Reports* 606.

Morel LE, 'The Dred Scott Dissents: McLean, Curtis, Lincoln, and the Public Mind' (2007) 32 *Journal of Supreme Court History* 133.

Morgan ES, *Prologue to Revolution: Sources and Documents on the Stamp Act Crisis, 1764–1766* (Norton, 1973).

——, *American Slavery, American freedom: The Ordeal of Colonial Virginia* (2005).

Morgan ES and Morgan HM, *The Stamp Act Crisis: Prologue to Revolution* (The University of North Carolina Press, 1995).

Morgan J, 'Rethinking Disorderly Conduct' [Forthcoming] *California Law Review*.

Morris AD, 'A Retrospective on the Civil Rights Movement: Political and Intellectual Landmarks' (1999) 25 *Annual Review of Sociology* 517.

Morris TD, *Southern Slavery and the Law, 1619–1860* (The University of North Carolina Press, 1996).

Motomura H, 'Immigration Law After a Century of Plenary Power: Phantom Constitutional Norms and Statutory Interpretation' (1990) 100 *Yale Law Journal* 545.

Murch D, 'Paying for Punishment' (*Boston Review*, 1 August 2016) bostonreview.net/editors-picks-us/donna-murch-paying-punishment.

Murphy C, 'Lon Fuller and the Moral Value of the Rule of Law' (2005) 24 *Law and Philosophy* 239.

Natapoff A, 'Criminal Municipal Courts' (2021) 134 *Harvard Law Review* 964.

Neuborne B, 'The Gravitational Pull of Race on the Warren Court' (2011) 2010 *The Supreme Court Review* 59.

Neuman GL, 'Back to Dred Scott' (1987) 24 *San Diego Law Review* 485.

——, 'Anomalous Zones' (1996) 48 *Stanford Law Review* 1197.

Ngai MM, *Impossible Subjects: Illegal Aliens and the Making of Modern America*, New Paperback edn (Princeton University Press, 2014).

Nieman DG, *To Set the Law in Motion: The Freedmen's Bureau and the Legal Rights of Blacks, 1865–1868* (KTO Press, 1979).

Nir SM, 'The Price of Nice Nails' (*New York Times*, 7 May 2015) www.nytimes.com/2015/05/10/nyregion/at-nail-salons-in-nyc-manicurists-are-underpaid-and-unprotected.html.

Nyquist M, *Arbitrary Rule: Slavery, Tyranny, and the Power of Life and Death* (2015).

Oakes J, 'The Political Significance of Slave Resistance' (1986) 22 *History Workshop Journal* 89.

Olmos S, Baker M and Kanno-Youngs Z, 'Federal Agents Unleash Militarized Crackdown on Portland' (*The New York Times*, 17 July 2020) www.nytimes.com/2020/07/17/us/portland-protests.html.

Onion R, 'Take the Impossible "Literacy" Test Louisiana Gave Black Voters in the 1960s' (*Slate Magazine*, 28 June 2013) slate.com/human-interest/2013/06/voting-rights-and-the-supreme-court-the-impossible-literacy-test-louisiana-used-to-give-black-voters.html.

Ontiveros ML, 'Noncitizen Immigrant Labor and the Thirteenth Amendment: Challenging Guest Worker Programs' (2007) 38 *University of Toledo Law Review* 923.

Onwuachi-Willig A, 'Policing the Boundaries of Whiteness: The Tragedy of Being out of Place from Emmett Till to Trayvon Martin' (2017) 102 *Iowa Law Review* 1113.

Orth JV, *Due Process of Law: A Brief History* (University Press of Kansas, 2003).

Ossei-Owusu S, 'The Sixth Amendment Facade: The Racial Evolution of the Right to Counsel' (2019) 167 *University of Pennsylvania Law Review* 1161.

Oubre CF, *Forty Acres and a Mule: The Freedman's Bureau and Black Land Ownership* (Louisiana State University Press, 1978).

Packer HL, 'The Courts, the Police, and the Rest of Us' (1966) 57 *The Journal of Criminal Law, Criminology, and Police Science* 238.

Pager D, *Marked: Race, Crime, and Finding Work in an Era of Mass Incarceration*, Paperback edn (University of Chicago Press, 2009).

Papke DR, 'The Black Panther Party's Narratives of Resistance' (1994) 18 *Vermont Law Review* 645.

Paquette D, 'Why the Most Outrageous Part of Donald Trump's "Hot Mic" Comments Isn't the Vulgar Language' (*Washington Post*, 7 October 2016) www.washingtonpost.com/news/wonk/wp/2016/10/07/the-real-issue-with-donald-trump-saying-a-man-can-do-anything-to-a-woman/.

Park K-S, 'Self-Deportation Nation' (2019) 132 *Harvard Law Review* 1878.

——, 'This Land Is Not Our Land' (2020) 87 *University of Chicago Law Review* 1977.

Patterson BE, 'Chicago's "Black Site" Police Scandal Is About to Explode Again' (*Mother Jones*, 8 December 2015) www.motherjones.com/politics/2015/12/rahm-emanuel-chicago-police-homan-square-scandal/.

Patterson O, *Slavery and Social Death: A Comparative Study* (Harvard University Press, 1982).

Peeples M, 'Creating Political Authority: The Role of the Antebellum Black Press in the Political Mobilization and Empowerment of African Americans' (2008) 34 *Journalism History* 76.

Penningroth DC, *The Claims of Kinfolk: African American Property and Community in the Nineteenth-Century South* (The University of North Carolina Press, 2004).

——, 'The Claims of Slaves and Ex-Slaves to Family and Property: A Transatlantic Comparison' (2007) 112 *The American Historical Review* 1039.

Pennington JWC, *The Fugitive Blacksmith, or, Events in the History of James W.C. Pennington, Pastor of a Presbyterian Church, New York, Formerly a Slave in the State of Maryland, United States*, 2nd edn (Charles Gilpin, 1849).

Perea JF, 'The Echoes of Slavery: Recognizing the Racist Origins of the Agricultural and Domestic Worker Exclusion from the National Labor Relations Act' (2011) 72 *Ohio State Law Journal* 95.

Peters, Jr J, 'Firsthand Account' in ED Lemont (ed), *American Indian Constitutional Reform and the Rebuilding of Native Nations*, 1st edn (University of Texas Press, 2006).

Pettit B and Western B, 'Mass Imprisonment and the Life Course: Race and Class Inequality in U.S. Incarceration' (2004) 69 *American Sociological Review* 151.

Pfaff J, *Locked In: The True Causes of Mass Incarceration-and How to Achieve Real Reform* (Basic Books, 2017).

Pilkington E, '"These Are His People": Inside the Elite Border Patrol Unit Trump Sent to Portland' (*The Guardian*, 27 July 2020) www.theguardian.com/us-news/2020/jul/27/trump-border-patrol-troops-portland-bortac.

Pippin SE, Wong JA and Mason RM, 'Perceived and Actual Consequences of the Foreign Account Tax Compliance Act: A Survey of Americans Living Abroad', *Advances in Taxation*, vol 25 (Emerald Publishing Limited, 2018).

Pocock JGA, *The Machiavellian Moment: Florentine Political Thought and the Atlantic Republican Tradition*, 2nd pbk edn (Princeton University Press, 2003).

Pope JG, 'Snubbed Landmark: Why United States v. Cruikshank (1876) Belongs at the Heart of the American Constitutional Canon' (2014) 49 *Harvard Civil Rights-Civil Liberties Law Review* 385.

Pope PJ and Garrett TM, 'America's Homo Sacer: Examining U.S. Deportation Hearings and the Criminalization of Illegal Immigration' (2013) 45 *Administration & Society* 167.

Posner EA and Vermeule A, *The Executive Unbound: After the Madisonian Republic* (Oxford University Press, 2010).

Price PJ, 'Alien Land Restrictions in the American Common Law: Exploring the Relative Autonomy Paradigm' (1999) 43 *American Journal of Legal History* 152.

Prowse G, Weaver VM and Meares TL, 'The State from Below: Distorted Responsiveness in Policed Communities' (2019) 56 *Urban Affairs Review* 1423.

Quadagno JS, *The Color of Welfare: How Racism Undermined the War on Poverty* (Oxford University Press, 1996).

Quillian L, 'Segregation and Poverty Concentration: The Role of Three Segregations' (2012) 77 *American Sociological Review* 354.

Rable GC, *But There Was No Peace: The Role of Violence in the Politics of Reconstruction* (University of Georgia Press, 2007).

Radin MJ, *Boilerplate* (Princeton University Press, 2012).

Rakove JN, *Original Meanings: Politics and Ideas in the Making of the Constitution*, 1st Vintage Books edn (Vintage, 1997).

Ralph L, 'The Making of Richard Zuley: The Ignored Linkages Between the US Criminal In/Justice System and the International Security State' (2020) 122 *American Anthropologist* 133.

Ramirez DA, 'The Mixed Jury and the Ancient Custom of Trial by Jury De Medietate Linguae: A History and Proposal for Change' (1994) 74 *Boston University Law Review* 777.

Rampell C, 'This Latest Trick From the Trump Administration Is One of the Most Despicable Yet' (*Washington Post*, 13 February 2020) www.washingtonpost.com/opinions/the-trump-administrations-kafkaesque-new-way-to-thwart-visa-applications/2020/02/13/190a3862-4ea3-11ea-bf44-f5043eb3918a_story.html.

Rana A, *The Two Faces of American Freedom* (Harvard University Press, 2014).

Ransom R and Sutch R, 'Capitalists Without Capital: The Burden of Slavery and the Impact of Emancipation' (1988) 62 *Agricultural History* 133.

Rao G, 'The Federal Posse Comitatus Doctrine: Slavery, Compulsion, and Statecraft in Mid-Nineteenth-Century America' (2008) 26 *Law and History Review* 1.

Rasmussen BB, '"Attended with Great Inconveniences": Slave Literacy and the 1740 South Carolina Negro Act' (2010) 125 *PMLA* 201.

Redford L, 'The Intertwined History of Class and Race Segregation in Los Angeles' (2017) 16 *Journal of Planning History* 305.

Reich CA, 'The New Property' (1964) 73 *Yale Law Journal* 733.

Reséndez A, *The Other Slavery: The Uncovered Story of Indian Enslavement in America*, 1st Mariner Books edn (Mariner Books, Houghton Mifflin Harcourt, 2017).

Ricciardelli L et al, 'A Snapshot of Immigration Court at Stewart Detention Center:' (2019) 20 *Critical Social Work* 46.

Richards LL, *The Slave Power: The Free North and Southern Domination, 1780–1860* (Louisiana State University Press, 2000).

Richardson HC, The Death of Reconstruction: Race, Labor, and Politics in the Post-Civil War North, 1865–1901 (Harvard University Press, 2001).

Roberts DE, 'The Meaning of Blacks' Fidelity to the Constitution' (1997) 65 *Fordham Law Review* 1761.

——, 'Race, Vagueness, and the Social Meaning of Order-Maintenance Policing' (1999) 89 *Journal of Criminal Law and Criminology* 775.

——, 'The Social and Moral Cost of Mass Incarceration in African American Communities' (2004) 56 *Stanford Law Review* 1271.

Roberts E, 'Welfare and the Problem of Black Citizenship' (1996) 105 *Yale Law Journal* 1563.

Roberts N, *Freedom as Marronage* (The University of Chicago Press, 2015).

Roberts P, 'Does Article 6 of the European Convention on Human Rights Require Reasoned Verdicts in Criminal Trials?' (2011) 11 *Human Rights Law Review* 213.

Robertson CB and Manta ID, 'Litigating Citizenship' (2020) 73 *Vanderbilt Law Review* 757.

Roithmayr D, 'Locked in Segregation' (2004) 12 *Virginia Journal of Social Policy & the Law* 197.

——, 'The Dynamics of Excessive Force' (2016) 2016 *University of Chicago Legal Forum* 407.

Roman M, 'The Black Panther Party and the Struggle for Human Rights' (2016) 5 Spectrum: *A Journal on Black Men* 7.

Royce EC, *The Origins of Southern Sharecropping* (Temple University Press, 1993).

Rugh J and Hall M, 'Deporting the American Dream: Immigration Enforcement and Latino Foreclosures' (2016) 3 *Sociological Science* 1077.

Rusco E, 'The Indian Reorganization Act and Indian Self-Government' in ED Lemont (ed), *American Indian Constitutional Reform and the Rebuilding of Native Nations*, 1st edn (University of Texas Press, 2006).

Ruskola T, 'Colonialism Without Colonies: On the Extraterritorial Jurisprudence of the U.S. Court for China' (2008) 71 *Law and Contemporary Problems* 217.

——, *Legal Orientalism: China, the United States, and Modern Law* (Harvard University Press, 2013).

Rutherglen G, 'Textual Corruption in the *Civil Rights Cases*' (2009) 34 *Journal of Supreme Court History* 164.

Ryo E, 'Less Enforcement, More Compliance: Rethinking Unauthorized Migration' (2015) 62 *UCLA Law Review* 622.

——, 'Detained: A Study of Immigration Bond Hearings' (2016) 50 *Law & Society Review* 117.

——, 'Fostering Legal Cynicism through Immigration Detention' [2017] *Southern California Law Review* 999.

——, 'Understanding Immigration Detention: Causes, Conditions, and Consequences' (2019) 15 *Annual Review of Law and Social Science* 97.

Ryo E and Peacock I, 'A National Study of Immigration Detention in the United States' (2018) 92 *Southern California Law Review* 1.

Saito NT, *From Chinese Exclusion to Guantánamo Bay: Plenary Power and the Prerogative State* (University Press of Colorado, 2007).

Salyer LE, *Laws Harsh as Tigers: Chinese Immigrants and the Shaping of Modern Immigration Law* (University of North Carolina Press, 1995).

Sampson RJ and Raudenbush SW, 'Neighborhood Stigma and the Perception of Disorder' (2005) 24 *Focus* 7.

Sances MW and You HY, 'Who Pays for Government? Descriptive Representation and Exploitative Revenue Sources' (2017) 79 *The Journal of Politics* 1090.

Sandefur RL, 'Access to Civil Justice and Race, Class, and Gender Inequality' (2008) 34 *Annual Review of Sociology* 339.

Santoro WA, 'The Civil Rights Movement's Struggle for Fair Employment: A "Dramatic Events-Conventional Politics" Model' (2002) 81 *Social Forces* 177.

Saunt C, *Unworthy Republic: The Dispossession of Native Americans and the Road to Indian Territory*, 1st edn (WW Norton & Company 2020).

Schaub DJ, 'Montesquieu on Slavery' (2005) 34 *Perspectives on Political Science* 70.

Scheflin A and Van Dyke J, 'Jury Nullification: The Contours of a Controversy' (1980) 43 *Law and Contemporary Problems* 51.

Scheiber H, 'Public Rights and the Rule of Law in American Legal History' (1984) 72 *California Law Review* 217.

Schlosser E, 'In the Strawberry Fields' (*The Atlantic*, November 1995) www.theatlantic.com/magazine/archive/1995/11/in-the-strawberry-fields/305754/.

Schuck PH and Smith RM, *Citizenship Without Consent: Illegal Aliens in the American Polity* (Yale University Press, 1985).

Schultz D, 'The Locke Republican Debate and the Paradox of Property Rights in Early American Jurisprudence' (1991) 13 *Western New England Law Review* 155.

Seale B, *Seize the Time: The Story of the Black Panther Party* (Black Classic Press, 1991).

Shalvi S et al, 'Self-Serving Justifications: Doing Wrong and Feeling Moral' (2015) 24 *Current Directions in Psychological Science* 125.

Shear MD, Benner K and Schmidt MS, '"We Need to Take Away Children", No Matter How Young, Justice Dept. Officials Said' (*The New York Times*, 6 October 2020) www.nytimes.com/2020/10/06/us/politics/family-separation-border-immigration-jeff-sessions-rod-rosenstein.html.

Shipherd JR, *History of the Oberlin-Wellington Rescue* (John P Jewett and Company, 1859).

Siegel RB, 'Equality Talk: Antisubordination and Anticlassification Values in Constitutional Struggles over Brown' (2004) 117 *Harvard Law Review* 1470.

Silver A, 'The Demand for Order in Civil Society: A Review of Some Themes in the History of Urban Crime, Police, and Riot' in David J Bourda (ed), *The Police: Six Sociological Essays* (Wiley, 1967).

Silver JR et al, 'Traditional Police Culture, Use of Force, and Procedural Justice: Investigating Individual, Organizational, and Contextual Factors' (2017) 34 *Justice Quarterly* 1272.

Sinha A, 'Slavery by Another Name: "Voluntary" Immigrant Detainee Labor and the Thirteenth Amendment' (2015) 11 *Stanford Journal of Civil Rights and Civil Liberties* 1.

Sinha M, *The Slave's Cause: A History of Abolition* (Yale University Press, 2017).

Sinozich S, 'The Polls – Trends: Public Opinion on the US Supreme Court, 1973–2015' (2017) 81 *Public Opinion Quarterly* 173.

Skogan WG, 'Why Reforms Fail' (2008) 18 *Policing and Society* 23.

Smith HR, 'Expedited Removal of Aliens: Legal Framework' (Congressional Research Service, 2019) R45314.

Smith RM, 'Living in a Promiseland?: Mexican Immigration and American Obligations' (2011) 9 *Perspectives on Politics* 545.

Snowiss S, *Judicial Review and the Law of the Constitution* (Yale University Press, 1990).

Soifer A, 'Old Lines in New Battles: An Overlooked Yet Useful Statute to Confront Exploitation of Undocumented Workers by Employers and by ICE' (2018) 19 *Nevada Law Journal* 397.

Soltow L, 'Economic Inequality in the United States in the Period from 1790 to 1860' (1971) 31 *The Journal of Economic History* 822.

Soss J and Weaver V, 'Police Are Our Government: Politics, Political Science, and the Policing of Race–Class Subjugated Communities' (2017) 20 *Annual Review of Political Science* 565.

Spooner L, *The Unconstitutionality of Slavery* (Burt Franklin, 1860).

Starr SB, 'Testing Racial Profiling: Empirical Assessment of Disparate Treatment by Police' (2016) 2016 *University of Chicago Legal Forum* 485.

Steinfeld RJ, 'Property and Suffrage in the Early American Republic' (1989) 41 *Stanford Law Review* 335.

Stevens J, 'U.S. Government Unlawfully Detaining and Deporting U.S. Citizens as Aliens' (2011) 18 *Virginia Journal of Social Policy & the Law* 606.

——, 'One Dollar Per Day: The Slaving Wages of Immigration Jail, From 1943 to Present' (2015) 29 *Georgetown Immigration Law Journal* 391.

——, 'The Alien Who Is a Citizen' in Benjamin N Lawrance and Jacqueline Stevens (eds), *Citizenship in Question: Evidentiary Birthright and Statelessness* (Duke University Press, 2017).

——, 'One Dollar Per Day: A Note on Recent Forced Labor and Dollar-Per-Day Wages in Private Prisons Holding People Under Immigration Law' (2018) 52 *Valparaiso University Law Review* 343.

Stewart EA et al, 'Neighborhood Racial Context and Perceptions of Police-Based Racial Discrimination Among Black Youth' (2009) 47 *Criminology* 847.

Strahilevitz LJ, 'The Right to Destroy' (2005) 114 *Yale Law Journal* 781.

Stuart F, 'Becoming "Copwise": Policing, Culture, and the Collateral Consequences of Street-Level Criminalization' (2016) 50 *Law & Society Review* 279.

Stuntz WJ, 'Plea Bargaining and Criminal Law's Disappearing Shadow' (2004) 117 *Harvard Law Review* 2548.

Tamanaha B, 'The Dark Side of the Relationship Between the Rule of Law and Liberalism' (2008) 3 *New York University Journal of Law & Liberty* 516.

Taylor K-Y, *From #BlackLivesMatter to Black Liberation* (Haymarket Books, 2016).

Tewell JJ, 'Assuring Freedom to the Free: Jefferson's Declaration and the Conflict over Slavery' (2012) 58 *Civil War History* 75.

Thompson EP, *Whigs and Hunters: The Origin of the Black Act* (Allen Lane, 1975).

Tillman SB, 'Ex Parte Merryman: Myth, History and Scholarship' (2016) 224 *Military Law Review* 481.

Tilly C, *Durable Inequality* (University of California Press, 1999).

Tirres AB, 'Property Outliers: Non-Citizens, Property Rights and State Power' (2012) 27 *Georgetown Immigration Law Journal* 77.

——, 'Ownership without Citizenship: The Creation of Noncitizen Property Rights' (2013) 19 *Michigan Journal of Race & Law* 1.

Tomuschat C, 'The Legacy of Nuremberg' (2006) 4 *Journal of International Criminal Justice* 830.

Travis J, Western B and Redburn S (eds), *The Growth of Incarceration in the United States: Exploring Causes and Consequences* (The National Academies Press, 2014).

Trelease AW, *White Terror: The Ku Klux Klan Conspiracy and Southern Reconstruction*, Louisiana Paperback edn (Louisiana State University, Press 1995).

Tushnet MV, *The American Law of Slavery, 1810–1860: Considerations of Humanity and Interest* (Princeton University Press, 1981).

——, 'An Essay on Rights' (1984) 62 *Texas Law Review* 1363.

Tyler TR, *Why People Obey the Law* (Yale University Press, 1990).

Ubbelohde C, *The Vice-Admiralty Courts and the American Revolution* (University of North Carolina Press, 1960).

Uhl L, 'Prosecuting Illegal Reentry Cases Where Evidentiary Documents Are Missing or Incomplete: Everything You Never Wanted to Know about A-Files and Removal Documents and Were Not Afraid Not to Ask' (2017) 65 *United States Attorneys' Bulletin* 17.

Uzgalis W and Zack N, 'John Locke, Racism, Slavery, and Indian Lands', *The Oxford Handbook of Philosophy and Race* (Oxford University Press, 2017).

Van Maanen J, 'Observations on the Making of Policemen' (1973) 32 *Human Organization* 407.

VanderVelde L, *Redemption Songs: Suing for Freedom Before Dred Scott* (Oxford University Press, 2014).

VanderVelde L and Chin GJ, 'Sowing the Seeds of Chinese Exclusion as the Reconstruction Congress Debates Civil Rights Inclusion' (2020) 12 *Tsinghua China Law Review* 185.

Vandevelde KJ, 'The New Property of the Nineteenth Century: The Development of the Modern Concept of Property' (1980) 29 *Buffalo Law Review* 325.

Verdier P-H, 'The New Financial Extraterritoriality' (2019) 87 *George Washington Law Review* 239.

Villazor RC, 'Rediscovering Oyama v. California: At the Intersection of Property, Race, and Citizenship' (2010) 87 *Washington University Law Review* 979.

Vinograd C, '2016 Presidential Debate: Donald Trump's Remark About Paying Taxes Raises Eyebrows' (*NBC News*, 27 September 2016) www.nbcnews.com/storyline/2016-presidential-debates/presidential-debate-donald-trump-s-remark-about-paying-taxes-raises-n655261.

Vladeck SI, 'The D.C. Circuit After Boumediene' (2011) 41 *Seton Hall Law Review* 1451.

——, 'It's Time to Admit That the Military Commissions Have Failed' (*Lawfare*, 16 April 2019) www.lawfareblog.com/its-time-admit-military-commissions-have-failed.

Wacquant L, 'From Slavery to Mass Incarceration' (2002) 13 *New Left Review* 41.

Wagner J, Dawsey J and Sonmez F, 'Trump Vows Executive Order to End Birthright Citizenship, a Move Most Legal Experts Say Would Run Afoul of the Constitution' (*Washington Post*, 30 October 2018) www.washingtonpost.com/politics/trump-eyeing-executive-order-to-end-citizenship-for-children-of-noncitizens-born-on-us-soil/2018/10/30/66892050-dc29-11e8-b3f0-62607289efee_story.html.

Waldrep C, 'National Policing, Lynching, and Constitutional Change' (2008) 74 *The Journal of Southern History* 589.

Waldron J, 'Is the Rule of Law an Essentially Contested Concept (In Florida)?' (2002) 21 *Law and Philosophy* 137.

——, *The Rule of Law and the Measure of Property* (Cambridge University Press, 2012).

Waldstreicher D, *Slavery's Constitution: From Revolution to Ratification* (Hill and Wang, 2009).

Walker JEK, 'Racism, Slavery, and Free Enterprise: Black Entrepreneurship in the United States Before the Civil War' (1986) 60 *The Business History Review* 343.

Wang AB, 'Border Patrol Agents Were Filmed Dumping Water Left for Migrants. Then Came a "Suspicious" Arrest.' (*Washington Post*, 24 January 2018) www.washingtonpost.com/news/post-nation/wp/2018/01/23/border-patrol-accused-of-targeting-aid-group-that-filmed-agents-dumping-water-left-for-migrants/.

Washington J and Olivares J, 'ICE Medical Misconduct Witness Slated for Deportation Is a U.S. Citizen, Says Lawyer' (*The Intercept*, 2 November 2020) theintercept.com/2020/11/02/ice-medical-misconduct-us-citizen-deportation/.

Wasow O, 'Agenda Seeding: How 1960s Black Protests Moved Elites, Public Opinion and Voting' (2020) 114 *American Political Science Review* 638.

Webb DA, 'The Somerset Effect: Parsing Lord Mansfield's Words on Slavery in Nineteenth Century America' (2014) 32 *Law and History Review* 455.

Weiher GR, 'Public Policy and Patterns of Residential Segregation' (1989) 42 *Western Political Quarterly* 651.

Welch Jr. RE, 'American Atrocities in the Philippines The Indictment and the Response' (1974) 43 *Pacific Historical Review* 233.

Welke BY, *Law and the Borders of Belonging in the Long Nineteenth Century United States* (Cambridge University Press, 2010).

Wells-Barnett IB, *Lynch Law in Georgia* (Chicago Colored Citizens, 1899).

West R, 'Toward an Abolitionist Interpretation of the Fourteenth Amendment' (1991) 94 *West Virginia Law Review* 111.

——, 'Paul Gowder's Rule of Law' (2018) 62 *Saint Louis University Law Journal* 303.

West TG, *Vindicating the Founders: Race, Sex, Class, and Justice in the Origins of America* (Rowman & Littlefield Publishers, 2001).

White GE, 'Reflections on the Republican Revival: Interdisciplinary Scholarship in the Legal Academy' (1994) 6 *Yale Journal of Law & the Humanities* 1.

White W, *Rope & Faggot: A Biography of Judge Lynch* (Alfred A Knopf, 1929).

Whitman JQ, *Harsh Justice: Criminal Punishment and the Widening Divide Between America and Europe*, 1st Paperback edn (Oxford University Press, 2005).

Wiecekt WM, 'Somerset: Lord Mansfield and the Legitimacy of Slavery in the Anglo-American World' (1974) 42 *University of Chicago Law Review* 86.

Wilentz S, *No Property in Man: Slavery and Antislavery at the Nation's Founding*, 2nd edn (Harvard University Press, 2019).

Wilkinson CF and Volkman JM, 'Judicial Review of Indian Treaty Abrogation: As Long as Water Flows, or Grass Grows upon the Earth – How Long a Time is That' (1975) 63 *California Law Review* 601.

Williams G, 'U.S. Expats Find Their Money Is No Longer Welcome at the Bank' (*Reuters*, 11 June 2014) www.reuters.com/article/us-banks-expats-idUSKBN0EM16V20140611.

Williams P, 'Alchemical Notes: Reconstructing Ideals from Deconstructed Rights' (1987) 22 *Harvard Civil Rights-Civil Liberties Law Review* 401.

——, 'Spirit-Murdering the Messenger: The Discourse of Fingerpointing as the Law's Response to Racism' (1987) 42 *University of Miami Law Review* 127.

Williamson J, 'What Washington Means by Policy Reform' in John Williamson (ed), *Latin American Adjustment: How Much Has Happened?* (Institute for International Economics, 1990).

Wilson C, *Freedom at Risk: The Kidnapping of Free Blacks in America, 1780–1865* (University Press of Kentucky, 1994).

Wood AW, 'Kant on Duties Regarding Nonrational Nature' (1998) 72 *Aristotelian Society Supplementary Volume* 189.

Wood GS, *The Creation of the American Republic, 1776–1787*, 2nd edn (Published for the Institute of Early American History and Culture at Williamsburg, Va, by the University of North Carolina Press, 1998).

Wright G, 'Slavery and Anglo-American Capitalism Revisited' (2020) 73 *The Economic History Review* 353.

Yoo J, 'Merryman and Milligan (and McCardle)' (2009) 34 *Journal of Supreme Court History* 243.

——, 'Settled Law: Birthright Citizenship and the 14th Amendment' (*American Enterprise Institute*, reprinted from *The American Mind*, 25 October 2018) www.aei.org/articles/settled-law-birthright-citizenship-and-the-14th-amendment/.

Young EA, 'Welcome to the Dark Side – Liberals Rediscover Federalism in the Wake of the War on Terror' (2004) 69 *Brooklyn Law Review* 1277.

Zeidman S, 'From Dropsy to Testilying: Prosecutorial Apathy, Ennui, or Complicity?' (2019) 16 *Ohio State Journal of Criminal Law* 423.

Zietlow RE, 'Giving Substance to Process: Countering the Due Process Counterrevolution' (1997) 75 *Denver University Law Review* 9.

Zinn H, *SNCC: The New Abolitionists* (Haymarket Books, 2013).

Index